PRAISE

STAFFORD WHITE

An eye-opening experience. – **Sunday Telegraph**

Unpretentious, human and thoroughly helpful…leaves no stone unturned. Buy it! – **The Daily Express**

Delightful! – **Daily Telegraph**

You hear his distinctive voice, easy, confident and encouraging. He writes reverently. – **Country Life**

Seekers of fitness for mind and spirit will find a wealth of information. A haven for the heart. – **The Times**

Spiritual substance without being force fed. – **The Sunday Times**

Recommended reading. – **Mind, Body, Soul**

Invaluable to stressed folk. – **Vogue**

Splendid! – **The Observer**

Mindfulness is very well presented, clear and simple. – **Padmaloka Buddhist Centre**

Brings new and valuable insight into life questions that beg for answers. – **Mirabella**

Stafford Whiteaker encourages us to step off the world at least occasionally. – **The Universe**

A celebration, a labour of love. – **The Listener**

Most notable is the inter-faith emphasis. – **The Tablet**

A joy! – **The Field**

Well researched without a hint of pedantry. – **Tatler**

Reconnect yourself to the deeper, more spiritual being you really are. – **The Scotsman**

According to Stafford Whiteaker experience yourself and your relationship to others and, if you are fortunate, feel a consciousness of the eternal. – **Telegraph Magazine**

You'll find peace and spiritual renewal. – **Here's Health**

Challenging practical suggestions which contain a great deal of spiritual wisdom. – **Fellowship of Solitaries**

Good Living in Hard Times

Also by Stafford Whiteaker

The Good Retreat Guide
Living the Sacred
The Little Book of Inner Space

Good Living in Hard Times

The Art of Contentment

Good Living in Hard Times

The Art of Contentment

Stafford Whiteaker

BOOKS

Winchester, UK
Washington, USA

First published by O-Books, 2012
O-Books is an imprint of John Hunt Publishing Ltd., Laurel House, Station Approach,
Alresford, Hants, SO24 9JH, UK
office1@o-books.net
www.o-books.com

For distributor details and how to order please visit the 'Ordering' section on our website.

ISBN: 978 1 78099 316 4

A CIP catalogue record for this book is available from the British Library.

Design: Stuart Davies

Printed in the USA by Edwards Brothers Malloy

CONTENTS

Acknowledgements

With thanks to Carolyn Cope, Kim Didden, Paul Jezewski and Niels van Hemert for the support of their friendship.

For my grandchildren:
Alex, Hannah, Joe, Martha, Tena and Tom.

INTRODUCTION

Much of our contemporary life is a substitute for former social habits. For example, mobile phones, texting, twitter, emails and other forms of communication have become substitutes for many of our face to face encounters. These changes have many advantages and are here to stay, but we pay the price of giving up many of the characteristics of our "reading' what the other person is actually feeling. We have voice, electronic images, or words alone to determine the state of mind and emotions of the other person talking to us. This diminishes our ability to fully understand the other person at that moment in their lives.

Our technological innovations outstrip our ability to equally revolutionize the way we think and act. We need more time to transcend our own collective genius. The level of thinking that creates the technological advances is not the same kind of thinking that we need in order to adjust individually and collectively to them. It is a dilemma of our species that has probably always been a problem for us since the beginning our history. In a nutshell, the old busy is never the new busy.

We should then, as Saint Bernard of Clairvaux advised, ride over the vicissitudes of daily life with the poise of someone sustained by values that are eternal. If we are to do this we must begin by turning our minds to more important ideas and ideals. Here are to be found the concepts of living which bring personal contentment and promote the common good. From such clarity about our lives we may find the grace with which to understand values which raise us to awareness of the eternal. Here reside the universal truths that open us to those moral and ethical standards which make for a life of love.

TRULY FREE – TRULY CONTENTED

In the middle of difficulty lies opportunity.
Albert Einstein

For the first time, we are dismantling the legendary Tower of Babel. The result has been profound. Our talk to each other is global, information is instantly and abundantly available, and we have so far maintained an almost complete independence from authority in the exchange of our opinions and information. We have given ourselves permission to say what we want when we want and different languages are no longer a barrier. Cyberspace exposure of hidden political realities and commercial agendas are slowly forcing a transparency on a scale never before available and it is global in scope. No one yet knows what form or shape the future system of governance will take, but it is almost certain not to be a continuance of the present hierarchical one but will most likely be horizontal in as yet an unknown structure.

With all this change comes an increased awareness not just of the present state of the societies in which people live but of themselves in a new role for justice and economic equality where the common good is also part of the vision. It is no longer enough for the individual to succeed. Society as a collective community must also benefit. Above all else the mass of people now around the world are rejecting the present substitution of market economics for all other values as the matrix of human ethics and life. This means a return to moral and ethical values which arise not from religious teachings but from the reality of secular experience.

In this book I have tried to place before you some of those values that make for such a life of dignity, believing that in changing ourselves for the better, we change society. We match our external efforts for the common good with inner disciplines that make for individual happiness.

Adapting to the rhythm of our time

Adapting to the Rhythm of our time is the sub-title of a delightful old cookbook by Edouard de Pomiane. It is very appropriate when explaining what my book is all about which is how to adapt to your present situation so that you may live a more contented life. This makes for your happiness, because you are at peace with yourself. If you are at peace you can work to make your community one of peace.

Living a contented life is like good cooking when you think about it. There are a few principles to follow if you do not want to spoil the dish. Finally, when you have achieved your aim you can share it with others. In this case, not a fine cake or a juicy roast of beef but the happiness, peace, and contentment that is the goal of a life well-lived. This is the perfect dish that pleases everyone you know. Such a life is a bowl of plenty not costing a lot of money but achieved by the care and attention to certain principles and values.

Make no mistake, there *are* good ways and wrong ways to live if you want a contented life. Since good living involves the whole person, its principles encompass not just mind and body but the spirit as well. This is not about religious beliefs although they often help. It is to accept that even when mind and body are crushed, the spirit can survive to guard and keep alive our will to live and to inspire within us a sense of hope. A moment's reflection on the lives of political prisoners or survivors of the Holocaust is enough for us to know the truth of the power of the spirit.

Those things we treasure most come not from our thinking but arise from that which we call *the heart* and which was once widely called *the soul*. Love, joy, peace, patience, kindness, generosity, forbearance, gentleness, faith, courage, rational self-restraint, and purity are the harvest that the spirit brings. These are things everyone wants in their lives and, being of the spirit, to possess them you need to choose to live by the spirit. This means the spirit is your rule of life. All you need do is open your innermost self so that, as Saint Ambrose said, you may see the riches of simplicity, the treasures of peace, and the sweetness of grace.

Such discernment brings moral and ethical values for daily life which are not just a matter of individual taste. It is not how you feel about something that counts. It is how you measure a situation and your actions in it by those values which constitute the structure of your lifestyle and by which you judge how well you are living. This is why contentment is an art.

None of what I suggest to you in this book is original but are those aspects of life values which have served men and women well for thousands of years through peace and war, riches and poverty, and political repression and democracy. These have stood the test of human history. Maybe some are out of fashion for the moment, but they eventually return in some form in every culture because by their individual practice they collectively make a society that is civilized.

When practiced, these principles for living give us true freedom – a freedom that comes only from within and that should be ours by right and not just by society's laws or religious teachings although both may confirm such liberty.

Adapting to the rhythm of our time is necessary if we are to achieve this fullness of being alive – but we cannot succeed if we succumb to those elements of modern living which diminish us and make us victims. Such examples as consumerism, materialism, and too much self-concern spring to mind. The difficult in avoiding what pulls us down is that we are often just too scared to try to be truly independent. We often know what we want but not what we need. We are confused as to what is our true poverty and what is our true treasure.

As with all good recipes you cannot make a fine dish unless you start with the right ingredients. The same is true for your life.

One must begin with quality and not quantity. The beginning is to turn the mind to more important ideas and ideals rather than be overwhelmed by transient petty details that derail your focus. Here is where you will find the right ingredients to put into practice the art of living a contented life.

You will find that throughout this book I repeat in shorter ways the values of a contented life which I discuss elsewhere as major topics. This is quite deliberate because all the ethical and moral values that make you healthy and rich are intimately related to each other much like the notes in music make up a melody and throughout such orchestration echo and repeat themselves.

Hopefully, this book will encourage you to take action for yourself through understanding what makes you poor, what makes you healthy and what makes you rich. Then, you must take action and practice such values and ethics of good living. Achieving this is difficult but the goal is the self-reliance which brings dignity to your life no matter your circumstances.

Modern life spoils so much that is pleasant. So, as the good cook Dr. de Pomiane would have agreed, let us see that it does not spoil the fine dish that is our health and happiness.

A new perspective

We face so many challenges today that most of us feel hard times are sitting on our necks or lurking just around the corner ready to jump into our lives. Yet, the primary enemy is not outside us but within. We are usually not aware of this. We long to make things different. We read self-help books. We try hard to practice a spiritual path or do meditation or get enough exercise or whatever the latest self-help idea is from the alternative healing, scientific, media, and commercial sectors of our society – not forgetting the abundance of advice on offer from a plethora of web wisdom gurus. Most of this has a tendency to either confuse us or make us fear the worse about the future, battered as we are by doomsday messages ranging from what we eat to the world ending soon according to ancient civilizations. This over-load of questionable advice does nothing to help us toward a contented life.

When we decide that we want true freedom, we must reject any system of economics or politics that seeks to control us other than that which serves the obvious and transparent common good of all of our society. What this means, as I said at the beginning of this book, is that the ethical and moral values by which we live are not just for our own individual benefit but for the common good as well. It is this individual action when we later come together collectively as a community that makes a force for change. The contemporary cry of our times is for dignity and justice whether it is in the popular uprisings in the Middle East or in the protestations of the Occupy Wall Street Movement. Although no doubt people will choose ideologies, it should mean we do not take up a particular political position or believe one way for society to live together is better than another. It should mean we believe in our lives being judged and helped by a system which is not based on the profit motives of capitalism, which has made the few rich and powerful and everyone else responsible for making this possible for them, or put up with any other system which caters for the few and does not bring justice, peace and the basics of living to everyone. It means we must put aside judgment of others and take up compassion for them.

Above all else in this individual and collective struggle you need hope based on values you believe essential to good living for yourself and your nation. It is hope that keeps the fire of motivation going even when you feel you are failing. It keeps you going when you stumble, lose your way, or just feel you want to give up. It is the adrenaline of the spirit, the powerhouse of being positive, the ingredient that stops you from staying in a state of disenchantment. This works for your community as well as for yourself.

We need to start by getting a perspective on what good living and hard times mean. Naturally, this differs from person to person. If you are a beggar hunting discarded food, the chance discovery of something really fresh and delicious is good living. If you have always wanted an expensive car or a big house or a fantastic highly paid career and such comes your way, then for you this could be good living. In other words, this means we are *momentarily* pleased by the way our life is going. As to hard times, these can range from being unemployed and living in some damp slum of an apartment to having just broken up with your latest partner. Everything is relative.

The list of what are good and hard times is endless but if you feel you are in hard times, then make no mistake that is where you are.

What I mean by good living is not momentary. It means to live fully the life you have *now* in a way which nourishes and makes possible the healthy and joyous union of your mind, body and spirit. This brings a sense of belonging and well-being. We may not always be happy for happiness is transient, but we can find contentment most of the time.

So good living is about the authenticity of our daily life. When you live this way you are living truly as you *are*. No illusions. No pretensions. No closed heart. No negative mind. Just *being*. Such good living is more than just contentment. It is a state of love.

What we achieve is measured in our present culture by our possessions and the degree to which we may consume the production of industry. To have is good. Those who do not have are losers. We have been slaves to this ethos for several hundred years now and it has become a global measurement of the progress of every nation. It has brought us material advantages and widespread discontent.

This measurement takes no real account of our health or

happiness, least of all our freedom. We go to work to keep ourselves and our families and this becomes more and more difficult to achieve. We are often bored, restless, disillusioned, and disappointed with ourselves and with life. If you have fallen on hard times and your employment does not seem to give you enough to live comfortably and you worry constantly about rent, mortgage payments, and the cost of just getting by, then this system which serves commercial interests so successfully, can actually kill you. Your health will suffer. Your relationships will start not to work. Your feelings of belonging to a community will be fragmented. Your successful friends will draw away. Your self-esteem will be low. The few will continue getting richer while you slowly sinking into a state of defeat. What meager benefits of health care you have will be tied to your job or be in a collapsing under-financed system. You will be expected to work more years for a pension and get less in the end than you need.

Finding a way to meaning in your life

The new morality emerging about how we live our lives, fathered by the change in global economics and born of necessity, does not just involve our own private life but the life we lead as members of a community, a society, and a world. Discovering and making these new relationships means changes in how we live, think and feel. We are all wary of change but it has been forced on us – many would say: *At long last*!

These days most people do not give much thought to personal moral obligations and issues. Such questions as *What does it mean to be honest?* are individually answered as a personal judgment. It is all about how you feel as an individual. This moral individualism does not secure any common agreement in our Western cultures since there is no single source of revealed or inherited or shared codes of behavior. The individual is essentially the only moral unit and every judgment is based on how we feel at any given moment. There is no commonly agreed framework of reference or obligations overall which collectively act for the good of society as a whole. We have laws but hardly understand or even know their moral or ethical origins. Change must and is happening and it starts with the individual – you – and not just with change in the political and social systems of your society.

The political and social philosopher, Slavoj Žižek, claims one of the main dangers of capitalism is that by the virtue of being global it encompasses the whole world and, thus, *it sustains a "worldless" ideological constellation in which people are deprived of their ways of locating meaning.* It is this finding of meaning that eludes us today. We are left to fall back into how we feel rather than having a framework of moral and ethical reference.

In such an environment you are left to make up rules for living as you go along. In these shifting sands of individualism it is impossible for society to achieve moral agreement. The end result is a fragmented culture where everyone tries to be as non-judgmental as possible but is confused about what may be right or wrong unless it should be murder, rape or child abuse. In the end there is a lack of moral discipline in the way society behaves. This leads neither to individual or community contentment with life. There is no consensus about what serves the common good. People of faith in Western cultures, who hope to live a code of conduct through moral and ethical values offered by their religion, fare little better than the unbeliever, because their society at large does not share their views and, thus, cannot often support them. Indeed, in the face of a wide-spread ideology of secularism, most believers try to go about life displaying as little evidence of the teachings of their faith as possible. The group dynamic of the culture is shared laws but not shared codes of everyday moral and ethical behavior. For example, no matter how momentarily shocked people might be after a terrorist attack or how fluent the indignation of politicians and the media after street riots, such events really only reflect the disapproval of people because they are unlawful. They do not result in any attempt to build a better moral and ethical framework to sustain the society and, thus, promote a shared understanding of what is right and what is wrong. The solutions which are sought are always economic, legal, or educational and never spiritual in nature. They cater for the individualism that is always inherent in reaching a secular answer to the problems of society. They always involve spending money instead of love.

What moral precepts we do have spring from somewhere. They do not just appear. Parents and schools are big influences, but traditional sources of moral ethics lurk in the shadows. We are trapped by the unconscious influences of a society steeped in centuries of religious teachings, a heightened contemporary consciousness of the right of individualism, and a wide-spread dislike of institutional religion.

Is it really necessary to have moral precepts in order to live well?

The answer must be positive if we are to have a solid foundation on which to build. Real values give us that groundwork.

What those values are is up to you, but in this book I have tried to put before you those things which over the ages in all cultures and great religions possessed the ability to make for truly contented living. Such living is an art and so moral and ethical values must be practiced on a day by day basis if they are to succeed. As I said, these matters belong in the realm of the spirit for they transcend the needs of the body and the thinking of the mind while catering for the needs of both.

Our spiritual life is not a haphazard affair. Creating this foundation for good living is serious and difficult and even more so in hard times, but its precepts are tools that can be used to create beneficial habits. They help us to strive toward ideals which transcend our economic, social, and political situations.

They bring us not just a sense of contentment with our life but that freedom which is called *dignity*.

After all, as another good cook, Elizabeth David, wrote: *What one requires to know about recipes is not so much do they work as what do they produce if they work?* What you are doing in this book is producing a life that is contented even though times are hard and you live, as everyone does now, in an increasingly disenchanted and cynical world.

The positive side to financial down-turns

Millions of people everywhere are discovering that there is a positive side to the financial plunge. They are being forced by new global economic circumstances to revalue their lifestyles and, much to their surprise, they are discovering riches which they never knew they had. Even the still wealthy are reviewing, if only very slightly, their conspicuous consumption. The economic water may be very cold and filled with the flotsam of worry and stress but the opportunity is there for you to swim to a different shore. A shore that is more secure, healthy and joyous with a contentment of being that no bank or politician or credit card company can take away from you.

How you swim to this shore will change your life. The first big dive into deep water is to reassess how you live and to become more self-reliant. It may surprise and shock you to find out what you *need* rather than what you *want* and how much you depend on outside sources to evaluate your life. Such discernments must arise from within you if they are to remain stable and sustaining. With every decisive stroke forward in your new way of living you get stronger and closer to that brighter shore. That place on the horizon of your new life is called *contentment*. It is the goal we dream of and when you find it, contentment will fill up your life like good wine in a beautiful glass. There is no quick fix in the art of such living.

We try our best and this is good

It is true that more and more people have been trying to live a different, less consuming lifestyle and that many movements have sprung up to help, such as organic and locally produced food, ecologically sound guides to greener living, and better health information. Magazines and newspapers are filled with advice about our carbon footprints and what we can do to save the planet. We buy self-help books that tell us there is an instant answer if we do this or that. We do try to do our bit. We put the scrap paper in one box, the empty bottles in another, the plastic in another. We cut down on waste food. We get a smaller car and try to use less petrol or go multi-fuel. We learn that healthy living does not happen at the doctor's office, but is achieved by the small decisions we make every day.

The average person does all this and more, yet usually winds up feeling that somehow it doesn't really account for much in the scheme of things. Life goes on as usual – or it does until a catalyst arrives as it did with the latest recession and subsequent real and potential revolutions arising from movements such as the Arab Spring in the Middle East and the Occupy Wall Street demos. But no matter what there are always good times and hard times. If we live contentedly in the hard times, we will surely live even happier in the good ones.

You are not alone and you are not "wrong"

You can suffer hard times through no real fault of your own at any time in any society. At the moment you may have fallen on hard times simply because you exist in a political and social system which made you a victim rather than a free, equal, and democratic citizen. You were just there, so you got caught. You may have done everything that was considered good and proper to a good life. You may have obeyed the precepts of capitalism but not become over-addicted to its consumerism. You had the right job, the right relationship, and put your priorities on concerns of family and friends. You felt safe and your guard was down. The long knives found you.

Solutions are local, not national

The American farmer, ecologist and essayist, Wendell Berry, puts great emphasis on the essentiality of local community and largely dismisses the contemporary notion of "the public". When we are trapped economically, our need of finding hope is not going to be met by "the public" except in temporary unemployment or housing benefits or some such other social support system, all of which is impersonal and basically faceless, whereas local community is not. Local community means family, neighbors and friends where you live. It is from these people that you will find the words, comfort, and energy to inspire your future.

We are repeatedly told by the media and research pundits that such "community" hardly exists and that the sense of family and its unity is enormously diminished – in fact rapidly disappearing. If we are looking at these things as we defined them fifty or a hundred years ago, certainly things have changed – but have they changed as much as the various social investigators and popular surveys would have us believe?

Nothing is new under the sun

When we ask ourselves some basic questions about living today, the picture we have been given seems at best only partially true and not nearly as bad as many would have us believe. For example, do sons and daughters love their parents any less today? Are we really estranged from our neighbours? Do we not belong in a place even if it is in a small apartment block where tenants come and go? An often repeated idea by the media and various books is that the paradox of modern life is that we may earn more money and enjoy a higher standard of life than previous generations, yet we work longer hours and are unhappier and more dissatisfied than previous generations. Is this true? The idea that previous generation did not get depressed, anxious, worried or dissatisfied with their lot is simply not true. Human characteristics have not changed much in millions of years. We continue to enjoy the benefits of fresh water, enough to eat, and shelter, but a large part of the world never has. For each obese American, there is a starving or diseased person who needs help. For each dissatisfied person, there is one who believes life is not so bad. We are told that the more we have the more we want. This is true but has it not always been so? The exploitation of people as "consumers" for the sake of money is not a new thing, only the scale of it. The trouble lies not in our human nature but in believing that many of our basic human characteristics are somehow "bad" or "sinful". In a secular society which has long since given up the concept of sin, it is hard to believe religion any longer prompts such belief. In any case, the capitalist economic system in which we live does not want us to be satisfied. It does not want us to be contented or not to desire the "more" of things. Contented people are usually poor shoppers.

How to judge the success of your life

In finding that peace and contentment for which we yearn, the problem rests with the way we judge the success of our life. The fact we may want "more" or to change things from time to time does not have to diminish our contentment because our sense of contentment is no longer measured by things outside of ourselves. When we understand and accept this even our desires are no longer problems but simply an element of our nature – not to be denied but to be kept in check and to be judged worthwhile or not by the morals and ethics around which we structure our behavior. These desires and the worldly standards by which success in life is measured do not then make up our value system and lifestyle. We are not blinded to reality. For example, if you feel self-esteem simply because friends flatter you, then you are accepting a value which is transient and has no lasting power in improving your life. On the other hand if you know flattery for what it is, your self-esteem is not involved and your inner peace not disturbed one way or the other – except perhaps to encourage you to have greater discernment in choosing your friends.

Such inner values and standards of living are difficult to maintain because the world is always inviting us to depend on contemporary ideals and fashions. We are asked to remain obedient in how we live and to leave judgments that matter to those who would govern our lives whether such are political, social or economic. However, we are not children and need to reclaim that full dignity which is the liberty of having our own standards for judging the success or otherwise of our lives.

Are you rich but just don't know it?

At this moment in your life you are truly rich. You may not think this is so and laugh at me, but I guarantee you that you possess great wealth. You may be going down the road toward claiming food stamps, receiving threatening letters about home repossession, and living surrounded by bad news from all over the world, yet I insist on saying *Fear not! You are rich! You have the will to live, an instinct to survive, and the courage to thrive.*

As if all this were not enough, you are rich beyond your wildest dreams for you are *alive*.

Understanding the values you live by

It is easy to understand that honesty or kindness can be part of the moral and ethical values by which we live, but it is less obvious that things like fresh air, playing, and sound sleep can also be part of such values.

However, closer examination of the things I write about in this book that make you poor or healthy and rich tell a different story. You will find how each thing is connected to enduring principles that enhance living, contribute to happiness, help build up the common good, and bring the possibility of contentment. For example, if we drink clean water it makes us healthier – but this is catering to the body which is only one aspect of ourselves. When we are truly mindful of that water it can lead us to think more deeply about this wonderful resource. In this way our minds become involved and eventually we may understand the spiritual dimension and significance of water. Then, water in all its forms can link us to the wider universe to which we belong. Such appreciation involving as it does our mind, body and spirit becomes part of how we choose to live. In this way, how we view and treat water is more than just an issue – it can become a moral and ethical value for us.

It is that straight-forward. We do not need to be philosophers or spiritual masters. We just need to seek positive changes in how we view our life and to find the grace to live those everyday values that bring personal contentment and social peace. Fresh air, sound sleep, eating real food, sharing, laughter, hospitality and other values discussed in this book make for a stable ease in living that raises you above your present circumstances. It is not just good living in hard times but good living *all* the time.

The reason you need to spend time on the things that make you poor is so that you can find what fragments your life. This enables you to deal with them so you are free to pursue those things which make you healthy and rich. Know your enemy is the key here.

Free will is your most powerful tool for change

Just as with all good cooking you cannot make a fine dish unless you start with the right ingredients, the same is true for your life. One must begin with quality and not quantity. The right start is to turn the mind to more important ideas and ideals. Here is where you will find the right ingredients to put into practice the art of a contented life.

At the moment you may not have freedom of action in determining the economics of your life but you do have free will. Here is the first basic ingredient for contentment. It is, if you like, the yeast in your bread of life. The rising up of your free will help you to succeed in hard times because what you can will for yourself is a change in the way in which you view your life. Here is where the mind and body are lead by your spirit.

This change of vision is not just to accommodate some passing situation no matter how difficult. It is to change the nature of how you look at the world and your life in it. It means nothing less than giving up the false security of how you presently live and to live afresh with values that are not about *having* but *being*. It is the recognition of the things that make you poor and the adoption of those things that make you healthy and rich. This is where free will becomes your most powerful tool for such life enhancing change. You alone must choose to act.

On the sense of independence

What is this curious sense of independence we all talk about? If it is about going and coming when one wants, even doves in the dovecot do that. If it is about playing music when one wants or going out without reference to others, then that is not about having independence but about *wanting to do what I want when I want to do it*. Little children do that. Constant movement in one's life dismantles any sense of stability. It usually defeats building structure and form in one's life and often brings no sense of lasting satisfaction. It is rarely productive in building lasting personal relationships.

This sense of independence for which contemporary people seem to have a great desire, can be a way of not admitting to yourself the need for constant diversion or novelty. It is a way of not living with yourself and of keeping your real feelings at a distance.

True independence should be a sense of the freedom of self, no matter where you are or what you may be doing. This kind of freedom arises from the inner being. It signifies that one is confident and assured as to who and what one is. It reflects an acceptance of self in the world and has nothing to do with social ease or good manners or being busy. This is why the political prisoner can be free and independent while locked away. *Know thyself* is the hardest goal in life. None of us can achieve it if we are constantly distracted.

Free yourself by the practice of the values given in this book. In this way you will find real independence.

The freedom that is hope

How is it that a man or woman unjustly imprisoned can still maintain hope? How can a person survive torture and still believe in any positive aspect of self or humanity? How did a holocaust victim manage to return to normal life? The answer is that hope was kept alive in their hearts. It is this kind of hope that was the fuel that kept alive the deep ember of life that was their will to live. If we lose hope, we lose everything – our ability to focus, find new values, concepts, understandings, and, finally, our compassion for ourselves and others. We must possess hope or all is truly lost.

Such hope is not necessarily based on some religious belief. If you have these kinds of beliefs and they sustain and give meaning to your life, then well and good. However, most of us simply cannot muster the religious perseverance to sustain such hope in the face of a situation which seems one of continuing defeat. Heroes are few and far between. Saints are even scarcer.

The place you need, the destiny you must work on, and where you must be reborn is *where you are at this very moment in time.* This is the place where you must find hope.

Despair is the same enemy whether you are unjustly imprisoned or simple trapped in a situation that brings you low. True poverty is being in a state of no hope and letting such despair rule your life. When our mind and body has been fractured and when our health is not at its best, what we need to know is how we can throw out despair and find hope to survive, heal, and come out in sufficient wholeness to begin again. The solution is to discover and put into practice a way of living that brings an inner sense of peacefulness. This is the state of being in which hope thrives.

The contentment of which I speak is not some kind of naïve or blind acceptance but an intelligent awareness that a essential part of your living a good life is in possessing hope which no one nor any situation can take away from you. A part of you that is never imprisoned. This is your spirit.

It is the spirit that is the strongest element in each of us so if your spirit can remain whole, then so can your mind and body. Invisible, ultimately indefinable, and not amenable to any of our scientific studies, the spiritual enables us, nevertheless, to have hope. With this one ingredient we can survive all the problems and injustices that the world throws at us. Here is the power you need to make it to that distant shore of contentment.

Hope is listening to your heart

Hope cannot exist in you unless your actions are fair and just. Inside every human being is a little voice. It used to be called the conscience and most people thought they had one or at least something like it. It told you what was right and what was wrong – or at least it made you so uneasy that you were forced to think about what you were doing. It was a voice urging discernment between what was positive and negative or morally "bad" or "good".

In Walt Disney's 1940 film of Pinocchio it took the form of a cricket called *Jiminy H. Cricket* who accompanies Pinocchio on his adventures, having been appointed by the Blue Fairy to serve as the official conscience for Pinocchio. He would warn Pinocchio not to tell a lie which would make his nose grow long. *Watch out! Careful now!* Jiminy would admonish.

While some people of faith still consider what their conscience tells them before they act, most of us today hardly listen to that little interior voice. We sometimes say, *Oh, I don't think I will do that – it doesn't feel right somehow.*

This intuition about what is the "right" action is what having a conscience is all about. It is when we decide not to do something that we feel is somehow "wrong". We may not even know the reason. We may not even know how it is "wrong". Such inner intuition is our conscience which is spiritual in nature and informed by our physical and emotional experiences.

Each of us has a Jiminy Cricket to help us along. When we listen to him, we are listening to what our heart tells us. *Listen! Listen!* This is what all of us must do. When you live a life of the values given in this book, you will find after a while that in such practice hope grows stronger and stronger. It wipes away your fears and makes your self-reliance a statement that satisfies your heart. You will find that like all crickets your Jiminy will sing too.

The harmony of the spirit

The benefits of paying attention to your spiritual life are legendary. It brings emotional, psychic, and physical healing. It connects us to the values we hold essentially true for our lives. It gives us a vision beyond just the tiny bit of the world we see and touch. Our bodies and our minds may be limited by time, but our spirit is an eternal force, as strong as the stars and as tender as a mother's touch. It is this spiritual aspect of ourselves which sustains a state of harmony within us and with everyone around us.

Do not waste your time discussing the pros and cons of religion or this or that spiritual path. Believe in God or believe what you will, but believe in something you surely will, for the existence of the spiritual is hard-wired into you. The form and belief it takes is up to you. Michael Graziano, Professor of Neuroscience at Princeton University, put it in a nutshell when he wrote that *eradicating religion is not possible. It is a fallacy that ignores the specs of the human machine. We are not rational entities. Religion grows on the social machinery in our brains.*

Unless you are a person of faith, I do not know where the grace you need to live a life well and with joy comes from and what this may mean to you, but I do know that the gratitude you will feel for a blessed life comes from within you. This recognition is your thanksgiving for being alive.

Spiritual desolation is the pitfall on our journey

Spiritual desolation happens when we turn away from the positive in our lives. Sometimes we become negative in such tiny ways that we are unaware of it until these negatives collect together like drops of rain and flood us with a sense of desolation. We then feel nothing is worthwhile, that life has no meaning and that all we do is futile and all our efforts at happiness are in vain. Our frustration and hopelessness grows so enormous that we decide finally that God, if he existed in the first place is permanently out to lunch. This makes for spiritual desolation. In such despair we have forgotten the universal and eternal aspect of our life, neglected the hope that knows no beginning and no end and, thus, we have denied love.

Hope and love are the promises of the eternal in our lives. Indeed, if we are divinely created and inspired as holy books tell us, then surely these two profound aspects of our humanity are the keys that open awareness of the universal oneness of life.

Thus, the vital action when you feel spiritual desolation and all seems lost is to flee from this desert of feeble self-concern and return as soon as possible to where you may recover in the embrace of the spirit. If you are a person of faith this means an immediate return to God. In any case whatever the inspiration, your return to the positive is a re-embracing of your spirit. This brings you hope.

The three thieves of our happiness

St. John Chrysostom declared that the worse pitfalls in our pilgrimage of life are anger, lust and over-consumption. These pitfalls, while not as important as spiritual desolation, defeat our hope of a more deeply realized life. Even fleeting happiness is quickly lost and contentment is never enjoyed.

Anger and rage exist not because of evil intentions and circumstances but because we are human. The most powerful expression of our anger is not our fist but our tongue. Here is the instrument of life and death. By it we praise or condemn. By it we lavish love or hate. Your spirit knows that hard words never bring peace but charitable ones revive every heart.

You can lust after anything and anyone. It does not have to be an object of sexual desire. In fact sexual desire might just be the easiest to give up. The Buddhist monk, Venerable Ajahn Sumedho, recorded the following about lust in his narratives of monastic life when he was a young novice and thought his new life of chastity would be too difficult to bear: *Food was highly restricted but one thing allowed was sugar. So then I found myself having a fantastic obsession with sweets while before I had not really cared about sweets at all. When word got around that we'd have cocoa, one could not think about anything else. I did not find sexual desire any problems in those days, because my obsessions were with sugar and sweets. I'd go to bed at night and dream about pastry shops.*

Lust in a million disguises underpins all obsessions and employs a full-time scout looking out for more of the same. This busy little searcher is called *Envy* who is always at work hunting for things we might lust after. Kill envy and lust is greatly diminished.

Anger, lust and over-consumption can be controlled by those moral and ethical habits which you have chosen to dictate how you live your life on a day to day basis. Repeated studies have shown it takes at least three weeks to establish any new habit, so don't think you can get to this new shore by just jumping in the water.

Begin to learn the art of contentment now

New beginnings are like sunrises when something unexpected may be illuminated. You are in such a place now. Learning to do anything well calls for practice and the same is true of the exercise of moral and ethical habits if they are to work. This means discipline and perseverance which most of us are not very good at now-a-days and inclined to dislike. However, even if you never reach perfection, keep trying.

Begin then to learn what to avoid because it makes you poor and what to practice because it makes you healthy and rich. None of us can be perfect in all these things but what matters is that we don't give up trying. Gradually you will move toward a place of contentment with your life. You may not acquire much. You may not find many material changes. Family and friends may think you indifferent to troubles when they see you rising calmly above your present circumstances. Accept all these as simply the scenery in your journey and pay them no heed. Continue to build up the values that will serve your true happiness. Fear nothing and be happy.

THINGS THAT MAKE YOU POOR

OVER-CONSUMPTION

The enemy of consumerism is a satisfied and content person, because she does not need to acquire anything more.
Lynn Casteel Harper, American Baptist minister.

We are as much consuming creatures as a monkey or a lion. It is in our nature to consume. How much we consume is about how we live out that natural instinct. In this era of increased plenty for so many people, we have created a situation of over-consumption. If you are having a hard time making ends meet, you might think you do not fit into such a category. After all, aren't you trying to get by on less not more?

Think again for the problem still exists in one form or the other for you. Regardless of our financial situation, we are slaves to consuming. It doesn't matter whether this is about food or possessions. Our lives are cluttered and this creates an enormous amount of "baggage" which we carry. It is a physical and emotional burden that none of us need or want in our lives. It costs money we do not have. Moreover, it makes us victims of a system that promotes profits, not our happiness and contentment. Doing something about such over-consumption is very difficult since we live in a society built around ever-increasing consumer buying. We are not encouraged to just *be* but *to have.* The result for most people is a false sense of security, a sense of lack of meaning to life or, if you are on hard times, a desperate feeling that you are a failure and being left on the sidelines of successful living.

We have become not just consumers of need, but consumers of greed. This disparity between what we need and what we want boils down into two categories of consumption: our food and our possessions.

Food and over-consumption

Everybody knows that the consumption of food is a basic fact of living. Paradoxically, the amount of food we buy has increased until we have reached a state of over-consumption so dangerous to our health that governments have programmes to help us. These are the same governments who support the economic system that created the problem in the first place. There is little we can do except to eat *real food*, which I discuss in more detail in the section on *Things that make you healthy*. Such personal action as I suggest is both a political statement that collectively could affect our economic system for the better and a change of lifestyle that helps us to live well even in hard times.

No matter the place, culture or religion, the procurement, preparation, and consumption of food underpins the economic and social life of every community. In isolated communities and in those suffering chronic poverty, most of the day is traditionally taken up with obtaining food by some kind of work whether directly agricultural or not. This is how it was a hundred years ago for our own forefathers. In our time, one estimate of progress that economists make is based on the hours we must work against the cost of basic foodstuffs. Over the last century the amount of time we spend working in order to get food has continually fallen as has the price of that food. *Hurrah!* you might say but the news is not all good.

The problem is that we not only eat too much food, we also buy too much. At every turn in supermarkets and shops we are urged to buy. In the end, we stuff ourselves and our kitchen cupboards full of food we don't need – and often we don't even use. If you doubt me, check out your cupboards now and see what is past its use-by date or what has been sitting there unused for years. I try to do such an inspection regularly so what is on hand is only for an emergency meal. I continue to fail to achieve this tidy, only-what-I-need cupboard. I particularly do not understanding how I always windup with two unopened out-of-date packets of dried bread crumbs or a half-eaten bag of crisps left over from the last World Cup Match – never mind the two jars of six year old peanut butter I found hiding behind a package of macaroni.

Don't think that obesity is only an American phenomenon. The European Commission report, *Health at a Glance Europe 2010*, showed that in Britain almost 25 percent of the population is obese with Ireland at 23 percent, and even the small states of Malta and Luxembourg manage to be on the list of the too fat countries. You might think that a national habit of eating a lot of fish and doing plenty of outdoor sports would let a country off this obesity list – but Norway and Sweden weigh in with some 10 percent of their people now overweight. The obesity health problem is now global. We *all* eat too much and most of it is junk or highly processed food.

Our attention to this problem needs not just to be directed at our own habits, but the eating habits we are instilling in our children. The simple fact is that our obese and over-weight children have a greater risk of developing heart disease, diabetes, cancer, arthritis, asthma, and even of premature death. The solution begins at home with us as parents. If we are finding the times economically hard then we have an additional strong motivation to start reducing our over-consumption and begin eating wholesome food. If you have kids, do it for their sake. If not, then do it for your cat or dog because chances are if you are overweight so are your pets.

Is over-consumption ever a good thing?

There are times when the over-consumption of food is part of good living. These are our feasts, fetes, and celebrations. When we enjoy ourselves in this way we expect to consume more food and drink than usual, because they are the essential components of any kind of party. We collectively hold special images about food when we celebrate. Such collectivity may be that of a nation, say Thanksgiving Day in America or of a family for a Wedding Anniversary or birthday or that of a religion like Christmas or the Festival of Lights at Hanukkah. On these occasions over-consumption has a proper place in our lives. Such food is the reward for honest labour. In Christianity, this translates into the spiritual principle that God *nourishes* the soul in exchange for our *good works* which are our acts of charity. Saint Paul pointed out that we should work for our food and not leave it to others to provide for us.

In this way a spiritual concept is interwoven with our concept of food as a special reward for work. Indeed, the so called *Protestant Work Ethic,* which has contributed greatly to the historic vigour of American material progress, springs from this religious principle. My father, an American, advised me that *if a man hires you for a dollar per hour, then give him your best full hour.* Mind you in those days a dollar went a long way. Now you can't even buy a burger for it. Still, the principle remains one that promotes our integrity and dignity. The majority of people need to feel independent and this is why long-term unemployment can have such a devastating effect.

In playing such a vital role in our celebratory and spiritual occasions, food marks out the characteristics of a family or community and serves to unify it. From the Christian Eucharist celebration with wine and bread to a neighbourhood BBQ party, our public consumption of food manifests itself in all aspects of our social existence. The anthropologist Victor Turner believes that such public celebrations involving food have a two-fold purpose. He feels it reinforces the structures of a community and at the same time creates a sense of community by those celebrating, increasing a sense of belonging with the effect of creating harmony. This is why we often feel happier and more positive after such celebrations. In the New Testament it is surprising how often we are told about Jesus going to some feast or banquet or wedding. He celebrated lots of good times with other people. He was a man poor in possessions but perfect in spirit. Happy occasions engender a spiritual energy which brings people closer together. Indeed, many couples who eventually marry met at a wedding or special event.

Sharing of food in this ritualistic and celebratory way is an acceptable form of eating and drinking too much, because such over-consumption is occasional, positive in its effect, and part of the weaving of our human social fabric. It is a special treat and not for everyday. The British broadcaster and author Joan Bakewell beautifully summed it up this way: *In houses and hotels, palaces and farmsteads, in tents and yurts, in hostels and care homes, on liners and yachts, in igloos and palm huts people come together for food. The moment they do, they are taking time out - from work, from endeavour, from hunting or trading, from learning or teaching, from making money, from spending money to enjoy one of the most primitive rituals known to man – the shared meal.*

Possessions

Most of us are over-whelmed with possessions. Half the stuff we have we don't need and are rarely if ever going to actually use. What can we do? In a Carmelite convent in Wales, I discovered how the sisters there managed to keep personal possessions to a minimum. It was rather drastic and not one most of us would even want to try – but it does contain the kernel of a splendid idea. Each year every sister had to move herself and her possessions into a new room – and here comes the crunch – *and get rid of ten percent of her stuff.* If you think this is easy, just try it. You will find you are more attached to useless junk than you ever thought possible.

People often claim one of the great benefits of moving house is the opportunity it gives to clear out junk. This can work except usually within a year the new place is just as badly loaded up with things we don't need or use. Cleaning up the garage, the store room, or the attic are jobs that we almost always find a reason to postpone. Unlike the nuns in Wales there is no Mother Superior who will order us to clean out the results of our over-consumption – yet if we do it the benefits are considerable and not just in making your home a neater, less cluttered environment. The benefits can serve the good health of our mind, body and spirit.

Too many possessions can be a great burden and not just in the physical sense. They can be part of the mental and emotional baggage we carry around and it is a weary load. Look around yourself now. How much of your litter could be thrown away? Open the clothes wardrobe. Does anyone *really* need that many clothes? Having all these possessions, even when they are expensive or designer inspired, does not make you richer. If you don't actually need them and don't use them, then they make you poor because their existence weighs you down. They are extra baggage you don't need to carry. If you want to feel really good about your possessions then sort them out, keep what you really need or like, and give the rest away. Some people would argue that, if you are on hard times, getting rid of possessions is the last thing you should do. Don't believe them. How are old handbags, shoes, sweaters, magazines, and all the rest of the things we keep but never use or wear anymore really going to help you live better in hard times? Does such stuff make you feel richer? I think it is more likely all this stuff is going to make you remember you don't have the money to buy new things and this can make you sad.

Simple living is what you need if money is scarce. Start getting a simpler life by clearing out and cleaning up wherever you live. A room is bigger if it is tidy. Two tidy rooms will increase your sense of peace. Do it to a whole house and you have space you never knew you had. An increased sense of space can bring multiple benefits. For example, a sense of order in your life is emotionally helpful. It increases physical comfort as well as bringing a feeling that your life is a calm one even if the world outside is chaotic.

A little bit of *regular* organization makes a home easier to live in – especially when you have kids. When my own children were small, each had a toy box in which at the end of the day they put the things they were playing with. To be fair I had a box too. So we were all equal in doing this family clean-up. A night-time raid on the fridge meant you did not fall over something on the stairs or step on a toy in the dark. In any case, if you want a good life, then whatever new routines, ideas, and habits you develop, you need to include your children if you have any. Please note that nagging your children to be tidy is *not* a good idea because it causes resentment and makes them unhappy. Do not command them but ask them to help you. Politeness is not something reserved for adults only.

How did we get to be such extra-ordinary consuming creatures?

Karl Marx had a few good ideas and plenty of bad ones about how society could best work. One of his better notions was that we suffer from what he called *false consciousness.* He felt this was a state in which as individuals we are ideologically blinded to the domination we suffer. For example, we succumb to over-consumption and do not recognize that we have been duped into buying into a system which exploits us. Thus, we are dominated and manipulated.

This is exactly what the present economic system does, based as it is on judging our society's progress and monetary health by how much people spend. If such a system worked, we would not have depressions, periodic massive unemployment, and recurring global monetary crises. We would not have people scraping by with an ever increasing number of people falling into poverty while a few people get richer by the minute. If such consumerism was a truly successful formula for society we would not be dispirited and scared of our future. Instead, we would be people of good spirit and high hopes. We would not be afraid.

This epidemic of consumption which the whole world now suffers has well-known psychological and sociological consequences. For example, there is an established connection between an excessively materialistic outlook and increased levels of depression and anxiety. Many professional investigators of the way we live argue that the real price we are paying for such consumerism is the loss of those essential things that make for a strong and supportive community life. Such essentials include our friends and neighbours. The author, Annie Leonard, believes with an increasing number of people including myself that our obsession with possessions is directly destroying the planet. The message to consume, consume, consume *is* that dangerous.

One important aspect that makes this worse is that we have become such over-developed consumers that when we are faced with really important and vital issues, such as climate change or depletion of natural resources, we decide as long as we stop buying *this* and buy *that* instead, then everything will be okay. In other words, we still consume but simply change what we consume when the basic and real problem is our habit of constant consumption. The extent of this kind of habit is more than individual or even national. It is world-wide.

For example, the creation of global carbon trading markets is seen as a great way to accommodate developing countries and still satisfy the economically advanced nations. Corporate business and financial traders see this as a potentially good investment while environmentalists dither, unsure if it is the best way to combat global warming. In reality the whole scheme is another way of changing consumption from one form to another.

We are still pursuing the same economic goals in the same formula. We appear not to know when or how to stop consuming the earth as if it was a gigantic supermarket of resource products. Sadly, there is no political or social will to change this fact. As Karl Marx suggested we are indeed blinded to our enslavement to a system that has seduced us into believing more is better.

Over-consumption and the spiritual life

Over-consumption is a formidable hindrance to the spiritual life. Such a habit used to be called *gluttony.* This word with its original meaning, which includes the idea of personal corruption, needs a return to daily use, because gluttony is not simply about over-eating and over-drinking. It is also about indulging ourselves so much that we lose all sense of satiety not just for food to satisfy hunger but for other important aspects of living that make us individually healthy and whole and contribute to the good of others. Gluttony in any form fills us up and suffocates our spirit. It is bad for us, our friends, neighbours, and community life. It is not possible to continue this way when you are trying to make ends meet. If you have encountered hard times then you need to understand that *more is better* is not the slogan you need. What slogan you need to understand is *less is more.* This goes against everything capitalism has taught you since you were born.

Here are a few questions to help you discern and test your current level of gluttony:

1. Do you have a compulsion to go shopping?
2. Do you buy lots of gifts for others to show them how you feel about them?
3. Do you graze all the time, nibbling this, drinking that?
4. Do you worry all the time about getting ahead in life?
5. Do you have a closet full of clothes you never wear?
6. Do you think keeping up with your neighbours is okay?

7. Finally, do you think you *deserve* to enjoy life?

If you answered yes to the first question, then you needed to go no further since you have already got a bad case of gluttony. Over-consumption is what you do.

What do the above questions really mean in terms of living a good life?

Possessions do not tell people how you feel. They may help, of course, to define your character in some way but do they represent the true feelings of your heart? Do they say aloud what you feel? For example, the lover who gives a bouquet of roses is much appreciated but then when did a gesture of flowers ever replace these three little words: *I love you?*

When it comes to food – question 3 above – what we eat is more than energy to keep life going. It is symbolic of life and an expression of love, because we cannot live without food and the preparation and serving of it to others and the taking of food together is a unifying force between people and helps forge strong bonds of affection and understanding. If you said *yes* to questions 4, 5, or 6 then you are a true modern consumer. The sooner you stop feeding the system with the limited money you have, the sooner you will start to live a good life because you will be freed from much of your consumer slavery. You will replace superficial values about life with moral ones that nourish who and what you are as a person.

In a world in which we believe we have endless *rights* and where our individualism comes before any sense of community or what benefits society, the last question is one few ask themselves today. As far as I am concerned if you think you have a right to material possessions then you have an overblown sense of self-entitlement. You are in deep trouble, because those who claim such as a right most often show little concern for others and a lot of resentment if they don't get what they want. No matter how much you have been seduced by commercial interests from cosmetics to cars into thinking you have a right to possess something – you don't.

We may all deserve happiness, that fleeting come and go sense of pleasure, but God and the Universe are not going to automatically supply it. We must make an effort too. When we stop being victims to a system that treats us as fodder for profits, when we refuse to over-consume, when we take the running of our lives into our own hands and ignore all the blandishments to buy and possess, we can begin at long last to live in liberty. We have told the god of indulgence to go away. We are guarding our happiness and our pocketbook.

NOVELTY

What does "novelty" mean today? It is a word we hardly hear anymore. Before the First World War, it was in common usage and often referred to odd little objects that were new and unusual – items not to be found in a general store of that time but in specialty shops. Special ribbons, buttons, silks or lace are just a few examples. Many British department stores still use the term to define a particular section where you might find such things. When I first arrived in London in the late fifties, I remember having great difficulty finding out where to buy a pair of leather gloves in the vast Army & Navy Store near Victoria Station. *You will find them in the Novelty Department, Sir,* was what I was told. I had no idea what this meant but after much searching I found this section of the store. The multitude of unrelated items on display, including gloves, was fascinating for someone just arrived from Mexico where every little shop sold just one kind of thing. For me, this Novelty Department was an Aladdin's Cave.

Such shops hardly exist anymore except online, but novelty is still with us. Now it means something that diverts our attention, entertains us for awhile, and general relieves the dullness or boredom of our day. In other words something novel is still that which for us is odd, unusual, and not available all the time. It is something new, entertaining and interesting which captures our imagination or attention. Unfortunately, such a novelty is time limited. It can be for a few days but it is usually only for a few hours before we long for something new. Our amusement span as well as our attention span grows shorter and shorter.

The days are long gone when anyone could write as did that amusing eighteenth century author, Sydney Smith: *What a pity it is that we have no amusements in England but vice and religion.* Today with contemporary social liberation little is left that anyone would call vice. Even the words *mistress* and *lover* have been replaced in ordinary conversation by that multi-definition term *partner*. As to religion, church attendance continues to fall and we mostly speak of *spirituality* as the word *God* is presently out of fashion in the West.

However, we still spend a lot of our time and money seeking the novelty of amusements because we suffer from a surfeit of possessions and information and so hunger for that which is new. Anything which diverts us from our routines and from our deeper feelings about our life. Some of this diversion, of course, serves a good purpose. Weekly swimming or gym workouts or games of badminton, tennis or squash do a lot not just for our health but for stimulating mind and spirit. It is when we continually seek new stimulation and constantly change from one activity or interest to another that novelty becomes something that makes us poor.

It is not just people living an ordinary life that can be affected by the need for novelty. It can be a problem even for nuns and monks who are suppose to be pursuing a life of inner tranquility and satisfaction. Novelty serves them in the same way as it does for you and me. The rituals and routines in such religious communities go on day in and day out – the same routines for years. So it is understandable that even nuns and monks should still hunger for that which disrupts the sameness of such daily life. A new guest, a visiting lecturer, some new music, a surprise at Sunday lunch – anything in fact which amuses and diverts is welcomed. We suffer from similar feelings and often for similar reasons arising from boredom with our routines.

Feeling bored is, therefore, something we all suffer occasionally, but when it becomes a dominant feature of our life, then we need to deal with it. Turning again to the religious life, when in early monastic days they had a monk restless for the novelty of change, the wise abbot would order the monk to stay in his cell. *The cell cures everything* was a common understanding in those days, having arisen early in the Christian hermit tradition.

This advice might enjoy a rewarding revival today in our own lives. Can you image saying to yourself: *Sit down. Stay put. Novelty is no solution. All will pass.* It could just work for you because what you are asking is that you *endure*. Endurance is about patience and waiting. How you feel will pass. It always does, because constant change is in the nature of how we think. Your mind, then your body will move onto different issues and feelings. This practice of enduring is a spiritual one and it brings calmness and acceptance.

Today, everyone seems to be looking for calmness. Acceptance and patience, which are essentials of calmness, are in short supply these days too. A woman I know up in a Welsh valley – and she is not the exception – can hardly sit still if someone is boring her. Her favourite expression as to how she feels in such a situation is: *I could have killed her!* She does not mean it literally of course, but she has a very limited supply of patience as do most modern people. Sitting down and not being distracted or entertained and just being quiet involve acceptance and patience. Like my Welsh friend, not only can most folk not do this, but they do now know *how* to do it. Patience like acceptance is not within their ability anymore, because novelty is the magic ingredient they desperately long for. It keeps them from any deeper awareness of how they actual feel about their life.

The evergreen novelties of sexuality & spirituality

Without doubt sexuality and spirituality can both act as novelties. Just as men and woman can find momentary novelty in the sexual thrills of chance encounters and in one night stands, so they can shop around and experience different spiritual encounters. Age usually helps dampen down the frequency of the sexual encounters but spiritual practices are having a field day for people of every age. Practically everything we read about has some spiritual connection, no matter how tenuous. When we constantly aspire *to find ourselves* or actualize *the real me,* spiritual practices from meditation and yoga to bible study and prayer groups can all turn into novelties. Just something else that amuses us for a little while. Many people become addicted to these new experiences and seek ever new ones. However, we miss the whole point of what a spiritual practice might offer us in terms of improved well-being and self-awareness if it is simply yet another novelty. In any case, the passing excitement of novelty, whether sexual or spiritual, often masks the real reasons we seek it. As I have said earlier, constant novelty keeps us in the dark about real awareness of ourselves. Equally, it demeans the deep feelings we may encounter in our sexuality and spirituality. It makes superficial what is profound.

The novelties of place

Our home should be our castle - a place of firm foundation, a safe refuge, and a defined space in which we are truly comfortable. This does not happen when you move house or apartment on a regular basis. Naturally some must do this as their work demands such change, but for most it is the answer to an inner restlessness. It is a seeking for the novelty that invites you to believe that the grass is greener in the next pasture. The solution is to move home yet again. It is a form of running away from yourself. The new place is attractive precisely because it involves novelty – new things to buy, new decorations to do, new arrangements to explore, new people and neighbours to meet. It is all exciting, but very emotionally and physically exhausting. In fact the level of stress in moving house is one of the greatest we face in ordinary living. In causing psychological distress it comes only after the death of a loved one in terms of severity, and well before those other major life events like loss of your job, grave illness, and divorce.

So when you undertake moving your home, think carefully. The next pasture is not necessarily greener or much different. From an economic point of view, such changes usually do not result in saving you any money. On the contrary, moving means finding extra cash above your usual out-goings. If you do move to a much cheaper rental property, eventually it may make economic sense – but you will still suffer some degree of stress. Unless your new home is just down the street, you lose immediate contact with nearby friends and family. This does not help you live a good life.

What does home mean to you?

In *The Wind in the Willows* tale, Mole loses his *Home Sweet Home* to the bad weasels. He is despondent for he is thrown out into unfamiliar surroundings. He has no place to call his own. We all need such a place whether it is a grand mansion or a humble cottage or a single room. It is said that home is where the heart is. So what *does* home mean to you? When you begin to answer this question you may find feelings that matter in familiar surroundings, friends and family members. The shops you use, the streets you walk down, the familiar faces you pass in the street, even big supermarkets – all these things give a sense of familiarity. This brings a feeling of security. It is a measure of the richness of your life if you recognize the importance of just being able to walk down your street and say *Good Morning* to people. They may not be close friends but you recognize each other as belonging to that same general place. This kind of familiarity builds up your feelings of belonging. One example I can think of is when you live in grand cities like London, Paris or New York. The area where you live becomes your *village* with its own special features, customs, delights, and problems. When my children were small, we lived in the Italian section of central

London. There were Italian shops and a local Italian Catholic church and school. It was noisy, alive with life and thriving in its own special Italian-English culture. Then one day the local authorities decided to raze all the old apartment buildings and little row houses and build office blocks. Gone were all the joys of living in *our* village. It had been turned from a living culture into a dehumanized, efficient place of profit. Before you give up your *Home Sweet Home* for the short lived novelty of a new place, remember that you need to belong to a place you know.

The roots that make us

Some years ago I wrote about the culture of place in a book, *Living the Sacred*. I find I have not changed my mind about its importance. I think that if we are to make our lives a celebration we must live in harmony with nature. It is helpful if we understand how much the environments where we grew up and where we now live affect us.

When someone speaks of *the environment*, it seems to me a foreign thing, distinct from anywhere I recognize. What I do have is a sense of place: *this* present place where I feel the cool night wind sweeping down from the Pyrénées, *that* childhood place where I remember the steam ferry leaving for San Francisco, *any* place where the cry of a barn owl brings forth the memory of my grandfather's farm. We are always planted in the present and in the past. Whatever you are when you are being yourself cannot be separated from where you are – that place of now yet also the past places of yesterday. This mixture of the present and past determines the vision and understanding you have of yourself in the world. It reinforces your sense of uniqueness while reaffirming that you belong somewhere. This helps enormously in making you feel that you and your life have continuity and reality.

Naturally, where you have grown up and where you now live

greatly influences the kind of roots you have. An urban living person does not usually feel the same as someone living rurally because her roots have grown in a totally human-made place. This makes it easy for the urban person to be alienated from nature and to have a sense of place that is defined by human life in the city. When so much seems human-made it can be hard to see that there is a universal perspective to life.

Somewhere between the rural and urban dweller is that twentieth century phenomenon, the suburban person. Rejecting the city life, finding fault with the harsher practicality and rough manners of rural life, the suburban dweller longs for a nature that is romantic but tidy. The result is nostalgia. Such a person usually wants the world to be *comfortable.* Since the essence of Nature is unpredictability and change, this makes the reality of the creation around us a problem for most suburban people. But such folks, like all of us, keep trying. British media often have articles about country type living in the city and suburbs. Not just city farms run for visitors, but windowsill herb and vegetable growing, country crafts done in town, making an allotment – in fact everything which bring a bit of country living into city or suburban life. The average French man or woman is well-known to keep alive the romantic flame of rural living in their hearts, escaping there as often as possible and defending it at all costs, yet still paradoxically clinging to an urban habitation.

Try asking yourself a few pertinent questions about where you live: Are you an Urban, Rural or Suburban person? What is the reality of the place you are in now? What does this mean to you? How does this connect you to other people? How does this connect you to Nature?

A better understanding of the roots that connect you to the place you live or the place where you would like to live will tell you a great deal about your true feelings. Such awareness is practical because it helps you rationalize where you are now and to try to make that a comfortable acceptance. If you already feel where you are is right for you, then rejoice at such a blessing.

Looking around for things to celebrate

No matter what your roots or your sense of place or how gentle or rough your neighbourhood, you can still celebrate whatever you find there: the colour and excitement of busy streets and the delight of the sheer glass walls of a skyscraper at sunset; the embrace of a small house with its familiar and supportive smells and memories; a place where the neat rows of tulips bloom with the same beauty as in the far land of their origin; a moment in the sun when the sweat of your garden labours burns into your eyes and you are grounded in the earth.

Reverence is born in accepting that we are of earth and knowing we are shaped by the land of our birth. Neither poverty nor great wealth changes this essential truth. Here is an important key that unlocks the door to contentment and discards the false promises of novelty.

DISTRACTION

From background music to mobile phone apps, today's supply of distractions is limitless. We can do so much– texting, tweets, emails, music apps, TV, online films and videos, electronic games, checking out websites and much more. We believe that most of this is in aid of keeping in touch with friends and events and being "busy" Actually, the reasons do not matter. We are people with the biggest choice in history of things and activities that can keep us occupied. Such occupations, however, are almost all some form of distraction. The ancient Roman Circus was used to keep the public entertained so they didn't think about what was happening politically and socially. Our modern distraction serves the same purpose. It diverts our attention away from important aspects of ourselves and those of our society to rather meaningless information or entertainment in the same spirit as the old Roman Circus events. I suppose that if Marie Antoinette, the French queen, who reportedly responded to her people's cry for bread with the suggestion they eat cake instead, were alive today she would just tell disgruntled citizens to go buy some new DVDs or watch a game show. Diversions give us temporary relief from a whole bag of emotional and relationship problems as well as drawing our attention away from important aspects of our life.

What I am calling distractions are regarded by most people as just part of the tools and past-times of contemporary life. Is my condemning such distractions nonsense? People have always liked a bit of distraction to make their lives more interesting or fun and to give some meaning to the dullness of most day to day life and in moderation that can do us little harm - but modern distraction has become an easy addiction. Here is the core problem and why modern distraction makes you poor. Like any addiction, it results in harm to mind, body and spirit. It is one of the major reasons we feel over-whelmed and that our lives are fragmented. Such feelings cannot lead you to good living even in the best of times.

Most retreat places, whether monastic, church lead, faith-based, alternative spirituality, or healing and therapy based, ask that guests not use mobiles, iPods and laptops. What they are trying to create for their guests by this rule is the opportunity not to be distracted and to find in just being quiet a sense of inner calm. Most people who are going on retreat find it very hard to give up these modern distractions because they are addicted to them. Such addiction can be social communication, music to ameliorate loneliness, or simply fiddling around on the web. Some people are so addicted to their distractions that they go home after the first day of a retreat. Think of a man using a crutch and you take it away. He is likely to fall down. The same thing happens when we are addicted to distraction and suddenly stop. The structure of distraction that we use to mask our inner feelings falls apart and we are left with a void. In that inner void we can encounter truths about ourselves. Some are good and some are dark. We don't like going to this interior place if it suggests we are not perfect.

Cutting back on distractions is not easy

What can we do to stop or at least cut down on distraction in our lives? For me the answer lays in living a simpler life. A life that is not filled with useless activities which serve no real purpose. A life where what we do and what we possess is what we need. More than a century ago, the American nature writer Henry David Thoreau wrote, *our life is frittered away by detail ... simplify, simplify.* In one single phrase he stated the real problem of distraction and the real solution to it.

Are you feeling fragmented? Do you feel your day disappeared in a flash and left you feeling unsatisfied? Are you always trying to catch up on what you have to do? How many times a day do you check your emails or Facebook or Twitter? Are you often short tempered when the kids interrupt what you are doing? When your mobile or landline phone rings do you *always* have to answer it right away? If such things are true for you, then perhaps you are in a state of distraction and, as Thoreau suggested, your life is being frittered away.

It is not easy to cut away the distraction in our lives. It truly takes courage to slow down the pace at which we live so we can live more simply. The solution to *simplify, simplify* is hard to do.

Here is what one young man said about the effects of his too-busy life style: *I suffered a pretty dramatic burnout several years ago. I was keeping a frenetic pace at work and in my personal life. I was working 90 hours a week at a stressful job. When I wasn't working, I was out socializing. I only went home to sleep for a few hours, and then I'd be up doing it all over again. My thinking at the time was "I'm young, I can handle it. Life is short, make the most of it! Unfortunately, the lifestyle caught up with me… At the age of 24, I crashed and burned… my "always connected" lifestyle got the best of me.* A lot of young people, if open about how they feel, might confess to similar feelings as this young man.

Advertising, marketing and media tell us it is great to be always connected. This advice helps sell products and services but does little to enrich our lives either as individuals or as a social community. The truth is that to be *always connected* is to be distracted and, worse, to be at risk of a kind of separation from the intimacy of family and friendships which depends in large measure on being physically together. Talking to someone on the mobile or texting is not enough. It is not as emotionally enhancing or as informative as a face to face conversation and social inter-action.

There is not an easy, quick solution to distraction as a lifestyle. No addiction is like that. If you want to live more simply so hard times turn into good times and you are feeling overwhelmed by life and unfocused, then you need some ways to help you recover from your addiction. There is no magic pill. No quick fix. You need to take appropriate action – and stick to it.

Tools for beating your addiction to distractions

As in all addiction recovery programmes, your first step to conquering your distraction habit is to admit you are in trouble and that you have a problem. When you have done this then move on to some techniques which will help you bridge the gap between how you are now and how you want to be in the future – which in this case is focused, fully present to the moment, unstressed, and not at all anxious with a sense that time is on your side. One outstanding practice to help you achieve this is being mindful.

Mindfulness

Mindfulness is being aware of the exact present time you are experiencing. It is the observance of what is happening right now in your life. Founder of the Mindfulness-Based Stress Reduction program at the University of Massachusetts Medical Center, Jon Kabat-Zinn's definition of mindfulness is direct and shows it can be practiced by everyone: *Mindfulness means paying attention in a particular way; on purpose, in the present moment, and non-judgmentally.*

But how do we tell the difference between being mindful and just thinking about something?

Bhante Henepola Gunaratana, founding abbot of the Bhavana Society, a Buddhist community in America, explains how different mindfulness is from either memory or thinking: *If you are remembering your second-grade teacher that is memory. When you then become aware that you are remembering your second-grade teacher, that is mindfulness. If you then conceptualize the process and say to yourself, "Oh, I am remembering", that is thinking.*

A Buddhist practice over the last 2500 years, mindfulness has become a proven tool in the West for helping to keep us focused on what we are doing, seeing or hearing at the time it occurs. It is a popular and increasingly widely known practice. It is now used in the field of psychological medicine and therapy. Scott R. Bishop of the Centre for Addictions and Mental Health and the Department of Psychiatry at the University of Toronto, claims that in the last 20 years, 'mindfulness' has become the focus of considerable attention by a large community of clinicians. He explains that because we are not really fully aware of our thoughts, they wander in an unrestricted way without purpose and that *having the purpose of staying with our experience, whether that's the breath, or a particular emotion, or something as simple as eating, means that we are actively shaping the mind.*

So in the practice of mindfulness we bring our minds into the here and now. We are alive to the moment. The experience we are having is what is important. This kind of focus is paying strict attention to the activity in which we are engaged and not allowing our monkey minds to go off leaping here and there through the endless jungle of our thoughts. Such focus keeps us in the present moment – the *now* of our life. This where you want to be because it limits how much you are distracted.

The book market and websites including excellent on-line courses are flooded with instructions to help you learn to be mindful. When you are focused in this way you do not feel overwhelmed because you are taking life a step at a time. There is no confusion and so an inner serenity can arise. This is an awesome help in hard times when we seem to have endless worries and must face dramatic changes to our lives. Maggie Jackson, a writer for the Boston Globe and author of *Distracted: The Erosion of Attention and the Coming Dark Age*, says, *The way we live is eroding our capacity for deep, sustained, perceptive attention – the building block of intimacy, wisdom, and cultural progress. Moreover, this disintegration may come at great cost to ourselves and to society ....The erosion of attention is the key to understanding why we are on the cusp of a time of widespread cultural and social losses.*

By limiting the stream of thoughts going in and out of your mind, you do not need to be distracted. You do not need to continuously respond to your family, friends, and the world at large. You can let go of the need to always stay updated. You can ignore your email in-box when you want to. You do not need to check out your Face book wall. You do not need to be always connected.

A quick sampling of current research on the benefits of mindfulness for body and mind shows hundreds of examples demonstrating its effectiveness. An American study from the Cleveland Clinic reported that mindfulness decreased negative emotions and increased well-being in people at risk from coronary heart disease. A Swedish study found mindfulness based cognitive therapy caused a 42 percent reduction in the primary symptoms of irritable bowel syndrome – a common modern Western complaint. Remission of depression, lessened time for substance abuse recovery, and higher thresholds of pain have all been shown as positive outcomes of mindfulness by research at respected institutions from the Massachusetts Medical School to Oxford University.

Mindfulness could be the answer to an addiction to distraction. It can help us to learn what we really need in life and give us the courage to discard that which is unnecessary, irrelevant, and unworthy whether it be habits of distraction or possessions – and, dare one say, even friendships that may fall into such categories.

The great thing about practicing mindfulness is that it helps to actually change your brain – and for the better! At long last not only can we shed the multiple distractions that fragment us, but we can start on a journey to wholeness in mind, body and spirit. Learning to be mindful is that important for surviving the hurdles of contemporary life whether in good or bad times.

Meditation

Meditation is a way of letting go of your worries and for releasing yourself from the constant activities, ideas and emotions of the mind and the body. It is a way to clear out the unquiet, to clean up the self and to use your inner space to become calm and refreshed and restart your life. If you want to learn to be mindful and get over an addiction to distraction, then meditation is a path that will lead you there. It is an ancient practice that has become a modern method for returning yourself to a calm and tranquil state. You do not have to be spiritually-minded or religious to practice meditation and to have positive benefits from it.

For example, I go to a weekly group meditation in my village. These men and women are from all walks of life. What they have in common is a sense of self-fragmentation and a lack of focus. Over the course of the last year, all have found benefits in the simple meditations we do together. These focus on emptying the mind of anxious thoughts and worries and finding an inner peacefulness and are not connected to any particularly spiritual tradition or religious path. Afterwards the benefits seem to last with people for a number of days. One of our group, Emily, a mother of two teenagers, summed it up this way: *I don't know what I would do without this group. I feel so much more calm and focused. Now when I do something I concentrate on it so I don't feel so over-whelmed by knowing I have lots of work and jobs to get through during the day. When I vacuum, I vacuum. When I cook, I cook. When I dig in the garden, I dig. When I sit down, I just sit! One thing at a time is what I have learned here. No monkey mind!*

Many people I have met over the years who could have benefited from daily meditation as a way of getting some calm into their lives were afraid to try it. They seem to think it is some sort of inner state from which they might not return - like jumping off a cliff. In one sense meditation *is* like a dive into unknown waters, but there is nothing to fear. The physiology of meditation has been well known through centuries of human practice and investigated by modern science if that reassures you. It is a safe and healthy practice.

What happens when you meditate?

In deep meditation, there is a sharp increase in the alpha rhythm of the brain with a concurrent decrease in the breathing rate and oxygen consumption. The heart rate decreases as well and there is a fall in the blood pressure. The skin has an increased electrical resistance. High lactate levels in the blood which are associated with stress fall. Yogic meditation masters can even control involuntary functions of the body such as pulse rate, digestion, metabolism, kidney activity, and body temperature.

All meditation has a single common ground which is the turning of your attention inward, away from external concerns which demand your attention. It involves concentrating your mind, often on one particular object or idea. The mind is slowly cleared of all thoughts. You let them gradually fade away until your mental involvement with thought is suspended. A clearer, calmer experience of yourself then takes place. Your attention has become inward rather than outward to worldly affairs.

The effect of meditation can best be summed up as a significant release from tension. It is a powerful gateway to self-realization.

Bobby Case is a character from Tom Robbins' book *Fierce Invalids Home from Hot Climates*. I think what he said about meditation is spot on: *Meditation hasn't got a damn thing to do with anything, 'cause all it has to do with is nothing. Nothingness. Okay? It doesn't develop the mind, it dissolves the mind. Self-improvement? Forget it, baby. It erases the self. Throws the ego out on its big brittle ass. What good is it? Good for nothing. Excellent for nothing. Yes, Lord, but when you get down to nothing, you get down to ultimate reality. It's then and exactly then that you're sensing the true nature of the universe, you're linked up with the absolute Absolute, son, and unless you're content with blowing smoke up your butt all your life, that there's the only place to be.*

The true purpose of meditation

The purpose of meditation is to move us forward in our search for the vision of the hidden self. It is a technique for purifying and awakening the spirit and is not, in itself, a form of spiritual salvation. You will not find meditation as a *final* answer to anything. But it is a classic and contemporary tool to the true self – that person you need and want to emerge fully into your ordinary day-to-day life. In this way you will find that self-containment and peace which means you do not need detractions. You live in reality without fear and with personal dignity regardless of your social standing, your job or lack of it, or your level of income whether it is high or low.

Many ways of meditation

There are many ways of meditation to achieve this inner state of the absolute – and maybe encountering that universal Absolute. It all depends on which meditation practice you chose. Different kinds of meditation may be useful for different purposes or for different people. In some practices you concentrate on breathing to focus your attention. Both Tibetan and Hindu spirituality insists on the importance of breathing – some ancient yogi texts tell us that all life is in our breathing. In other meditation techniques, there is visualization where colour, shape or form is pictured in your mind and held in attention. Some forms of meditation focus by concentrating on a candle or a stone and many use a mantra or phrase which is repeated over and over again. There is a Zen sitting meditation where there is no object of concentration at all. You just sit and try to be aware of your changing thoughts and feelings as they pass through your mind. Zen priests in Japan doing this kind of meditation may increase and sustain their alpha rhythms of the brain more than ten times longer than the average person who meditates. There are walking meditations where concentration is on the body and the processes involved as you move. Vigorous whirling and dance movements as in Sufi religious practice are also techniques of meditation.

Immediate benefits of meditation

The most immediate benefit of any meditation should be that you feel more calm and relaxed. It is an excellent way of combating stress. It should increase your ability to concentrate and generates a sense of a calm centre from which you may direct more of your energy into living more creatively in your personal talents and gifts. As we discover more about ourselves, our tolerance of others usually increases. Meditation can take you into different aspects of consciousness where new insights may come to you.

A bridge to sanity

At any one moment thousands of successful business people are leaving one role and taking on another. It may be a home-loving husband who must become a powerful corporate leader when his plane lands in another country. It may be a world-renown public relations executive who leaves her media conference where her every word must be guarded and carefully judged to drive home to be an open-hearted loving mom. This constant need to switch roles is common today. It is so stressful that such people can easily suffer from acute anxiety attacks. They need a bridge between one role and another, between being in one place and arriving somewhere else. They need a way to adjust their sense of values and self-performance to fit the frequently changing circumstances of their life. Meditation can help enormously to act as such a bridge. It can be practiced in the time between one role and the other to quiet and adjust the emotions and, thus, the body. The spirit finds in those few moments of peace a renewed energy.

Meditation is not anti-Christian

The rituals that may go with meditation are still regarded with suspicion by some Christians. Many church goers see meditation as anti-Christian, forgetting or not knowing the heritage of their own religion which includes contemplation as a form of meditation to better open the heart to the Holy Spirit. Others fear being somehow *taken over* by bad non-Christian elements if they are involved in any ritual like breathing exercises or focusing on a lighted candle. Our fear of the unknown is deep and abiding and includes refusing to let go of nonsensical ideas. Yet the unknown is always present in life from the hidden motives behind our actions to the events in the future which none of us can foretell. Rituals too are an everyday part of living which serve social, psychological and unifying purposes. Our lives contain a multitude of these rituals from the way we set the table for a meal to the village fete or how we always straighten our desk before beginning work. They also serve our spiritual purposes. The rituals or practices that go with a meditation are important ways to focus on your feelings and values, so through meditation you can reach your inner world, where new discoveries about yourself wait for you. Such stillness is a pathway to God for it dismisses the distractions and cares of this world and opens the deeper self to keep company with that which is universal and eternal.

Meditating is a habit. You need to practice it often so it becomes one

Ten minutes spent releasing your tension before beginning each day will assist you in your ordinary living and when you are seeking calm. Unless you live in a very isolated place you are likely to find a meditation group to join where you can learn meditation techniques. It is also possible to learn these from any of the many books about meditation which are available now. In addition you will discover on the internet a wide selection of audio-tapes, video-pods, DVD's and blogs to help you mediate.

Postponement does not do much for you in getting rid of an addiction to displacement. There is nothing like starting at once with something good. Here are a few simple exercises to help you start meditation.

Remember it is in our nature to have a mind full of different thoughts, images, colours, plans, sorrows, joys, memories and ambitions. Some linger, some speed through, but all need to be put aside in meditation so that the mind is focused in complete singularity.

Meditation 1: *Feeling is not thinking*

This is an exercise to get in touch with bodily sensations. First sit comfortably in a chair. Close your eyes. Feel your back against the chair, then your chest as it expands with each breath. Become aware of your arms, then legs, feel the soles of your feet touching against the ground. Visit different parts of your body. Visualize them. Gently let them go. Sit now within the calm embrace of your body. Let ten minutes slip by…then the next time try it for twenty minutes. Do this every day – twice a day if you can.

Summary

Take off shoes and socks
Sit comfortably with eyes closed
Visualize your body
See in your mind your back
Feel your chest expand as you breathe
Sense your arms, then legs
Sense the soles of your feet on the ground
Focus on the calmness of your body

Meditation 2: *Simple relaxation*

Here is an easy way to get you relaxed. Sit with your eyes closed for 20 minutes. This can be at home or in an airplane or train or just in your parked car. Turn off any sounds like a radio or TV. Switch off your mobile. You are going to discard and avoid distractions for a whole 20 minutes. You may think this is a just a short time- but when you try it, you will be surprised to realize that 20 minutes when you are still can seem a long time. If you have trouble sleeping and can't stop thinking or worrying, try doing this meditation just before going to bed at night.

Summary

Find a quiet room or somewhere you can be alone and not interrupted
Sit down
Breathe gently and regularly
Repeat a mantra of one word, such as *peace* or *one*
Do this for a set length of time from 10 to 20 minutes

Meditation 3: *Focusing the mind*

Concentration clears the mind of the coming and going of too much activity. It can be learned easily and quickly becomes an advantageous skill. It is developed through focusing your mind on a single subject to the exclusion of all else. To do it, you must anchor your point of attention in the present moment. Something which is here and now. What you chose to focus on is up to you. It can be a visual object, say a flower or a lighted candle. When you are paying strict attention to the object, you then focus on your breath as it comes into and leaves your body. The intention is to cultivate a non-distracted and undivided point of attention.

Concentration subjects

1. A visual object – a candle's flame, a flower, leaf, a symbolic shape or object, a cloth of pure colour.
2. A single sound such as a repeated word or phrase or a repetitive single chant or prayer. This can be from a CD.

You breathe by counting numbers as in a Zen manner or by just paying attention to the passage of air in and out of you. In, out, in, out, in, out.

Meditation 4: *Ch'i awareness: the breathing techniques*

The Chinese art of *T'ai Chi Ch'uan* springs from Taoist Physical Culture and has been handed down over some 10,000 years. It is a proven way of improving health through improved circulation. This brings tranquillity to the entire nervous system and, through its demand for concentration, a deep sense of peace. It is a system of meditation practice that is meant to lead to the ultimate harmony of the entire person, giving a balance between negative and positive forces -the famous *Ying* and *Yang* medical and philosophical concept. The word *Ch'i means* intrinsic and ultimate energy and comes from the Chinese word for air, energy, power or life. The simple warming up exercises and breathing exercises of *T'ai Chi Ch'uan* will help prepare you for meditation.

This exercise can be done standing or sitting. If you sit, you may use either a chair or sit cross-legged on the floor. Then relax the entire body. Let go of all worries and thoughts drifting in and out of the mind. Now imagine an invisible string pulling up from the top of your head to an invisible point high above you. Place your hands flat on your abdomen and while keeping yourself upright, let your shoulders drop as low as they will go. Take a deep inward breath through the nose, not letting the air fill your lungs and chest but allowing it to sink deeper so your belly swells out. You are sending your breath deeply into the area beneath your navel. This lower abdominal breathing called *Tan T'ien Ch'i Hsi* not only activates vitality in your gut, but it acts as a massage by the expansion and contraction of the abdominal muscles. This improves blood circulation to your liver and aids body metabolism. Having sent your breath down to the belly which in Chinese alchemy is called the *lower cauldron* – an appropriate name since this area is traditionally considered an energizing centre of your being – you now exhale through the nose. As you exhale press your hands firmly against your belly so that you force stale air out through your nose. Repeat this sequence six times.

Summary

Sit or stand erect but do it in a restful pose
Relax your whole body, letting tension go from each part of it
Calm your mind, letting all worries go
Put hands flat on abdomen
Drop shoulders
Take a deep inward breath through the nose

Let breathe sink deep so abdomen swells out
Exhale through the nose while pressing hands against abdomen so stale air is forced out through nose
Repeat sequence six times

The path of Yoga meditation

Yoga classes are available throughout most of the world. There is hardly a village or small town in England, Germany or France that does not offer a weekly session of yoga. Such classes are easy to find as well in America. Most of the people going to such classes go for exercise, seeing yoga as a way of keeping fit which of course it can be. Although most yoga teachers tell them, students often forget all about yoga as a way to awaken the spiritual. They rarely get beyond learning to do the various physical movements and, of course, in themselves these are good for you. Indeed, Yoga has many different philosophical expressions and a multitude of different physical techniques taught by various yoga schools and masters.

However, Yoga stems from the Hindu faith and teaches that the real purpose of life is to know God and that this knowledge becomes possible when the latent spiritual faculties of the mind are awakened by the practice of meditation. The sage, Shri Mangalnathji summed it this way: *God-realization is the purpose and goal of life; perfection, everlasting peace and freedom, are its fruits. When God-realization is once acquired, there is no fall from this exalted state of consciousness. There is no gain higher than this.*

Simplify, simplify, simplify ... the way to a life empty of unnecessary distractions

Marcus Aurelius, an emperor of ancient Rome and whose letters are still in print today because of their insight into human nature, which has not changed much over the centuries, wrote: *Most of what we say and do is not essential. If you can eliminate it, you'll have more time, and more tranquility. Ask yourself at every moment, 'Is this necessary?'*

When you ask yourself this question about your possessions you can begin to throw out or give away what is not either beautiful or practical. What you have left will be an uncluttered environment of simplicity. This makes for an easier life. You let go of unrealized and often unrealistic goals that confuse and complicate your life. You can replace them with the simple goal of contentment.

Keep asking yourself the same question that the Roman emperor asked even with all his vast wealth and power: *'Is this necessary?'* When you act on the answer you can simplify your life. Such simplification means you no longer need to be addicted to distractions. They no longer are part of your life or at least they play a very minor and much diminished role. Eventually you will positively avoid them.

Keys to simplifying your life

In his gem of a book *Timeless Simplicity*, John Lane who helped found Schumacher College in England, lists the following as the foundations of a simpler lifestyle:

Frugality
Rethinking your belief system
Following what bring you bliss
Working for fulfillment
Culling the unnecessary
Reducing expenditure
Setting limits
Careful consumption
Adopting a positive attitude
Taking life at a slower pace

Simplicity then is more than living less expensively – it is the cheapest and quickest way of living comfortably and at peace with yourself.

Stillness – the power of doing nothing

If you truly want to live a good life in hard times, then learn to sit down and do nothing. Learn to be idle. There is fantastic power in just doing nothing. Do you honestly really believe you came into this world to work and worry about the next hour, day, week or year? To live in anxiousness, feeling fragmented and full of fear? I claim none of us are born to such hardship. Stillness and just doing nothing is the corrective action we need to dispel this myth of human existence that brings so much suffering. Society may disapprove and call you lazy if it should see you just sitting around apparently doing nothing. But you are doing something very important. In fact, it is crucial to a contented life. You are finding in stillness and non-action an inner calm that will strength every task and problem you face.

When you sit still you become more powerful through the easing of inner tensions. The body can relax. Sensitivity to your surroundings grows – surroundings you have hopefully made simple and pleasant even if only a single room. Here are some guidelines or little thoughts that break the usual rules of what we are taught to believe about how we behave. They all help you do nothing:

You do not have to be busy
Time means nothing
You do not have to achieve anything
Play is what you were made for
Ignorance is bliss
Sitting down is not being lazy

For extra measure, you can add:

> **Relationships are always hard work**
> **True love exists but if not with you now, it is just somewhere else at the moment.**

It is a wonderful thing just to do nothing. Children and monks do it all the time. The first are divine in the purity of their natural state. The second are seeking to regain that same but lost state. Both know that being deliberately busy means the joy and beauty of the world pass you by. Perhaps this is why most children dislike the routines of education and why monks must learn to be still.

When doing nothing is what we do, then there is no distraction. This is practicing an important aspect of the art of contentment.

SUBSTITUTION

Substitution is about replacing one thing with another. It may be something physical or emotional. In such emotional replacing we have sublimated one feeling for another. Often the replacement is more socially acceptable or makes us feel more secure about ourselves. It can increase creativity in the artist. For example, when a poet puts into written words his feelings of love about which he finds he cannot speak. Where such substitution or sublimation can go wrong is when it is done contrary to one's own ideals. For example, many corporate executives make business decisions which as parents and members of the community they would judge disadvantageous to society.

Harry Stack Sullivan, the pioneer of interpersonal psychoanalysis, defined such sublimation as *the unwitting substitution of a partial satisfaction with social approval for the pursuit of a direct satisfaction which would be contrary to one's ideals or to the judgment of social censors and other important people who surround one.* Such substitution might not be quite what we want, but it is the only way that we can get partial satisfaction and still feel secure at the same time in how we are acting. All such sublimation is complicated. We don't stop to think why we do it or at what emotional expense. In fact, most of the time we are unconscious of our acts of such sublimation, because our need for this kind of substitution is so constant and so urgent that most of the time we are unconscious of doing it.

Substitution, therefore, plays a big part in our lives. The biggest substitution is addiction. Addictions come in so many forms that listing them would be futile. Everyone knows the four most common ones of alcoholism, smoking, overeating and drugs. Each of these has their own special problems when it comes to breaking the habit, but all addictions have much in common. For instance, addictions can help us manage stress or give us a sense that we have control over our lives, but when someone manages to overcome one addiction, they often pick up another. One example is that it is common for people when they stop smoking to start over-eating. Of course, part of this is a physical response but it is also linked to the need for a substitute to sublimate other, usually difficult, feelings.

Some people are considered to have addictive personalities. When they overcome one addiction, they will usually quickly find another to replace it. There are a number of medical opinions about this aspect of addiction. With alcoholism questions arise if those who suffer from it have a genetic predisposition to addiction or to alcohol itself or if it is a form of allergy or response of the body which easily slips into addictive need for some people. Recent medical thinking has moved addiction away from focusing on the psychological aspects toward consideration of it as a physical illness, because we know now that substance addiction affects the brain with actual organic changes to this organ and its functions. This casts further light on how truly complex addiction can be, involving as it does the whole person. It also helps us to better empathize with those who suffer such addiction. When we start to treat such addiction as a medical illness as we do, say, diabetes then compassion is generated. Such compassion is helpful to the suffering person and is equally helpful to ourselves since we are becoming more loving and forgiving and these are positive for our well-being.

One aspect of addiction that is often over-looked is the pleasure it brings. After all, we humans are hard-wired for pleasure seeking and for relief from our anxieties. How we play out this aspect of being human is what is important. It can either help our life to be happy or it can ruin it. Pleasure in and of itself is not the final answer to leading a contented life.

However, regardless of the psychological and physiological profiles of addiction, for most people addictions are crutches to deal with stress, anxiety, and the need to feel in control, or support other emotionally based issues. These are the kind of substitutions we all know a lot about. All are expensive habits which in hard or good times you can do without.

Unless we can get to the bottom line of why we have an addiction – and admit we have lost control over the situation – we will not find long-term recovery.

If you are facing hard times, then here is the golden opportunity to get rid of any addiction from which you are suffering. Your goal can be as simple as just giving up a habit to save money. It does not have to be something difficult like giving up smoking – although that would be a great idea. It can be cutting back on soda drinks or coffee or not buying pre-prepared food.

Finding out why we substitute in our life is the big step toward resolving it. In doing so, we improve the quality of our health and emotional well-being. Along the way we will probably also improve our relationships – after all what woman likes sleeping with a guy who stinks of beer or a man who finds the love of his life sitting in front of the TV in a haze of smoke?

Major addictions like hard drugs need mega-help, but it is also the little addictions of our everyday living that can handicap us in our struggle for a balanced life. In our local meditation group we each pick an angel card with its message at the end of the session. *Surrender & Release* is one of my favourite cards because *surrendering* to something which is negative in my life like an addiction means I have become aware of it. This awareness can bring an action or response that *releases* me from such captivity. Less addiction lightens the baggage we carry in the journey of our life story.

Pets as substitutes

Many people do not like animals around them, especially living in the house. There is nothing wrong with this. For millions of other people, animals are a part of their immediate family. These pets are in the home for a number of common reasons like the children want them or because we like walking a dog. In the end such pets usually become our friends and companions. They are part of our families. Despite the poor economic situation in the USA, Americans currently spend almost 50 billion dollars on their beloved animals.

Everywhere in the world stories abound on the benefits of animal companion for human health. Some psychotic patients who refused to speak will talk to dogs. Others who refuse to move will often reach for a dog so they can pet it. Karin Winegar, whose book *Saved: Rescued Animals and the Lives They Transform* chronicles human-animal relationships, says of such profound human-animal inter-action: *We've seen this from coast to coast, whether it's disabled children at a riding center in California or a nursing home in Minnesota, where a woman with Alzheimer's could not recognize her husband but she could recognize their beloved dog.* One of the foremost scientists investigating the relationships between dogs and cats and their owners is Rupert Sheldrake and his numerous books and articles on the subject are fascinating reading whether or not you own a pet.

Wonderful as they are, pets are not a substitute for our inability to sustain a human relationship. If this happens then the pet has become a substitute for a missing human relationship that we want or need but which we seem incapable of having or managing. This kind of pet substitution is not good for you. Once, when I was in a full anxiety state over a failed relationship, I wrote that a cat can be the ideal companion rather than an unsatisfactory and troublesome partner. *At least we know where we stand with a cat,* I claimed. Anyone who has a cat knows that the opposite is true of this marvelous creature. What it showed was that, typical of most of us, I turned to my pet relationship for comfort when my human one failed. Substitution was the name of my game.

We may admit to not understanding the way other people

behave but most of us cannot resist feeling we understand our pets. Some of the nicest sayings we have are about cats: *When the cat's away, the mice will play. A cat has nine lives. A cat may look at a king.* These tell us, of course, more about human nature than about our cats. In all our folklore, surely none can be more in the realm of fantasy than some of the old remedies in which cats were the major ingredient – another case of pure substitution. They certainly showed little real knowledge of a cat's behavior and tolerance. For example: *To cure an infected eye, stroke it with the tail of a black cat.* Better still: *To cure a cold, stick your finger into a cat's ear for fifteen minutes.*

When pets become substitutes for people

However, just because a cat or other pet may give companionship and ameliorate loneliness does not mean it is a substitute. It becomes a substitute when its role dominates our life and how we think and react not to animals but to other *humans*. Years ago I was involved in a national pet charity that helped save abandoned dogs and cats. Their annual fund-raising campaign was never directed at animal lovers but more insidiously at men and women who actively hated other people. Such people were their cynical target. While it is nice that people should want to give money for the welfare of animals, pause for a moment and reflect on why somebody would leave millions of dollars to aid animals when all around them are children, sometimes their own, in need of help. Motives can be suspect when pets become substitutes for other things, especially for other humans.

Sometimes then as in the case above, our feelings about an animal mask a deeper personal emotion we feel that is not related to the creature in question at all. For example, I had a friend visit me who writes about animal welfare. She is famous in her home village for taking in any dog that may be in need, even offering daytime hospitality to dogs so they won't be lonely when their owners are at work. Needless to say, her cottage is filled with dogs. They are all friendly and sweet just as she herself is - but she leads a rather solitary life in which dogs seem her only sustainable relationship. Once when visiting me I began to understand the deeper reasons for her need to rescue dogs. I call her visit *The Barking Dog Story.* Here is what happened:-

The Barking Dog Story

We were sitting peacefully before a cozy fire when a neighbouring dog started barking. It went on for awhile. For me it was just an annoyance breaking into a pleasant evening. Not so for my friend. Suddenly, she turned to me. *What are you going to do about that barking dog*? she demanded.

Nothing, I answered. *It is missing its owner,* I explained. *He runs the local grocery shop, his daughter is away at college, and his wife who helped him in the shop has left him. It's a mess. He has had to change his working hours so he is later than usual in coming home. The dog isn't use to it yet, so he is telling us by his barking that he is unhappy with the new situation. He will settle down to the new routine after awhile.*

Not good enough, she told me. *If it was a baby crying you would do something! You don't understand how I feel.*

So I got up, put my coat on, went out into the dark to investigate. The dog, an old Golden Retriever, was sitting by the gate of his home. When he saw me he wagged his tail and gave me a friendly dog-smile. I spoke a few reassuring words and returned home.

Just as I thought, I told her. *The dog is fine. No problems – he just has to get use to his new routine. After a few nights he'll adjust.* I picked up my newspaper to read it. As far as I was concerned the barking was explained, the dog's problem was transitory, and we could continue our cozy evening.

She stared at me. *You don't understand how I feel. If I lived here I would speak to the owner and offer to have the dog stay with me when he was at work.*

My protest that the dog would not get use to his new routine if she were to do this was of no avail. I explained also that if the dog was removed he would lose his role in the family as guardian of the house. Nothing would pacify her. How she *felt* was what was important. She simply could not or would not comprehend that her feelings were about herself and not about the dog. My friend could not allow the real situation to surmount her feelings of anxiety. I realized no appeal to her intelligence would work.

Whatever the reason, this dog barking triggered some deeper feelings that had nothing to do with animals and their welfare. In this particular case, I knew from her life story which she had told me that maintaining an intimate human relationship was difficult for her. Commitment was something she readily admitted was not something she could do. She could take just so much intimacy with another person before withdrawing to make it a more superficial, light-hearted friendship with boundaries she could make and keep. This way she was in control of her emotions. Unable to sustain for long any intimacy with another person, she had found a perfect substitute in dogs where she could remain in command.

This is not an uncommon form of substitution when we are reluctant to deal with anxieties and incidences in our past which prevent us from deeper human relationships. We are scared about what might happen and being scared about the unknown future and scrambling to stay in control does nothing to improve the quality of your life whether you are rich or poor. We do not really trust other people. More importantly, we actually do not trust ourselves. Substitution in this case takes away our liberty. One is not free.

Are you a substitute person?

A substitute person is someone you keep in your life or someone who keeps you in his or her life not out of love, but because you or they substitute for something one of you needs. Maybe you are fun to go shopping with, but you never see the person otherwise and when you are together, the talk stays definitely on the surface. Deeper feelings or personal situations are not discussed. You are there because you are fun to shop with. You may be that single woman or man who gets invited when an extra female or male is required at a dinner party. You are there because of your gender not because you are appreciated for yourself. If you act as a substitute person, how you are really feeling is not at all important. The original you, the real you, is not being loved or respected. You are being used, just something to fulfill some need that really has nothing to do with who you are. You are a substitute person.

Nobody *wants* to be a substitute person. Yet many people are just that. Who and what we are is original and unique. It is this whole person that is not wanted. Only part of us is wanted – the fun part or the good listener part or the help me move house part, or the extra pair of hands part, or the you cheer me up part. Celebrities often suffer from this for it is only the public self that is admired and wanted.

Why do we allow this to happen? Usually because we are afraid of losing that other person's presence in our life. We are afraid of rejection if we insist on being taken as a complete original person, warts and all. When we accept being a substitute person on a regular basis in a relationship, we are accepting that we will never be able to fully share our hopes, dreams and beliefs with that other person. We accept that he or she is never going to love us just for ourselves. In the end, this makes us sad. Most of us know instinctively that only relationships where we are loved and respected for our true selves are worthy of a life where honest feelings matter.

Restoration

Substitution has a cousin called *restoration.* This cousin is a powerful and positive tool for you. Restoration here means you look back on your story and see where you once did something that was fun. For me, this was painting in water colours – something I was not very good at but that I really enjoyed. One day when I was feeling especially blue, I got out the paints and some paper. In no time I was enjoying myself. In a few minutes the blue clouds in my head had blown away. My situation had not changed but my thinking had. I had restored a forgotten pleasure.

I don't believe there's one human that couldn't successfully use restoration in at least one area of her life. Just think how much it would mean for you to restore laughter, fun, and some joy into your day. Realities may not change but how you view them will. Restoration can work wonders. Think back on your story. What use to be fun? Who use to make you laugh? What activity brought you pleasure? Try some restoration. It need not cost anything.

What can we substitute for love?

The answer is, of course, nothing! When we substitute material possessions in place of love in our lives, we create dissatisfaction. Our inner feelings tell us this replacement will never work. Things can not love us. The more we try to substitute possessions for the love we need, the more we go around in a circle of increasing unhappiness. This eventually changes how we view our life – and that view is almost always negative. If times are hard for you, the last thing you need is to deliberately increase your unhappiness. By remembering there is no substitute for love but that we all need love, we can begin to focus on those aspects of our lives in which human love may be found – our family, friends, neighbours, and community. This is a good beginning whether times are abundant or not.

Spiritual substitutions

It is no surprise that spiritual beliefs in all their various forms and practices can be a substitute given that we are an inseparable union of mind, body and spirit, all of which are constantly interacting. Religious and spiritual beliefs and practices can fortify and give meaning to our lives, but it can also be a substitute when we use it to mask our deeper feelings so we do not have to deal with these in an open and honest way.

Deacon John Manutes, an American Orthodox Church deacon, talks about his own spiritual substitution in this way: *Another obstacle which I am personally fond of is spiritual substitution. That is to say, I don't need to pray today or tonight because I have done other things that should please God. For example, I worked on my sermon quite a bit today, or I spent a few hours preparing for a Sunday school class. Or, I was at church today from 8:30 this morning and won't get home until about 1:30 or 2:00 so I'm making the rest of my day all to myself. This is rationalization at its finest and I have been pretty good at it in the past.*

The rest of us are good at this kind of rationalization as well whether in spiritual matters or that directly concerning our bodies or minds. How often I say to myself, *Oh, I ate a salad at lunch so it's okay tonight if I chill out on a burger.* Even more frequently, *I went for a long walk today so I don't need to do my yoga.* Even worse is when I feel a bit lonely and can't find a friend to visit so I arrange a coffee date with someone I know will bore me but at least I'll get some company. I come home feeling more down than when I started out. We all substitute one thing for another and rationalize our actions with endless reasons.

To be mindful about how we live, we need to cut out as much rationalization as possible for it is false thinking. It prevents us from bringing into the light our real feelings and needs. So substitution which increases rationalization is not helpful for good living.

Keeping up with fashion

The majority of men are reputed to be unconcerned with keeping up with fashion, which is part myth and part truth, depending a lot on the guy's age. Older men turn into pumpkin shaped guys with a waistline they thought they would never have. Gone are the broad shoulders, the impressive expanse of chest, and the ripples of a hard belly. Of course in their heads, most men at every age still believe they are desirable and as good as ever – *good as ever* usually implying they can still perform okay in bed. Men do outgrow lots of the elements of youth. It takes years but it happens. Some become wise and gentle. Most have few illusions about where life has taken them and why. Most are decent, good partners, fathers and friends. But the majority never admit to a decline in penis performance. Sure some take a pill and perform. I knew an 83 years old architect who regularly took Viagra for his much younger wife's pleasure and it was an essential part of their happy marriage. So there are forms of substitution that can be important. In this case, what nature no longer automatically provides, science will. Some, of course, might not call this substitution but restoration.

But let's return to the subject of fashion where I started. Most men are not much interested in it in spite of male cosmetics, hair gel, designer stubble and popular various "looks". Women are the ones who are *à la mode*, following trends, talking with girl friends about the latest colours, styles, lines, and designers. If you are a woman who closely follows fashion and tries hard to keep up with it in your wardrobe and buys popular magazines like

Grazia and *Vogue* to see what the newest look is, then having a fall in income or losing your job or just simply having to cut back on how much you spend on your personal appearance can be a real emotional set-back in your lifestyle. Such a change that appears so superficial is often not as it calls for a woman to take a totally new view of herself. All of us know how hard such a fundamental change is.

However, if you do feel uncomfortable wearing last seasons' outfit and you simply cannot afford to buy something new and this truly upsets you, then you may have become a slave to fashion. This is not good because it is a substitution for how and who you are. It means fashion controls you and not the other way around as it should be. You have become too involved with being a person who impresses friends, family, neighbours, and people on the street you will never know – and in the process perhaps running up too much credit card debt.

It seems to me futile to tell any woman to forget fashion. *Looking good* is surely a positive aspect of being female. The avenue to explore is how to feel this way about yourself and keep within what you can afford. This is the wardrobe challenge that faces you if you want to live well with much less income. It helps enormously to tackle this problem with a girl-friend. It is also fun. Learning to make your own fashion statement is a big step in becoming more aware of your own personal identity. This is self-liberating.

Liberty to be yourself

It is the freedom from substitution that brings us more liberty to be ourselves, to express who and what we are, and how we really feel and view the world. This individuality is not selfish or self-centered. It is a freedom that allows us to love others because we love ourselves enough not to substitute the superficial and false for what is real. When times are tough and money short and worries mount up, the more real we can make our lives the more dignity we give to ourselves. Too much substitution makes us poor in spirit and in our vision of life. It does not bring contentment.

EXPECTATION

Most expectations make you poor because they usually make you disappointed. Disappointment does not lead to a richer, more fulfilled life. A sense of hopelessness, low self-esteemed, depression, or a history of failed relationships can often rightly be blamed on our expectations.

There are a number of ways in which expectations are part of our daily life. They can be about what we expect of ourselves or of others. They can be about choice or consumption. Expectations can be the engine that drives our sense of entitlement. At any moment of the day we have expectations of one sort or another. Of all the things that make us poor, I believe that our expectations perhaps do the greatest damage, because most of the time they leave us disappointed with life. For this reason they stand in the way of our being able to love without reservation and it is this kind of unconditional love that most enriches our lives.

Self expectations

The expectations we have for ourselves are mostly either too high or too low. If you expect too much of yourself, always setting high goals whether at work or at home and you are always struggling to achieve them then your expectations for yourself are too high. My mother told me once that she was disappointed with her life. It was not enough that she was a successful wife, mother and scientist, because her self-expectations lay elsewhere. In her case, she had always expected to be a brain surgeon. Now dreams are great and we need them even for something wildly improbable but only as long as such dreams do not become an unfulfilled expectation that makes us discontent and disappointed with our life. Why continue to set yourself up for failure?

If we are to find contentment with our life, we need to sort out our self-expectations. The way to do this is by getting to know your real self- not the one your family or friends can only partially know. It's an awareness of your deepest self you are after. What you dream. What you like and dislike. What you believe and hope - and most important how you feel in your heart. *Know thyself* remains the best road to finding expectations that not only please you but are within your ability to accomplish. One guideline is certain: do not try to fulfill the expectations your partner, family, or your friends may have of you. They may have wonderful intentions, but it is *your* life.

Therapists in psychological medicine often find that the origin of many clients' depression or anxiety has been triggered by unmet expectations. Surprisingly, such persons rarely consider that having the expectation was what caused the problem in the first place. Even when they claim the expectation they have is reasonable and justified, the only way to alleviate their suffering is by the process of them letting the expectation go. Frederic and Mary Ann Brussat, who have been covering contemporary culture and the spiritual perspectives of everyday experience for some forty years, give an amusing example of expectations which puts things into perspective. It is the story about a man hunting rabbits: *One day when he was out in the woods, a rabbit ran past him and collided with a tree stump, knocking itself unconscious. The man couldn't believe his good fortune as he put the rabbit in his game bag. Every day for the rest of his life, he came back and watched the stump, waiting for this to happen again.*

We may not be out hunting rabbits with our expectations, but what about the widower who remarries and expects his new wife to be as domestic as his first one? What about the expectations we have that our holiday is going to be our best-ever and when it turns out differently we decide we did not enjoy it in spite of the fun we actually had? What about all the expectations of caring, intimacy, and good manners we carry into a new friendship? What about all the little daily expectations we load up into our private relationships. Our sexual encounters are usual one big expectation and often less realized than we desired.

It is one thing to be hopeful and be satisfied with what we get. It is another to have expectations and feel unfulfilled when they are not met. From time to time, I have facilitated gay men's spirituality retreats. There are always a number of older men in the group who are still looking for *Mister Right* with the same expectations for a partner that they had when they were young. They continue to be disappointed. We all know women who never find a life partner because they have expectations that no man can meet. Such people continue to dream but usually end up living alone. Sadly, our various expectations can be a big block in achieving a good life and they are difficult to change – but we can do it.

Expectation and choice

We have been lead to believe that we can find, buy or live *the* best. If only we have enough expert information we can make the best decision for the best product, way of life or lover. We are drowning in "expert" opinions from every form of media, label, institution, and association. For example, we expect to find the perfect partner and, if it does happen, we have online dating to guide us to the "best" choice of person. This does not mean we have given up our expectations but simply quantified them.

It is not just in relationships where we expect perfection – in our homes we expect the *perfect* kitchen, the *ideal* bathroom, the *most comfortable* sofa. The list of our contemporary expectations seems endless and these are heavily reinforced by the media in both articles and advertising. We expect to chose and possess the best. This includes every aspect of our lives from lovers, partners, friends and family to inanimate objects. How can we not be disappointed?

How too much choice expands our expectations

The Economist magazine recently ran an article about the tyranny of choice, showing what hard work it had become simply to chose one brand over another in a supermarket. Here is their excellent summary of the present situation: *Wheel a trolley down the aisle of any modern Western hypermarket, and the choice of all sorts is dazzling. The average American supermarket now carries 48,750 items, according to the Food Marketing Institute, more than five times the number in 1975. Britain's Tesco stocks 91 different shampoos, 93 varieties of toothpaste and 115 of household cleaner. Carrefour's hypermarket in the Paris suburb of Montesson, a hangar-like place filled with everything from mountain bikes to* foie gras, *is so vast that staff circulate on rollerblades.*

This magic land of choice in supermarkets now extends to every area of our lives as long as we have money to spend or a credit card in our pocket. Each product tries to seduce us to choose it with all the power that modern marketing can muster. It does not stop there of course. We can choose how we want our bodies to look. There are a variety of noses, mouths, breasts, legs, and bellies to choose from. Botox takes care of wrinkles and lifts. Implants, and liposuction in a variety of methods are there for you. Just choose. Even the soul seems to have choices. A couple of religions to pick from were not enough for our modern age. Now we have a cherry bowl of spiritualities *and* religions to pick over.

This is not freedom.

You are not liberated by such a bewildering choice of things.

You are being confused.

Confusion is not part of living a good life, because heart, mind and body are not calm.

Over-choice like over-consumption is a modern form of enslavement.

Such a wide choice in everything we do or buy is hard to deal with if you have limited money. When this is the case we have every reason to buy wisely. Such wisdom is not found in marketing claims or in books or in articles in magazines. It is found from your own experience and based on salient facts like price for quantity comparison.

What this all means is that our lives are no longer simple and it is simplicity which you need in order to survive in hard times. You do not need to fill your life with online surfing, chatting, tweeting, and face booking, adding apps and online site choices to your ever expanding horizon of decision-making. This kind of endless personal decision making results in our living in a constant state of expectation. Such expectations have been inflated to such an extent that people think the perfect choice exists. It does not.

Daniel L. McFadden, Nobel Laureate and Presidential Professor of Health Economics at the University of California, believes that consumers with too many options face *the risk of misperception and miscalculation, of misunderstanding the available alternatives, of misreading one's own tastes, of yielding to a moment's whim and regretting it afterward combined with the stress of information acquisition.* Barry Schwartz in his book *The Paradox of Choice* says choice no longer liberates, but debilitates. In other words you wind up confused and a slave to materialism, all because of your expectations.

Expectations of the society we live in

Any society, like America, which places such enormous emphasis and priority on material success, is bound to be a society in which the majority of people do not believe they have achieved such a goal. Only a relatively few make it to the ranks of the rich and powerful. The rest of us have to be content with life as we find it. It is very difficult to feel such contentment when one is pushed from all sides to achieve, to earn more, to get more, to be more – and the goal posts of this competitive game are always being moved. This has produced such a widespread anxiety in society to succeed in material ways that in France, for example, the academic standards have been lowered so more and more young people pass the Baccalaureate which gives them a right to go to university. Ever increasing numbers do go and equally increasing numbers fail after the first year because the academic standards where higher than their abilities. So before they even celebrate their twenty-first birthday they have run the race for social success and failed. This disappointment gives a sense of personal failure. It dramatically lowers self-esteem. The same kind of thing happens with work. It is no longer good enough just to have a job- one must have a *career*.

The Oxford English Dictionary defines *career* as an individual's course or progress through life. It is usually considered to pertain to remunerative work. The word itself comes from the Latin word *carrera,* which means race. The example of usage the dictionary gives is the term *rat race.* You are not a rat so why act like one?

Perfect love has no expectations

Perfect love is when we love someone unconditionally. This means we have no expectations of them. We accept them just as they are – the best and the worst, their blue and bad days and their glorious moments. We love the person with our whole heart. We hold nothing back. We have no expectations just total acceptance.

Isn't this the way any of us want to be love? Just for ourselves. When this happens, expectations have no role to play. They don't exist.

If you want to live a contented life in which you have love for yourself and for others, then put aside your expectations, grow in your tolerance and acceptance of yourself and others, and put aside all judgments. Then and only then will you be at peace and truly rich.

BAD NEWS

Did Adam swim and was Eve created from a fin in a watery Garden of Eden? Some scientists believe that before we were members of the Great Ape Family, we were fish in the ocean. If we did develop first in the sea as this Darwinian scenario suggests, then I don't think we were fish but sponges.

I say this because we humans are in a constant state of absorption, soaking up like a sponge everything that is going on around us. Whether we like it or not we are, thus, continuously connected to everything else. We seem to be born hard-wired for this kind of state of being. For example, at the Mall I sit on a bench, gratefully putting down my shopping bags and giving a sigh of relief. The stranger sitting next to me comments on how crowded the Mall is this afternoon. We chat for a moment – nothing serious but this stranger who I will probably never meet again, makes a little comment on the dress of the passing teenagers. What she says awakens memories and with them comes a reminder of choices I made when I was that age. The stranger without knowing it has cast a net into my mind and pulled up into my consciousness thoughts that will change how I feel this afternoon. Maybe I will remember things and be sad or perhaps recall some times that made me especially happy. This brief, seemingly so unimportant chance encounter, has affected me.

The influence of strangers, as well as the people we know, is overt but also subtle. It is continuous in our lives and happens all the time to everyone. The old saying that no one is an island is true from the moment we are born. No one is truly separate from the world around them. From flecks of invisible dust in the air we breathe to giving birth, we are in a sponge-like state of influence – *everything* affects us whether we like it or not. This influence is total – mind, body and spirit.

So why are we so careless about what we deliberately and consciously bring into ourselves? Why aren't we on guard?

One good example of such carelessness is the fashion for a daily diet of news about the world, almost all of it negative, disheartening, and unhelpful to anyone.

Our daily dose of negativity

My first reaction at this morning's news was anger. I was filled with the desire to do something, anything to take some action that would help. The cause of these feelings this morning just happened to be the announcement that Israeli commandos had boarded and killed some 20 people on one of the charity boats trying to deliver aid to Gaza, the Israeli blockaded Palestinian territory. What possible positive purpose did my knowing about this far off event have on my life? None, as far as I can figure out. Yet there I was, a willing volunteer to being enraged, frustrated, depressed and having my view of life changed in a way that was neither healthy nor an enhancement to good living. It certainly did not help either the ordinary people of Israel or Gaza.

The poison arrow of gossip

Everyone knows that bad news travels fast and that no one is particularly interested in good news unless it should be something hugely important like a cure for cancer. We thrive on emotional stories and gossip and in this Celebrity Age we can have hours every day of peeking into the private lives of thousands of people we will never meet. This all seems fun until we wonder why we feel let down, depressed or more negative about life in general than we really have reason to be. The cause is bad, sad or just down-right scandalous news and the cruelest of images. We may be entertained by such news but an over-load has disastrously negative emotional results. A diet of bad news makes us poor not just in spirit but in how we view life and other people, in the state of our physical health, and in how we see our own lives.

A person who gossips all the time about other people in a negative or scandalous way has a reputation that makes us careful of what we say when we meet him or her. We are on our guard because we know that gossip can damage our reputations, make others think less of us, and even damage our dearest and closest relationships. Gossip is dangerous because it is almost always bad news. Yet, we indulge ourselves in this very thing every day by participating in an overload of gossip in all its forms via the media from television to online editions and blogs.

Information and gossip overload

We receive five times as much information everyday now as we did in 1986. This does not take into account the massive amount of information we pour out via emails, twitter, text messages and other forms of social networking. Dr Martin Hilbert at the University of Southern California has calculated that every day the average person has the equivalent of 600,000 books stored in various forms, from their computers and microchips to the strip on the back of their credit cards.

Every country has its own special pattern for bad news. In France, the newspapers have hardly come to the end of the summer holiday swimming fatalities when they begin the list of autumn victims who ate poisonous mushrooms. No sooner have these delicious but fatal dishes had their turn in the national spotlight, than the newspapers tell us of how many people were shot during the opening of the new winter hunting season. Only murders, the possibility of a political leader having Alzheimers, or a celebrity divorcing will take precedence over these annual bad news articles.

Having not yet learned my lesson in the bad effect of bad

news on my day, I could not resist finding the headlines on the internet. What I found in the first few minutes this morning did nothing to make me feel happy about myself or the world:

50 Left Dead after Mutiny in South Sudan
2000 Dead in Philippines Quake
Killing of Missionary Rattles Texas
New Cancer Drug Does Not Work
Tanker Fire Forces Residents to Evacuate
Volunteers Abducted in Indian Tiger Reserve
Contamination from GM Alfalfa Certain
New Thai-Cambodia Border Fighting
300 Killed in Egypt
Fires Rages near Perth
Police Evict Eastern Island People
Pregnant Woman Murdered in London.
Wildfires Wreak Homes In Cyclone-Hit Australia
11 year old girl raped
Bomb kills 60 in Iraq

Do any of these headlines make you feel happy? None of this news is probably within our own community. None of it is close enough for us to help the victims except perhaps through the giving of money which is an emotionally detached act. A safe way of feeling you might think – but it is far from being safe for you, bearing in mind that everything enters our mind, body and spirit.

The reason we persist in turning to such news is that it somehow seems to connect us to the society we live in and to the world community at large. In reality such connection is meaningless. We are simply voyeurs on someone else's tragedy. If it made us happy, all would be fine, but its effects are negative.

A friend once complained how sad he felt after watching the evening news on television. When I asked him why he persisted in something that upset him, I thought his reasoning was fairly standard for people these days. *I need to keep up with what is happening,* he told me, *I like to be a good citizen, do my part, and knowing what is going on is being part of the community. I feel it is my duty as a good citizen,* he told me.

How could knowing there was an earthquake in the Philippines and 2000 people killed or the news that four out of five Congolese women were raped during a civil war possibly make him a better citizen in Idaho where he lived? How could any bad news from afar serve except to make him feel helpless and full of despair? It is this feeling of helplessness combined with a sense that nothing changes in the senseless cruelty of nature and humanity. So much seems rotten when you dig deep enough. This kind of daily scenario affects our brains. It not only changes our outlook on life but it desensitizes us to violence and cruelty which is what most bad news is about in one form or the other.

The effect of bad news of violence on your kids

We naturally want to protect our children from the evils found in every society from bullying in the playground to hit and run drivers to paedophiles. Yet, we allow them to watch television's violence and gruesome images, and to play electronic games which involve killing or destruction to score a win.

One hundred forty-six articles in respected professional behavioral science journals, representing 50 studies involving 10,000 children and adolescents from every conceivable background, have all demonstrated that viewing violence produces increased aggressive behavior in the young. As early as 1972, the American Surgeon General's report on *Television and Social Behavior* discussed such effects on children and young people which included effects on learning, emotional development, and aggressive behavior. Clear grounds were established to warrant taking remedial action on television programme vigilance but almost a half century later nothing has been done. Even worse, most parents while limiting television viewing time still do not regard most television violence and electronic games as harmful to their children.

Such exposure to violence desensitizes our children and ourselves to violence and cruelty. We become gradually less and less sensitive to the bad news, overload of horrible images, and violent entertainment filling our contemporary lives.

Lt. Col. Dave Grossman, an internationally recognized scholar, author and soldier, is one of the world's foremost experts in the field of human aggression and the roots of violence and violent crime. A member of the American Board for Certification in Homeland Security and of the American College of Forensic Examiners Institute, Col. Grossman often explains to his audiences how desensitation works. He calls this desensitization process *The Methods of Madness*. It is worth noting that such methods by the US Army includes the use of ordinary video games to desensitize young recruits because it can significantly increases their kill rate when they enter the battlefield. For example, application of such conditioning techniques using images of violence before they were sent into the war zone increased the rate of gun fire of soldiers up to approximately 55 percent in Korea and around 95 percent in Vietnam.

Here are a few of Col. Grossman's comments about this type of military training: *How the military increases the killing rate of soldiers in combat is instructive, because our culture today is doing the same thing to our children. The training methods militaries use are brutalization, classical conditioning, operant conditioning, and role modeling...Brutalization and desensitization are what happen at boot camp. From the moment you step off the bus you are physically and verbally abused: countless pushups, endless hours at attention or running with heavy loads, while carefully trained professionals take turns screaming at you. Your head is shaved, you are herded together naked and dressed alike, losing all individuality. This brutalization is designed to break down your existing mores and norms, and to accept a new set of values that embrace destruction, violence, and death as a way of life. In the end, you are desensitized to violence and accept it as a normal and essential survival skill in your brutal new world.* He then goes on to relate this breaking down of mores and norms to what is happening to our children – and, of course, it happens to you and me as well:

When young children see somebody shot, stabbed, raped, brutalized, degraded, or murdered on TV, to them it is as though it were actually happening. To have a child of three, four, or five watch a "splatter" movie, learning to relate to a character for the first 90 minutes and then in the last 30 minutes watch helplessly as that new friend is hunted and brutally murdered is the moral and psychological equivalent of introducing your child to a friend, letting her play with that friend, and then butchering that friend in front of your child's eyes. And this happens to our children hundreds upon hundreds of times.

Bad news makes us numb

The effect of media bad news and violence in all its many forms is to lower our responsiveness to real violence. Bad news makes us numb. Who can forget his or her first horrified reaction to people leaping from the burning twin-towers, but now on re-run of these scenes our emotions may still be stirred but not at the shocking depth of our first encounter. We are desensitized to the event by its sheer repetition. Like sponges we have absorbed the worse and have emotionally and mentally learned to live with it. But this living with it comes at a high price for we lessen the redeeming virtues of our innocence and personal boundaries. This loss does not have just a physical and emotional effect on us, but one which disturbs at a deep spiritual level.

Rumors are dainty morsels that sink deep into one's heart

We are bombarded by rumours and warnings of looming disasters. Take climate change as an example. The nations of the world now gather annually to discuss a global agenda for climate change. The goal is to improve the prospects of the living planet and its biodiversity. The nations talk but do not agree on any hard plan. Profits come first. Economic growth remains the golden yardstick of all measurements.

Why should this continue to be the case? Thomas E. Lovejoy, a professor of environmental science and policy at George Mason University in America, seems to hit the nail on the head in answering this question. He claims the major reason for lack of progress is that the biology of our planet is largely ignored in human affairs and, further, that its critical contributions to our well-being is not taken into account in our formal economy. He gives an example, telling us that we take no account of the fact that between 40 – 89 % percent of the annual income of the world's poorest people comes either indirectly or directly from nature. We continue to exclude the benefits of the ecosystem and its biodiversity in our considerations of how to repair and renew our plundered planet.

When all these various rumours and warnings of impending disasters sink deep into our heart, they generate fear. Fear is in the very nature of our primitive responses. History shows that every king, dictator and politician knows this and exploits it to our disadvantage. Fear is a powerful enemy of our happiness. The deepest fear we have is our fear of the unknown. This is why change is so difficulty for most people. It is for this reason that Christian Scripture tells us: *Fear not, the Lord is with you!*

Beware of what you emotionally eat

It is said that words of a gossip are like choice morsels set before us which when swallowed go down to our inmost parts. Bad news in all its forms is just such a plate of poisonous morsels. Ration how much you nibble if eat it you must. As to fear there is nothing you can do about the past for it is gone and nothing you can do about what may happen in your life or that of your society in the future. So why should you worry and fret and fear?

A good way to stop such needless waste of your energies is to give up listening and watching bad news. Just remain innocent and tend your life with loving care so that your mind and heart are at peace. This is good living no matter who you are or where you live or what you possess. Make a notice for your television: *No news is good news.*

MONEY WORRIES

Worry over money boils down to simply having enough of it. The crunch comes when you start to examine what "having enough" means. It can mean you don't have enough for the electricity bill or to pay the mortgage this month. It could mean that you just can't buy what you want when you want it. When people talk about money, one thing is certain that it is relative to them and not to you or anyone else. Having enough money is different for each person and each family. In our culture, few habits are as deeply engrained as the desire to own things and few delights score so high on our personal agendas as getting a bargain or having invested wisely. If you have been living high on capital or credit, the fall into lower income hurts. The cutting back on what you spend, whether it is a little or a lot, is emotionally hard and often results not just in worries but in panic attacks and depression. Paradoxically, such depression is known to bring on more shopping!

About money

This proverb is credited to the Chinese and has been passed around the world for years via the internet. The reason it is still going around the globe is because in every country people agree with its essential truths. The problem is remembering it when you fall on hard times and long for those extra few dollars.

With money you can buy a house but not a home.
With money you can buy a clock but not time.
With money you can buy a bed but not sleep.
With money you can buy a book but not knowledge.
With money you can buy a doctor but not good health.
With money you can buy a position but not respect.

With money you can buy blood but not life.
With money you can buy sex but not love.

Money baggage

To become aware of what money means to us, we need to deconstruct our financial lives. First, why do we think about our money like we do? Since most of our concepts about our money come from those we encountered in our childhood, we have to dig deep into our own history to understand what beliefs we really have about money and finances.

There are questions we can ask ourselves to uncover these hidden beliefs that affect our behavior about money. For example, how have desire or even aversion to money played a role in shaping your relationship with money? As a child from a deeply religious Christian family, I was so guilt-ridden about making money because I was taught to think of it as the sin of greed that as an adult I could make almost anything my goal except money. Our past experiences and our present attitude about money shape how we act. The wealthy sometimes hide their riches. The poor pretend to have more than they do. Many hide their debts. Our money is a powerful part of our life story. How has it affect your relationships? Kristi Nelson, a consultant with the Centre for Mindfulness in Medicine, Health Care and Society, feels when we hide what is true about ourselves and money; we can become "class imposters", living a life that does not reflect the truth about us. She declares time, energy and love to be real forms of currency as much as cash. What we do with these intangible resources tells the truth about what values we hold.

If you are carrying around money baggage, then there is no better time to unload some of this emotional junk than when you are in hard times. Do this assessment of how you feel about money *before* you start to work on a budget. Then you will approach with greater clarity and a more practical mind how you are going to handle what income you have.

Depression and money worries

Earlier I wrote that money worries often bring on depression. Most developed countries now accept that depression represents a major public health challenge but few governments have had the political will to link directly personal economic well-bring with health and to give this aspect a high priority in their economic and employment planning. Yet, the average person readily ranks money problems at the top of their list of the causes of depression. This belief is not new. More than twenty years ago, a survey by the National Depression Campaign found 88% of people believed money problems to be a prime trigger for depression, with work problems coming in second followed closely by marriage problems. With the latest global economic and banking crises, rising unemployment, and national government austerity measures, a contemporary survey would most likely show the same kind of results about the popular belief of a link between income and depression.

How money worries increase spending habits

It does seem odd that when a person is worried about not having enough money they will often start spending more. It is a reaction that may not make good sense but it does happen and often more with women than men. With more woman than men suffering from depression this perhaps comes as no surprise. Professor Karen Pine of the University of Hertfordshire in a survey she did found that 79% of women said they'd go on a spending spree to cheer themselves up if they were in a financial crisis. This, of course, supports what many women would admit *can* happen when they use shopping to avoid or remedy negative feelings or dissatisfaction with their lives. *Go shopping* is a slogan that carries a lot of weight psychologically with many women as every product manufacturer and shop knows. Since going shopping distracts us, there is a kind of liberty when we are in a consuming mode. The problem, however, remains once we return home and put down all the bags of goodies and find we are further in debt.

Credit cards: the smooth-talking enemy

We usually forget that credit cards are an instrument developed by capitalism for increasing our spending. They have succeeded in changing our thinking about money and how much real money we have so that most of us live in a land of financial make-believe. Cutting up credit cards and using cash is one of the scariest things we can do. Our whole system of living is geared to using credit. In Britain banks now speak of eliminating cheques altogether since 70 percent of their clients don't use them, preferring cards. I know people who deem this a great convenience because when the credit card bill comes in they pay it off. No credit charges. No balance or interest. No debt problem. This is great if you can do it but the majority of us have a credit card balance to pay off - yet we still keep on using them. The temptation to add to your credit debit is ever present. In British supermarkets, they ask at check-out: *Would you like cash back?* This is pushed as a convenience for us – but it is just another way of putting us more in debt. We not only charge up what we have bought but can get real pocket money to continue our spending and the raising of our debt balance.

The problem seems to be that we don't make the connection between credit cards and real money. Even in business people use to dealing in large sums of money begin to forget that it is real and not just figures on an accounts page or an expense receipt. A woman friend, who worked for a global Dutch corporation where vast sums of money were spent every day, suggested a way of bringing home the reality of money to executives responsible for budget planning. She wanted them to be given cash to spend instead of just scribbling down monetary figures which she felt became unreal and unrelated to the reality of credit and debit. You might try the same thing when you next start to work out your spending plans. It is surprising how quickly cash in hand can be spent when the money is no longer just figures on a page or debit lines on a card statement.

Cash is best in hard times

Most suggestions about getting your finances in order tell you to start making budgets. You may be able to do it but personally I never could stick to a budget. I also never could seem to do that piggy bank thing where you put so much aside each week for the basics like electricity or gas. What I did find helpful was switching from credit to cash. Then, I had to think about the money I was spending because an empty pocket is an empty pocket unlike credit cards where more credit always seems to be available. At one point in my life when I used credit, the card companies kept upping the amount of my credit until it was more than two years of my current income. Eventually between just three cards I could have bought a small house with the credit on offer to me. Fortunately, I didn't do it.

So if we don't have cash, we can't spend. Paying later for anything is not a good idea either. Temptation is always hard to beat. As Oscar Wilde famously put it: *I can resist anything but temptation.* So if you can't cut up the cards, then give them to a friend to lock away until a later date- a *much later date* like five years from now. Whatever cash income you have, that is it. Don't use credit. Don't borrow. There are always ways to cut down on spending. Don't add extra money worries to your life and your family when times are hard.

Is money the root of all evil?

The phrase *money is the root of all evil* is one which most people know whether or not they are a person of faith. It derives from a saying attributed to Jesus. The phrase is found in the Apostle Paul's *First Epistle to Timothy* in the bible, but there its meaning becomes different by the addition of just one word. This little word is *love*. Paul actually wrote: *The* love *of money is the root of all evil.* So it isn't money itself that causes the problem but our love of it. Some authorities even attribute this biblical saying as more accurately translated from the original Greek as *the love of money is the root of all sorts of evil.*

Now we are getting someplace because it isn't about money as such that is the problem but our attitude to it. So it is that our love of money can bring all sorts of negativity into our lives. This can mean changes to our values or confusion in our feelings and our relationships to other people. For example, one of the most common matrimonial problems is about money matters and we all know how much disharmony can be caused in a family because of financial disagreements.

Let's just call it greed

A word that for centuries defined this kind of love of money and possessions was *greed.* It is not a word much used today by people or the media, but tell me what else is the root cause of a financial scam or a banking meltdown because someone could not resist making a few extra million dollars? I think we should bring back this unloved word. Of course the reason it probably is no longer in fashion is because it reminds people of rules and regulations and moral codes which they feel interfere with their liberty to do as they please. If you are neck- deep in debt, you have given up your freedom already, so why not start using the word *greed* when you talk about people who love money too much? When you read about business people or politicians who cheat on expenses, accept back-handers, or secretly represent corporations in order to increase their profits or when the banking industry takes unacceptable risks and then asks the public to bail them, let's use the word *greed* to describe them. If Paul is up there in heaven he will be smiling down at you. It will also serve to remind you of that simple but powerful message in the saying: *The love of money is the root of all sorts of evil.*

The advantages of down-sizing your home

One of the biggest assets we have is the space in which we live. It may be a house, an apartment or a room. What matters is that this space is ours. This is what makes us king or queen of the castle no matter how society may judge our social or economic status and regardless if we have slipped into hard times. This sense of our own space is very precious to our emotional, physical, and spiritual health. Such space is our refuge from the outside world with all its conflicts and demands. It is where we may find peace.

There may be no social value in down-sizing where you live, but the economic benefits can be huge. Less space can give us a greater sense of freedom. A small house or apartment not only can loosen up cash or lower mortgage payments but it may mean less cash out-goings.

There can be a deep psychological benefit to such down-sizing because what you are doing is liberating yourself from some of the work and economic burdens you have been forced to carry.

Here is what the American M.D. Creekmore on his popular *Living in Small Spaces* blog had to say about why he down-sized: *When people ask why I live the way I do, I smile and say it's all about the money… I could sell my life to the company for an hourly wage, the*

30 year mortgage and new truck in the driveway. I have lived this life and I hated it. The long hours, the overbearing yapping brown nose boss. And the stress. I worked for years at my last job, the pay was good, the hours long and the pressure felt like a barrel of bricks crushing my chest. I worked second shift, usually ten hours a day six days a week. Work, sleep five hours get up and go to work again, the drudgery was nearly unbearable. Every day I felt like I was going to cry, this was no life. After the company moved abroad, I had to figure out how to make ends meet. Finding another job paying as much was impossible at the time, my only alternative was to live on a lot less money.

Living in less space, keeping your life simple and making ends meet because you need and want less not more can be a happy solution when you are economically oppressed by a commercial system you are powerless as an individual to change.

The temptations of a bargain

A bargain is only something you *absolutely need* which is being sold at a price lower than usual. A bargain is not simply a lower price on something you might like to buy. So real bargains should be few and far between in your purchases. The slogan to remember is: *If you don't need it, don't buy it.*

Here is a game that a friend and I use to play when we were broke. She called it *Purchase Avoidance.* The winner had to cook dinner. The idea was that we went to the shops with the goal of finding things we *really* wanted but did not actually need. We would look at the object, sigh over it, and discuss its merits or glamour. If we did not buy it we won a point. Whoever avoided buying and got the most points, won the game. We had a lot of fun shopping and *not* spending money.

The passing of time often takes the emotional pressure off us. So when you next feel you have to buy something, wait for awhile. Don't do anything. Give yourself a week to think again about the purchase. This waiting period when we put spending on hold can change our feelings and often our needs.

Spending surprises

Surprise expenses are unexpected bills that arrive when you don't expect them. This means a lot of stress and anxiety. It is hard to save for these. I think the best way forward is to find out what you paid last year in such surprise expenses, such as an extra doctor's bill for a child or a visit to the dentist or a vet for the cat or what you need for family birthday gifts, then add it all up, divide by twelve months, and you know what you might need to set aside monthly. No sudden surprise expenses means less stress. All we can do is try to be prepared as best we can. This helps enormously in lessening the surprise factor when we are struggling to make ends meet. If you are able to do this set-aside, then do try it.

Stopping the stress of money worries

If we want to stop getting stressed out about finances, we need to stop emotional spending. We need to learn the difference between *want* and *need* and between *having* and *being.* We need to stop letting triggers to spend send us off to the shops. These triggers can be our children's demands or those of our partner or ourselves. Learn to recognize and deal with such triggers.

SELF PITY

Rise and shine or rise and whine?

Self pity is all about the ego. It is self-centered and usually contains a lot of anger about life. Self pity is comforting behavior that is just another form of obsessive thinking. People who are full of self-pity are whiners and nobody likes them. They are totally boring. We all have met the mother who constantly complains about the way her children treat her or the classic grumpy old man who sees everything in a negative light. Looking on the dark side of things all the time is going to lead you into despair. Making self-pity a habit is going to make you isolated and lonely because you do not have time to give attention to anyone but yourself.

Self-pity is a psychological state of mind. It is a thinking pattern where we have not accepted a situation we do not like. Normally we find these situations unacceptable because we do not have the ability or capacity to deal with them. We believe we are victims and seek to confirm it by having other people feel sorry for us. When such sympathy is not forthcoming, it will be actively sought. Self-pity of a temporary kind is common since everyone likes to have a little moan and groan. This is okay as long it is transitory and passes as soon as we are on our emotional feet again, ready to deal with our situation in a positive way.

Self-pity is boring

What poison is to food, self-pity is to life. Oliver C. Wilson

People who feel sorry for themselves usually have to tell other people about it. This kind of sharing is one of the most boring conversations anyone can listen to. If you suffer from self-pity you will lose friends and irritate everyone around you.

Ask yourself if you phone up friends all the time just to complain. Do you talk endlessly about your life? Do you always sound unhappy and displeased with life when talking with friends and family? Can you always find some excuse for things going wrong except to blame yourself? If these are true for you, then you are into self-pity.

Please remember this: Just because you live in hard times does not justify boring everyone to death about your situation.

Listening with your heart

The legendary Marlene Dietrich once said that grumbling is the death of love. The reason is that we have stopped listening to others. Eventually, they think we no longer care about them and their lives. When that happens love crumbles. Surprisingly the people we most demand listen to our complaints about life are the people who are most immediate in our lives – a wife, husband, partner, adult child, parent, or sibling. It is as if knowing us best, somehow they will understand best. They may well understand but your *poor me* attitude to life will leave them not wanting to be around you for too long. When you stop grumbling, moaning, and playing the martyr, you can open your ears to what people are saying and your heart to what they are feeling. Learning to listen to other people is one of the best ways to disarm your overwhelming concern for yourself. When I say *listen,* I mean we try to fathom what the other person is really saying about themselves – how they feel, what matters to them, where they are in their life story, what their needs may be. Everyone likes to have someone listen to them in this way. It is comforting and gives them a chance to safely express themselves. Don't offer advice. You don't have to make any comments. In fact the less you say the better. What they want is friendship. With such a focus on the other person, you can give full attention to someone besides yourself – and be much less boring as well.

So you can change the selfish habit of self-pity by simply shutting your mouth and listening to the other person. It is that easy.

Keep up this habit of listening to the other person and before long you will experience two things that help you live a contented life. First, you will gain a reputation for warmth and caring which makes everyone feel great including yourself. Second, your view of the world and yourself will change to a more realistic one. This is a positive tool for effectively dealing with problems that may arise in your life. In addition, everyone we meet has something unique to teach us about life. Try to find that jewel of wisdom in the other person. Keep listening for it.

The martyr in all of us

Some people believe there is a little boy waiting in every man and a martyr waiting inside every woman. In any scenario being a martyr is just one more example of self pity. Being a martyr is to feel sorry for yourself whenever you can so that everyone else also feels sorry for you. *Poor you* is the centre of attention. At the drop of a hat you can turn any conversation onto your life. Given five minutes chat and you are deep into the poor me. We can all tell stories about martyrs we have known. Most of us avoid them at all costs unless of course the martyr should be a member of your family. In that case, think of something else as they rattle on about how badly you or life is treating them. They have made a wardrobe of expectations about you in which to dress up their over-sized ego and their own expectations of what life should be bringing them. Think of the infamous stage-mother syndrome. Consider how many adult children feel they have somehow disappointed their parents. If you should be guilty of such martyrdom, stop it now. It is an emotional addiction that makes you sick, friendless, and difficult to live with. Martyrs are usual lonely, unhappy people full of disappointments about their own life and full of the need to control those they say they love. Mother birds teach their babies to fly, then kick them out of the nest so they can be independent in a life of their own and make their own mistakes and successes. A lesson in letting go that we humans do not seem easily to learn.

The helping hand

Here is a way that almost always works for those who suffer chronic self-pity. You find a friend or just anyone who needs help that you know you can offer. It may just be driving them to the shops if they are elderly or babysitting for a couple of hours when a single mum needs to keep a dental appointment. Someone near you, a friend, member of the family or a neighbor, can use your helping hand. Such action lifts you out of your self-pity because you stop thinking about yourself for awhile. You discover many other people are in a worse situation than you.

Just because you have fallen on hard times does not mean you are a victim or that you are in a helpless situation. Look around and see how many other people are true victims whether it is from poverty, crime, or illness.

Taking action

One good way not to fall into the trap of feeling sorry for yourself when you are feeling down is to get busy - some physical activity will do - anything from making a cake to washing the car as long as it involves body action. This will get your mood to lift from darkness into light. The author, D.H. Lawrence, famous in his day for writing about lust and sex, said that when he got the blues thinking about the future, he would start making marmalade. *It's amazing how it cheers one up to shred oranges,* he said. Then added: *Or scrub the floor.*

Let your inner child rule

Laughter can bring an awareness where you can see self-pity for what it really is. Being foolish, joyous and silly – all are great for drawing you away from self-pity and for realizing that life is both ups and downs – yesterday was lousy, today is better, and tomorrow? Tomorrow has not come to the party yet and who knows what she will wear? Diamonds of opportunity in her hair? A fabulous dance of love? Another detour on life's journey? A disappointment that opens a surprising new door? Since tomorrow has not arrived, why worry about her? In any case, there is nothing you can do about it.

Why not be child-like once in a while as a way to see the world with more innocence? When like a child you have little regard for tomorrow and live for the moment you will rediscover an unexpected ease with the world and the joy found in small things as when you were a child. As adults we do not always have to be grown up and aim all our efforts on wisdom and maturity. It is okay to clown. It is okay to let out your inner child to play. Why not be fifteen going on fifty? Who cares anyway? Still, there are lots of people who do not think the spontaneity of a child should ever be an adult action. For example, in a recent New York Times article about the founder of Wikileaks, Julian Assange, it relates with a serious, somewhat derogatory tone, how he suddenly started to skip in front of the journalist group he had been meeting with – and that two of these distinguished journalists were so startled that they stared speechless. Can this really be the reaction of such experienced and worldly news writers? To make matters even more pointed the article went on to comment that Assange had a bit of Peter Pan in him. Did this make him less a force for transparency and public truth in political matters?

So be prepared if you sometimes let your inner child out to play for some people to consider you eccentric, a bit of a Peter Pan, and a free spirit – but pay no attention to them. Just keep remembering that the central message is to lighten-up if you are seeking contentment.

Make hope your habit

What is self pity but the giving up of hope? Hope in your life, your family, friends, and yourself. It is a disastrous stratagem of self-denial to avoid dealing with how you really feel. Self-pity is a mental state in which you hide, playing out the role of victim. The signs are easy to spot as we all know people who indulge in this habit – a habit that makes them poor in spirit and leaves their friends in dismay. Such a person cannot stop talking about themselves – and it is rarely good news, but usually complaints about their situation or partner or just whatever might on that day might be making them unhappy. There is hardly ever any news from this war zone of self-pity that makes us feel good.

The famous American, Helen Keller, who through a fever as a baby became totally deaf and blind, overcame her disabilities, got a degree from Radcliffe College, and helped change the way her society felt about people with disabilities, had this to say about feeling sorry for yourself: *Self-pity is our worst enemy and if we yield to it, we can never do anything wise in this world.*

You may not have such profound disabilities as Helen Keller but at this moment in your life things are looking down. Times are scary and employment and income are fragile. This is the very moment when you must not indulge in self-pity. You can be as brave as Helen was. Believe it. You can still inspire people by how you behave. Such courage and the holding out of hope to others costs you not one penny. What it does cost is enough discipline to pay attention to the spirit of hope which rests in your heart and the heart of every human. Forget despair which displeases God. Forget the messy everyday details of your worries. Make hope your habit. Rejoice in the midst of plenty. Even better rejoice in the midst of hard times.

Make very morning a bright new day

Remember that self-pity of a real emotion. It numbs us for awhile and we enjoy the attention we get from others because we are in a sorry state but self-pity paralyzes your life and defeats your attempts to live well and happily. It makes you poor. There is no fast miracle cure for self-pity. It takes time and effort to get out of this lifestyle habit – but it can be done. When you do stop it, problems will be put into focus, your life will become easier if for no other reason that you are less uptight about your situation. Your life will go more smoothly and the people around you will feel more relaxed with you.

Seeing things more clearly always helps us to live a fuller, happier life no matter what our financial or other personal circumstances. So tomorrow when you wake up tomorrow, don't rise and whine but rise and shine! Be glad to be alive.

THINGS

THAT

MAKE

YOU

HEALTHY

CLEAN WATER

Water is sacred for we know we cannot live without it and making it holy is to show our greatest human respect. It is a metaphor evoking a multitude of different meanings in our religions, national myths, and in the stories we read to our children. It should, therefore, be one of the values in your moral and ethical framework for living a good life.

In all the great faiths of the world, water is the sacred element of purification. This includes Christianity, Islam, Hinduism, and Judaism. So sacred and important is water in our lives that a saying or *Hadith* of Islam relates that the Prophet, blessed be his name, declared a man who withholds superfluous water is one of three types of people whom Allah will neither talk to nor look at on the Day of Resurrection. In the Qur'an it is stated that living things are made of water and water is often used to describe Paradise. It is recorded in the Gospel of John [NT 7. 37-39] that after a great festival where many people were gathered, Jesus cried out to them: *Let anyone who is thirsty come to me! Let anyone who believes in me come and drink!* And again we read in the Old Testament *From his heart shall flow streams of living water.* [Isaiah 44.3 2.21., 19.34] Christians refer to Jesus as *living water* or *the water of life* simply because without water we cannot be alive and for them Jesus is that water which opens the spirit to the fullest, most alive life in God. Water is mentioned over 400 times in the bible.

We are water

Up to 60% of our body weight is composed of water. Your brain alone is made up of about 70% water and it constitutes about 83% of your blood. Take water away from your body and you would collapse like a balloon letting out air. You would not exist. In fact, all earthly existence depends upon it - the ecosphere, atmosphere and the biosphere are all linked intimately by water which interacting with solar energy determines our weather. It is this ever changing pattern of climate that brings us the physical and chemical elements necessary for life on our planet. Yet, in the Western world, we take this essential life-giving source for granted. We don't think about water if we have it.

Health benefits of water

Water is the human body's principal chemical component and most of us do not get enough of it. You need to be sure you have a big enough water intake to maintain good health. You need this water to carry nutrients to your vital organs and help them pass out toxins. This also gives moisture where you need it, for example in your nose and throat. Dehydration can be a severe condition in the very young and the very old whose bodies cannot sustain normal functions without enough fluid. Even a mild case of dehydration in the young or in the elderly can lead to fatigue.

How much water do you need?

It is very fashionable now to carry a plastic bottle of water around with you. One sure sign of the active modern woman is her bottle of water. We have formed this habit of drinking water on the go for several reasons. Continuously nursing a bottle of water satisfies a psychological craving for constant oral intake while at the same time it means no caloric intake for weight gain. Secondly, our deliberate exercise, such as jogging or gym workouts, means we need to have a ready source of water replacement. Finally, the bottle of water is a fashion accessory.

Naturally how much water we need varies according to our weight, height and gender but an average adult needs to drink about 1.5 liters of fresh water a day in addition to the water contained in food or other beverages. This helps replace the water we process internally and lose through urinating, breathing, sweating and bowel movements. If you consume about 2 liters of water through drinking it straight or in coffee, tea, and other beverages plus consuming a good diet, you should supply all the fluid your body needs. Many of us simply do not get even close to this goal.

The role of water in the elderly was recently highlights when it was discovered that a glass or two of water could frequently restore balance in elderly folk when they felt dizzy. Most old people do not drink enough water whether at home or in a care facility.

Don't wait until you feel thirsty

With so many soft drinks, frequent cups of tea or coffee, and poor eating habits, we often lose touch with feelings of thirst just as we have lost touch with the feelings of real hunger. Children retain this feeling for the need for fluid and frequently ask for glasses of water. When they want something to drink – and when you feel the need – then drink plain fresh water.

Don't wait until you feel thirsty to drink as by that time you are probably already slightly dehydrated. This is not good for your health and the older you are the less sensitive you are to your body's dehydration and your brain gets lazy in sending you signals to drink up. In 37 percent of Americans the thirst mechanism is so weak that it is mistaken for hunger.

Drink extra replacement water if you are exercising or working physically hard. Illness can cause us to lose more fluid from the body so if you are sick, drink more water. Since about 20 percent of our total fluid intake comes from food, a good diet with lots of fresh vegetables and fruit fulfills part of your water requirement.

Clean Water Tips

Drink tap water, not bottled.
Drink a glass of fresh water with each meal and between each meal.
Drink more water before, during and after exercise or hard physical work.
Substitute sparkling water for alcoholic drinks at social gatherings whenever you can.
Treat every glass of water as a wonderful, magical, holy gift.

A limited resource and a wasted one

We turn on a tap and there is our supply of clean water! How lucky we are since some 40% of people lack clean water. That means at least a billion people on earth don't have access to this indispensable resource. Unsafe water, which many people are forced to drink as it is the only water available to them, brings diseases that kill more people every year than all forms of war and violence. In the developing world such dirty water related diseases are the single most common threat to good health with an estimated 25,000 people dying *every day* from such illness.

Most of us know when we see images of our planet in all its lovely blueness that this colour is from earth's coverings of water – oceans, seas, rivers, lakes, and also the gentle stream that you found on a hillside last year. But of all that water, just 2.5% is fresh and of that amount only about 1% is unfrozen and therefore available. Water is a scarce commodity yet we continue to treat it as an unlimited resource. We may worry about the water bill, but we still run washing machines, dish washers, baths, showers, garden hoses, fast car wash-up places and, of course, endless golf courses. We pollute water all the time with industrial waste. We continue to use fertilizers and pesticides on our fields and gardens which leach into water sources and make fresh water undrinkable. We treat water with contempt as if the supply was endless. It is not.

As the population increases and our pollution and degradation of the planet continues in the name of convenience and economic growth, the amount of water available to us decreases. This decrease is now accelerating and is most notable when it comes to fresh water. *Le Monde Diplomatic* predicted in 2010 that if trends continue in just fifteen years more than 1.8 billion people will be living in regions of water-scarcity and two-thirds of the world's population could suffer *water stress*. This term *water stress* in ordinary language means *dying of thirst*. It is a painful, desperate way to die and takes about three days. In Britain, it is a way to death by dehydration on offer by many hospitals for those patients whose recovery is considered hopeless. It is called *The Liverpool Pathway* and was recently suggested by the professional staff to a friend whose ninety-one year old mother was in hospital. Happily, my friend took her mother home where the old lady is happily drinking as much water as she wants.

Where does all the water go?

The biggest user of water in the world is agriculture in terms of sheer volume. The agro-industrial sector is a user who appears not to care for it has low use efficiency while enjoying the privilege of subsidized water supplies.

We are often unaware of the waste of available water. For example, where I live a lot of corn is grown. Corn has a big appetite when it comes to water. Every year during the hot summer, the irrigation machinery works day and night. Our greatly increased consumption of meat means we need more corn for raising beef, but even so this use of water around me is used in an irresponsible way – and it is no different elsewhere in Europe or in America. Most irrigation machines spray water through the air. Some 10% of this water evaporates in the air before it even touches the plants or the soil. The farmers have invested huge amount of money in this irrigation equipment, usually through loans that are either subsided or that they cannot really afford. It does not matter that irrigation systems which run among the plants on the ground are more efficient. It does not matter that they plow so deeply and cut so mercilessly into the soil that they turn up the clay to the surface which should remain below the top soil in order to hold water. Being on the top the clay hardens in the sun and the water when it comes simply drains down into the more febrile soil, which not being clay, cannot hold the water. Hence, the need to constantly top up the corn with water by irrigation. It does not matter that the French government has run field trials showing that plowing to less depth means using less water. Our old habits die hard even when we know we need to change them.

Most of these same farmers, not just in France but across Europe, also pay little heed to warnings to wear masks and covering clothes when they spray chemicals, minerals, or some fertilizers on the soil. So if they do not care about their own personal health, why would they worry about the amount of water they use? In any case the water is subsidized and around where I live they throw pipe from pumps into the local streams and rivers and suck up as much water most of the time as they want. This profligate use of water cannot continue and governments are being forced now, including France, to rethink the implications for society of publically funded water subsidizes and public operated irrigation systems. Such expenditure has traditionally dominated national agricultural budgets.

For instance, in parts of Asia, including China, Indonesia and Pakistan, irrigation in the past has at times consumed more than half of all agricultural investments. India with its enormous population spends more than 30 percent of all public money on irrigation. Yet, India's insistence on updating ancient farming practices which conserved the available water by modern agricultural – industrial methods has been disastrous, resulting in little regard for the soil and the waste of enormous amounts of available water. The story is the same in Europe and the Americas. A quick glance at some statistics for available fresh water for different parts of the world between 1950 and the year 2000 confirms how rapidly we are reaching crisis point in water supplies: Africa from 20.6 down to 5.1; Asia from 9.6 down to 3.3; Latin America from 105 down to 28.3; Europe from 5.9 down to 4.1; and North America from 37.2 down to 17.5. At the same time the population increases and more people need water. Seven billion of them at the last count.

For now you have water, but one day you may turn on the tap and find nothing comes out. Blame yourself, your politicians and opinion formers, and an economic system based on profits not people.

Food security means using more water

The link between water and the security of our food supply is an intimate one with about 40 percent of the world's food production coming from irrigated land. As we eat more meat than ever before, our animals now require some 64 billion liters of drinking water *every* day. This is increasing year on year. No international or national official organization would disagree with the claim that water availability and irrigation is key to the success of future food security for the world. Yet, when it comes to fresh water, there are no global international policies in place at present and national ones are failing or are mediocre at best. This policy neglect as well as that for food itself, contributes to many of our major social, economic and environmental problems. Once again the collective society of the world lacks the political will to act on the known facts – but we can arrange global economic trade and financial summits at the drop of a hat – or rather at the drop of share markets.

For now if you live in developed countries you probably have the food you need, but one day you may find the cupboard bare.

Bottled water

You do not need bottled water if you live in Europe or North America. Your tap water is good enough. In fact some bottled water is not as pure as your local tap water. In spite of this the bottled water industry, composed of multinational corporations and supermarkets, have so convinced us that we need bottled water that it is now the world's most popular drink. Years ago when you dined at a restaurant with top food, you not only ordered good wine to go with the meal but also selected a special bottle of plain or fizzy water. Now it is so common to order bottled water at a restaurant meal, you need to ask for tap water if you want it. Cool springs flowing from green mountains to bring you pristine water are frequent images on those bottles of water lining every supermarket shelf. These images invoke goodness, health, and freshness. The reality in most cases is that the water is so filled with chemicals to purify it and so factory processed that it does not even have the memory of a mountain spring or river or stream. In a spiritual sense, if not a scientific one, it is dead water.

In addition to all this, bottled water in the way it resources water and processes it contributes to environmental problems. Recently, we were told not to reuse the plastic bottle the water comes in as the plastic in sunlight and heat leeches chemicals into the new contents which are unhealthy. It seems the more we imagine our habits lead to what we think is a better world and a better lifestyle, the further we get into bad stuff.

Stick to your local tap water. It is good enough and fresher and often more pure than bottled water.

The poverty connection between water and health

The poorest countries are forced to over-exploit their water resources based on the disastrous concept that economic growth is the single most important measure of a nation's progress. However, the poor without access to good fresh water are not always in some distant land. If you are one of the urban poor in Detroit or New Orleans, you may well have a problem with accessing good water and proper sanitation. True, you do not see people struggling with buckets of water from distant wells in these cities- but old buildings and poor sanitation are not the prerogative of developing countries.

Over population has, of course, contributed to the urgent need for more of everything – but plenty of so called developing countries have rich cultural heritages and former life-styles and social values which did not lead to unrelenting poverty, disease, and lack of food and water. In 1910 when a member of my family arrived to start a new life in South Africa, she recorded that the local native people were among the most fit and physically beautiful she had ever seen but within fifty years disease, slums, and lack of natural resources along with European food had become common place among them. Not all of their decline in health and fitness, she pointed out, came from racial exploitation but from a profound change in their food and social values and customs from native ones to those of Europeans. Other examples are plentiful from Latin America to Asia. We feel we must industrialize, that better business is somehow equated with social advancement and that national gross product is the measurement which counts most. The price for this way of running a society seems to be more disease, more poverty, more lack of fresh water, and the rapid disappearance of the integrity of local ecosystems on which people have always depended.

If you are reading this book, then you are not one of these deprived people. You are living in a bowl of plenty and probably just need to be aware of it. Start with drinking clean water – the gift of God's good earth and the beverage of universal life.

FRESH AIR

When I walk my dogs I sometimes sit under a tree and let the dogs roam about smelling histories which I will never know. The trees I usually sit under are just behind the cemetery wall so naturally it is quiet. I watch the cows in the nearby field. The wind blows the grass. The leaves above me whisper in chorus. I take a deep breath and feel very lucky for the air is fresh and sweet here, but elsewhere, perhaps where you live now, it is not so fresh. It is clean air we need for good health – and sunlight too. Seek it wherever and whenever you can.

Benefits of fresh air

The list of the benefits of getting fresh air into your body and mind is almost endless. It makes you realize we were born to breathe! Here are just a few of the many direct health benefits of fresh air: dilates your lungs and cleans them up; improves your blood pressure and heart rate; strengthens the immune system; stimulates your appetite [this does not mean you will eat more]; helps you sleep better; and alters the brain's chemistry positively – particularly the levels of serotonin which helps you improve your mood and promotes feelings of well-being. Fresh air clears and cleans our lungs, bringing more oxygen to our body cells. This gives us more energy. Oxygen also brings greater power and smoother functioning to the brain so we think better as we breathe better. We have more stamina too and our muscle strength improves.

No matter what age you are, breathing fresh air helps your over-all body functions and maintains good health, not just of the body but of the mind and spirit as well.

There is no substitute for fresh air

Re-circulated air, workplace air, canned air, air conditioning, heated air, any air "system" – these are not fresh air. Indoor or outside, wherever we go the air has dust and some level of pollution. Many indoor places of work or shopping have imported air. No matter how fresh such air may seem to you, it is no such thing. Fresh air is found outdoors such as in a park, garden, countryside or someplace where there are trees and grass and no cars. Sadly as we become more urbanized around the globe and more people live in cities, there is a decreasing access to fresh air unless people make a real effort to get some. They move from indoors at home which has dust and fumes to cars with closed circulation of air to shopping malls and supermarkets with air controls and providers. The effort to find fresh air can be difficult and often almost impossible for millions of people.

Fresh air cannot be found just anywhere outdoors these days. Not all of us have the privilege to be near trees, rivers or close to the mountains where we can fill our lungs with clean air. However, every one of us should make the effort to seek fresh air on a regular basis. You cannot live without it and you can't get enough of it. Seek the freshest you can find.

Are you suffering from stale air right now?

Here are just a few symptoms you can suffer from breathing stale air: feelings of nausea, headaches and dizziness; irritability; anxiety; and depression. As if these were not bad enough, stale air can bring conditions for catching more frequent colds. Most of us when we get any of these symptoms forget to consider the air we are breathing.

Consciousness has been raised about pollution now and air quality reports are readily available to everyone. Indoor air pollution and urban air quality are two of the world's worst pollution problems. The effects on your health even in relatively low levels of air pollution can be substantial. It costs the public a lot of money too. A British Columbia Lung Association investigation showed that just a one percent improvement in air quality can produce almost thirty million dollars in savings every year. The World Health Organization (WHO) estimates that there are some two million premature deaths caused each year due to air pollution in cities around the world. According to German scientists, people breathing in the fumes of heavy traffic regularly have a higher risk of heart attack. If you think jogging helps, don't do it in traffic. This will actually *reduce* the flow of blood to the heart and can trigger a heart attack even in normally health people. Poor old Los Angeles suffers up to triple the amount of particles in their air than most cities with consequent dire health effects. Air pollution has increased dramatically in our times. Fifty years ago the air was so clear in Mexico City you could see the surrounding beautiful mountains. Now the pollution is so bad you would be lucky some days to see the top of nearby office blocks. If you live in a major city you are at a higher respiratory and cardiovascular disease risk than the country dweller, but both need to be conscious of their intake of fresh air and their exposure to air pollution.

Why is air pollution so harmful?

We all know the throat restricting fumes of car exhausts and construction equipment. Even in the country the bellowing clouds of dust from tractors, smoke from crop and forest clearance, and vehicles driven over dirt tracks makes us aware of how many things we do that pollutes fresh air. An invisible enemy in this bad air is Ozone. No, don't look up at the sky for the Ozone holes you have read about – look down at your feet. Ozone forms at ground level when nitrous oxides and hydrocarbons react with sunlight. The reason we have to worry about the Ozone up in the sky is because up there it helps protect us from ultra-violet rays, a major cause of skin cancer. So Ozone can be a good guy, but when inhaled ozone reduces your breathing capacity. This makes you cough, gasp for air, and feel like you are choking. Other common symptoms of air pollution are burning eyes, and chest tightness. If you suffer from emphysema, heart trouble, or asthma, it is all much worse.

The good news is that when the air pollution goes and you get good air in your body, then the symptoms of air pollution are quickly alleviated for most of us.

How to prevent or lessen air pollution affecting you

The first thing most authorities recommend if we want to avoid air pollution when levels are high is to stay indoors as much as possible during the day. This is hardly the right prescription for your general health and if you suffer from depression you need as much sunlight as you can get. Unless medically advised otherwise, the best thing is to remain indoors only when the pollution levels, especially Ozone, are *exceptionally* high. Consult local radio and newspapers and the internet. If you go out on such days, try the early morning or after sunset when Ozone pollution is reduced.

How to get your supply of daily fresh air

The next time you feel any bad air symptoms, don't start medicating yourself, taking to your bed, or start moaning about it all, just try the following ten tips about getting that healthy intake of fresh air on a regular basis.

1. At night open your bedroom window- just a crack will do. Keep warm while you sleep- but leave the door open

as well so the air circulates.

2. When you have a break at work, try to get outside in the open. Just stand there and take some deep breathes. This helps you relax and gives you a chance to become mindful of the present moment. Don't think about your work or what someone just said to you or worries about home. Free the mind while you give liberty to your lungs.
3. When you are at home, do as the French do and open the windows when the weather is good and the air pollution low. Five minutes is enough. If you live in the city do it early in the morning before the traffic builds up or late at night when there are fewer car fumes.
4. *Never* smoke or allow smoking in your home or car under any circumstances.
5. Make certain any machines in your home like washing machines, gas cookers, or dish washers are properly ventilated. This includes any heating units, vacuums or other equipment which also should be regularly checked to see that they have clean filters.
6. Clean and sweep chimneys every year.
7. Exercise regularly.
8. Take a few moments each day just for deep regular breathing. Fill your lungs and grow more conscious of your breathing.
9. Avoid using scented candles, air fresheners or any artificial perfumes in your home. These popular but totally unnecessary products are full of chemicals. In France the government advises against them at any time where babies or young children play and sleep. If they are not good for your baby, they are not good for you. As well as filling your air at home with chemicals, they waste your money. The idea that burning a scented candle will somehow have a psychic effect on your mood is among the more doubtful ideas promoted by the media and alter-

native spirituality hotshots.

10. If your great-grandmother in all her heavy long dresses could do it, so can you – a good straight spine when you are walking and sitting helps open the chest and the lungs – you can breathe deeper for more oxygen. When you walk, let your arms swing free. It opens the chest and lungs.

Go green for good air

Plants are air-filtering and help absorb carbon dioxide from the air and produce oxygen. Some plants are better than others at this job. Below is a list of plants that includes those NASA in their *Clean Air Study* found helpful to clean the air in space stations. We are on earth. Earth is spinning in space. We are, therefore, on a space station – so get some of the plants listed below for your home or work place.

The recommendation of NASA suggests using between 15 and 18 such houseplants. The containers need be only about 6-8 inches in diameter. This may sound like a lot of plants but it really isn't when spread around the house from room to room. In an apartment or flat you are creating an indoor green space as well. This contributes not just to fresher air but your sense of well-being. It is not necessary to spend a lot of money on these plants. Start with a few and try to raise some of your own or exchange plants with friends. It is more fun than shopping for them and, somehow, plants you have grown or are given have a history that gives them individuality. In my garden, I treasure most the plants friends and family have given me. Each reminds me of someone I care for – such small, and admittedly often sentimental details, helping to build up a sense of contentment with life.

Plants have to be watered, of course, so make this action an opportunity to become more mindful. Focus on the plants when you water them. Consider their wonderment and beauty and make them a part of your contentment. This observation helps us to be mindful of the wonder of creation and such passing enchantments with the ordinary things of life always enriches us.

Areca palm (*Chrysalidocarpus lutescens*)
Bamboo palm or reed palm (*Chamaedorea sefritzii*)
Boston fern (*Nephrolepis exaltata* "Bostoniensis")
Chinese evergreen (*Aglaonema modestum*)
Cornstalk dracaena (*Dracaena fragans* 'Massangeana')
Dendrobium orchid (*Dendrobium sp.*)
Dumb cane (Camilla) (*Dieffenbachia*)
Dumb cane (Exotica) (*Dieffenbachia*)
Dwarf date palm (*Phoenix roebelenii*)
Elephant ear philodendron (*Philodendron domesticum*)
English Ivy (*Hedera helix*)
Gerbera Daisy or Barberton daisy(*Gerbera jamesonii*)
Golden pothos or Devil's ivy(*Scindapsus aures* or *Epipremnum aureum*)
Heartleaf philodendron(*Philodendron oxycardium,* syn. *Philodendron cordatum*)
Janet Craig dracaena(*Dracaena deremensis* 'Janet Craig')
Kimberly queen fern (*Nephrolepis obliterata*)
King of hearts (*Homalomena wallisii*)
Moth orchid (*Phalenopsis sp.*)
Peace lily (*Spathiphyllum* 'Mauna Loa')
Pot Mum or Florist's Chrysanthemum (*Chrysantheium morifolium*)
Red-edged dracaena (*Dracaena marginata*)
Rubber Plant (*Ficus elastica*)
Selloum philodendron(*Philodendron bipinnatifidum,* syn. *Philodendron selloum*)
Snake plant or mother-in-law's tongue(*Sansevieria trifasciata* 'Laurentii')

Spider plant (*Chlorophytum comosum*)
Warneck dracaena(*Dracaena deremensis* 'Warneckii')
Weeping Fig (*Ficus benjamina*)

SOUND SLEEP

This morning I got up tired and filled with negative feelings. I did not want to go to work. During the long night, I had checked the time again and again, walked around the room, gone to the bathroom, tossed, turned, and finally felt God had forgotten me. As I stared into the darkness, I felt like the Psalmist pleading: *I cry by night and I find no peace*. My saving grace is that when I got up so fatigued from lack of sleep I knew that there were millions of people feeling the same way. So what I write is to help me as much as you. I keep reminding myself to practice what I preach. That's a tough challenge but here we go:

How much sleep does a healthy person need?

We must sleep or our health can be seriously threatened. All the research that has been done shows that sleep deprivation can cause a long list of problems from trembling hands, blurred vision, and dizziness to anxiety attacks and depression. Writing in *The Proceedings of the National Academy of Science*, a team led by Dr Luis de Lecea claimed that sleep continuity is one of the main factors in various pathological conditions that affect memory, including Alzheimer's and other age-related cognitive deficits.

The period of sleep we need for a healthy and balanced life ranges from 4 to 10 hours depending on the individual. Influences include our genetic make-up and that is why you sometimes read that famous people, such as the former British Prime Minister Margaret Thatcher, could sleep just a few hours and still be efficient at their work and remain healthy. While there are no set hours that can be considered normal for everybody, it is still the quality of the sleep that counts. No matter how short or long the time you sleep, it must be sound sleep.

Do not sleep too much. Long hours of sleep can increase the

risk of heart disease, obesity, diabetes, high blood pressure, depression and reduce the efficiency of the immune system. As in all our daily habits, the need is to strike a balance, aiming for that which is the best one for you as an individual.

Quality counts

We spend about one third of our lives sleeping. It is not just the time we sleep but the *quality* of the sleep that counts. This quality of sleep refreshes and restores the body and mind. It helps us to live a calmer and more balanced life. Problems of sleep are almost always about the quality of your sleeping. However, all sleep is *not* the same.

Sound sleep is deep, unbroken sleep night after night in which your health is maintained through healing of your mind and body and from which you awake naturally refreshed. Years of sleep research shows that it is not lack of sleep that actually troubles most people but sleep which is *broken*.

Worry doesn't do any good

The more we worry about sleeping the more it is likely to be broken and not sound sleep. The outstanding principle of improving the quality of your sleep is to change the way you think about sleep. Just that change of viewpoint is enough to start improving your sleep.

The Institute of Psychiatry at Oxford University is one of the most distinguished such medical association in the world. One of its members, Professor Richard Tilleard-Cole, knew a great deal about our sleeping, publishing many scientific papers on the subject and lecturing to other scientists about it. He told me this: *The secret of successful sleep is not to worry about it. The calmer the mind, the calmer the body. It gets on with its job. You sleep. So never worry about not sleeping. Unless you have some rare disease, you will eventually sleep sooner or later.*

Nothing much in the way of recent sleep research seems to have improved upon his advice. We know a great deal about what sleep is and how it works, but not one definitive method to get us to sleep when we cannot seem to do it. What all of us sufferers want to know is how do we follow the professor's advice and get our monkey minds to be *calm*?

Calmness first

Working with imagery is one such potentially powerful tool in helping you to sleep well. You can think of green pastures or other pleasant scenes, even the traditional counting the number of sheep jumping the fence may help. The point is to get your mind away from negative thoughts and worries to imagery and thoughts which are peaceful. In the long term, it is the solving during your waking hours of these negative feelings and emotions that is the best remedy for insomnia which is another term for broken sleep. Anxiety, fears, restlessness, worry, and over-stimulation can cause insomnia. For most of us the Professor's advice to be calm is hard to achieve, but we can keep trying to make such tranquility our goal, especially at bedtime.

Classic events that make for broken sleep

In acute illness or after an emotional shock, we usually can't sleep well. We lose the pattern of our sleeping. Our physical rhythms have temporarily changed. We have displaced our normal routines and often our surroundings, losing a sense of place and of belonging.

One of the most common such experiences is the trauma of grief. Losing someone we love penetrates us so deeply that our mind and body find difficulty coping. Without sound sleep the situation can become grave and threaten our health. Grief can put us in free-fall and our lack of sleep wounds the body and mind and derives us of hope in the future. Grief is a disastrous state for anyone, but one of the aspects of life that is an essential part of being alive and certainly of having loved. Some say such loss is the price we pay for love. In any case it affects us in mind, body and spirit and this includes our sleeping pattern.

Sometimes during life changing events such as a death, divorce or loss of a job, we need help in sleeping so that we can enjoy our nightly time of recovery and refreshment which we especially need. Before bedtime, think about trying herbal teas or warm milk, meditation, or an hour without television or phone talk. If your doctor suggests you take some medication to help you sleep during this disturbing period of your life, it can be a good idea. You do not need it for long so you will not become dependent on it. It is only a temporary measure until natural sleeping patterns return. Treat it as such with the guidance of your medical advisor. Do not start popping non-prescription sedatives.

Spiritual aspects of sleeping

The medical treatment of sleep problems and disorders is a relatively new field of health care. Millions of tired people complain of what they call *light sleep* and millions more will put their sleep problems down to daytime stress. In order to really tackle these sleep problems we need to see ourselves as a unified being of mind, body, and spirit. Unfortunately many health care workers still routinely separate out the different elements of this intimate union and try to treat one as separate from the whole. This reinforces the idea of duality, rather than promoting the reality that everything is connected – there is no here and there, no them and us, no mind disconnected from the body, no mind or body disconnected from that which we may call the spirit of the person. Such duality has helped us to ruin just about everything in our lives from the way we treat each other to the way we treat our planet to the way we view God. Most research shows that the problems of sleep are almost equally divided between mental ones and physical ones and that both are inseparable in effecting sound sleep. If we are to have sound sleep we then need to understand and cater for issues of both mind and body. This is not possible unless we include the spiritual element.

The idea that our sleep has a spiritual dimension which plays a vital role in true health is hardly new. John Chrysostom [354-407 CE], an early and still famous Christian whose eloquent writing remains in print today, had this to say about using the night to regain the rhythm of life: *If you are willing to reflect on the meaning of night, you will also discover the infinite providence of the Creator. Night restores the tired body and relaxes limbs which are tense through the efforts of the day. By means of rest, night helps them regain their rhythm. And not only that. Night sets you free from sorrow and relieves your worries. It often reduces fever by making sleep a cure and by changing itself into a doctor's assistant. That is the importance of night. It is so great that often if you cannot benefit from your rest you will not have the strength to face a new day. At night, as in a time of truce, the exhausted soul and the worn out body regain their energy and are prepared to take up their daily activity again. On the other hand, if we prolong the day into the night, we are condemning ourselves to being useless because gradually our strength is wasted.*

I especially like his alluding to sleep as a time of truce, as if we were at war with ourselves when we are awake which, of course, most of us are.

So there are spiritual factors at play in your sleep problems too. For example, many people now live alone. When they go to bed feelings of loneliness can easily arise. The body cannot relax because the mind is fretting - and the only proper place for fretting is if you are making lace. Since this is not what you are doing, the result of such unease is a sense that nobody really cares about you. This is not an uncommon thought and teenagers can suffer from it as easily as the elderly.

An absence of hope can be at the root of such feelings. Such lack of hope is spiritual in nature for it is not something we can buy or create simply by making an intellectual decision about it. Hope arises from our will to live and is one of the single most important motivational powers we can possess. It gives invisible but real strength that sustains us when the world around us is full of injustice, maltreatment, war, and other cruelties. There is no *vain hope* for all hope is an energy that permits us to survive – and it also helps us sleep for it ameliorates those feelings of being lost and forgotten. Such hope is grounded in faith that the universal life of all living things is essentially good. This brings positive feelings about the future. If we have such hope, we may turn more easily away from negative feelings toward trusting that all will be well and that we are important in our own right. This sense of trust and self-worth springs from that hope which has been called the Mother of Charity. This tells us that to hope is to love life. When we go to sleep this way with the spirit of hope in our hearts, we have put ourselves into a more tranquil state where the responses of a calm body and mind may arise. We accept our present situation without fear, anxiety or despair. This state of inner grace leads us to the sound sleep of a soul at peace. We have used the night to regain the rhythm of life.

Time keeping is not part of sleeping

A term that is widely used by those who research and treat sleep problems is *closure*. This term means that the person trying to go to sleep has not closed down or shut off emotional thoughts and worries. They are still occupied with concerns of their waking life. In effect they have not finished with their day time life.

One of the most important things that can affect our not closing down when we go to bed has to do with time-monitoring patterns of thinking. These include lots of time checking actions from looking at the clock when you turn out the light to waking during the night and checking the time. A friend of mine is so pre-occupied with what the time is that she gave up wearing a wristwatch because she found herself constantly looking at it for no reason. But still her obsession persisted. During the day she is neither early nor late for an appointment. Not by even a minute. At night she awakes often, turns on the light and checks the time. The same routine every night and she always asked herself the same questions. How much had she slept? How long was there left for her to sleep? Needless to say, she suffers from broken sleep. Yet, she finds it impossible to stop her time watching behavior. One day forgetting momentarily that she did not wear a wrist watch I asked her what time it was. She opened her handbag and took out a small alarm clock.

Old habits die hard. This is good to remember when you are trying to change any of them in order to live well in hard times.

As the experts tell us, the secret to sound sleep is to break the lock time monitoring has over you. If you are to achieve this and get sound sleep, then three important and critical issues need to be solved. The first issue is poor sleep *quality*. The second is *behaviour patterns* which defeat going to sleep in the first place. The last are *closure issues* such as time monitoring. It is possible to tackle these one by one until your sleeping pattern is normal.

Preparing to sleep

Here are some things to prepare you for sleeping well.

Put to one side any work – even reading – that you brought home from your daytime employment. As Leviticus in the Old Testament wisely said, *there is a time to hold and a time to let go.* Work does not belong in your bed. I classify paying your household bills as part of work. Do not do them just before you go to bed. Paying bills is opening a can of worry worms. Avoid this and any other potentially stressful activity near bedtime.

Resist drinking alcohol just before bed and the same goes for smoking if you are still a slave to it. The metabolizing of alcohol by the body has an alerting effect. Skip other stimulants too like coffee or tea.

Schedule any vigorous exercise like gym, jogging, or running at least five hours before you go to bed. Vigorous exercise causes your body temperature to rise and the natural chemicals and actions of your body which make you feel sleepy will not start up until your temperature drops. If you are going to give the dog an evening stroll just before bedtime, make it a short one.

Some prescription and over-the-counter medications can interfere with sleep. Blood pressure medication and birth control pills are ones to check out. Some dieting pills can interfere as well, but hopefully you are eating a balanced diet with fresh food so you do not have a weight problem.

Sleeping pills are not the solution. Doctors are often far too quick to prescribe them and the over-the- counter self-medications are equally a bad idea. They quickly lose their effectiveness and they can become addictive, if not by their ingredients then psychologically.

Make the bedroom an inviting place. As the poet Marlowe's passionate shepherd wrote…

By shallow rivers, to whose falls
Melodious birds sing madrigals.
And I will make thee beds of roses
And a thousand fragrant posies.

It would be wonderful to get such a bedtime invitation every night but chance would be a fine thing! So we need to create our own delightful place of rest if not of romance.

Get yourself a decent bed. That means a mattress that suits your back and feels right for you. Even though warned continuously by the media and health advisors that the reason most people suffer back problems is due to worn out or too soft a mattress, millions of people continue to ignore this fact. An old friend of mine complained of her aching back. When I asked about her mattress, she would not admit it had anything to do with her complaint. *After all,* she told me, *my father and grandfather slept perfectly well on it and had no back trouble.* I drove her immediately to the Mall to buy a new mattress.

In these hard times, if you cannot afford a new mattress then get a board or a door. Put it under the mattress so that it becomes firm again. Never buy second-hand used mattresses. You don't know its age and history – or even if the cleaning really did get rid of uninvited little guests. Think mites and bed bugs.

Start making your bedroom a restful place by eliminating the clutter. Hang up the dumped clothes, put away the books and magazines, clean up the top of the bureau, and shut the wardrobe doors. Make the room tidy as if a house buyer or your mother were inspecting it. You may ask why you need to do this since you won't see any of the mess in the dark anyway. But there is a point to this apparently useless effort. You need to make a sleeping space that is physically and psychologically helpful in calming your mind, body, and spirit.

For example on the purely physical side, if light bothers you then be certain to block light coming through your windows. Even moon light, gentle as it is, can keep people awake. If noise from neighbours or outside disturbs you, wear earplugs. After awhile, you will get used to them. Modern ones are really effective in blocking sound – and they are cheap to buy.

When you tidy up your bedroom you are performing a little ritual. This will help emotionally to distance you from negative thoughts and worries and get you into the present moment which is about getting ready to have a good night's sleep.

Lavender is an ancient herb traditionally used for relaxation and bringing on sleepiness. You do not need to splash on expensive essential oil of lavender or spray the room with a lavender scented mist. A simple lavender sachet under your pillow will do. You can make it yourself without too much fuss. If you don't have any in the garden, a friend may. If not, a small bunch in its cotton envelope lasts for months. Whenever I think of buying any flowers, I recall the old Chinese saying *a country where flowers are expensive is not yet civilized.* This seems to me to be as good an indicator of a community's well-being as any economist's survey. So perhaps your spending a few pennies on some lavender is a social and political statement as well as a purchase for aiding sleep.

If you read when you get in bed, read a book that is easy, entertaining and which does not fill you with angst. A nice romance or a high adventure tale is better than some book about the war in Afghanistan or why the stock market will crash yet again. Reading at bedtime is to relax you, not fill your mind with worrisome stuff.

If your partner is causing you to lose sleep, for example by chronic snoring, then consult your health care advisor. Do not put up with being disturbed. Your lack of sound sleep will eventually affect your mood and that will have a negative effect on your relationship.

Sex and sleep. No matter how exciting other places might be, the bed is still the most favoured place for sex. Since orgasms increase endorphins which can help you fall asleep, don't deny yourself this lovely way to dreamland. Believe it or not, a recent survey of 10,000 English men revealed that 48 percent actually fall asleep *during* sex.

Meditation helps get you relaxed. Breathing exercises for a few minutes before turning out the light often reduces stress. There is no particular trick to the breathing – just concentrate on your breath as you draw it in and exhale. Feel it. See it. Repeat for at least five minutes. Tame the monkey mind.

The position in which you sleep does not matter and is not under your control. You may prefer to start by resting on the left or right side or lying flat on your back or belly. It is said that lying on one's right was the tradition of the Prophet Muhammad, peace and blessings be upon him. In any event, you will turn in many positions on the bed during the night and you will not know it. This is not restless turning in which you are half-awake, but the process of sound sleeping.

During the day various activities stimulate us, but at bedtime maintain a consistent routine. Our mind and bodies like healthy routines and no more so than when it comes to meals and bedtime. A balanced rhythm of these essential daily events brings well-being.

Nap time is not just for your baby or old folks

Mid-day is the prime time for catching a cat-nap, snoozing off, or enjoying a Spanish siesta. A half-hour nap during the day is worth almost two hours of regular night time sleeping, so if you nap then remember you may need less sleep that night. As to your work, midday is when we are at our least efficient. We seem naturally to slow down then. In Japan, offices and factories often have designated nap spaces to encourage people to sleep at midday, thus increasing their productivity in the afternoon hours. In Europe and America we are unlikely to find such enlightened employers, but in your lunch break you can go to your car or take a folding chair somewhere and just sit relaxed or stretch out best you can, close your eyes, and let yourself drift away. Even if you do not sleep, the relaxation will improve your afternoon's efficiency.

Sleep & lose weight

Studies have shown that those on a diet who slept an average of 8 ½ hours a night for two weeks lost 56% more body fat than those dieters who only slept 5 ½ hours which is less than the average duration of sleep. The researchers put this down to the sleep and wake cycle, believing that in sleep deprived people hormones are triggered which tell the body to feel hungry. A recent report in the *International Journal of Obesity* showed that lower stress levels also predicted greater weight loss. While a much more detailed study with a larger number of people is needed, these preliminary results suggest that if you are on a diet then sleeping well is going to aid weight reduction. The core message is eat less, move more, and sleep well.

Dreaming

To sleep, perchance to dream – William Shakespeare

Sleep brings dreams. Some are wonderful. Some are nightmares. We have no control over them. All the world's literature and religions speak of dreams and dreaming. Scientists still find dreams and their purpose a mystery. I am glad that they remain puzzled. Researchers have invaded so much of our private lives with their endless quest for definitions that at least our dreams are still safe for the moment. We need the hidden life and private secrets that our dreams so often explore.

Historically we have always had this curiosity about dreams and every culture has speculated over what dreams could mean. Psychology has had a go for years about such meanings. Culturally, dreams have been treated as messages from the gods, as predictions of the future, of belonging to the occult or religion. Prophetic dreaming containing divine messages is common to hundreds of societies throughout history including our own. Is God speaking to us in our dreams? No one can say but many prophets have claimed it. Is it the conscious mind which is at rest, giving the unconscious a nightly chance to rise up to active life? Is it our mind getting rid of unnecessary clutter from the day? Are our dreams foretelling some future event? Do they express our hidden desires or emotions? Theories abound and there is no agreed biological definition of the true purpose of dreaming. No one knows all the answers to the many questions about dreams. What we do know is that dreaming is an inseparable part of being human.

Other creatures appear to show the same sleeping states as humans. Who has not seen a sleeping pet dog start to twitch and paw the air as if in chase? We commonly just assume they are dreaming. I like the idea that my two canaries dream on their nightly perches, perhaps of wings fluttering in a grand sky that for their safety they cannot do in their waking hours.

A very pleasing concept of sleep has been put forward by Dr. Deirdre Barrett, a psychologist at Harvard Medical School. Known for her research on dreams, she has described dreaming as simply us thinking in a different biochemical state. She believes people continue to work on all the same problems in that state as they might when awake. This includes just about anything from musical composition and math solutions to work and relationship problems. The American Nobel Prize winner John Steinbeck summed it up this way: *It is a common experience that a problem difficult at night is resolved in the morning after the committee of sleep has worked on it.*

This gets better all the time for having called a truce in the war of our awakened self, we now have a Peace Committee to work it all out.

Our need for day dreams and sleep dreams

In any case when we enjoy sound sleep we dream and this is good for our health. We need also to dream when we are awake for it is all our dreaming – asleep and awake – that can open the vistas of our creativity and help us to understand ourselves. Since dreams affect our moods, they serve to act as a kind of virtual reality of how we feel. No artist or entrepreneur would want to give up dreaming for it is a step in realizing a vision.

Each of us needs the hope in the future that dreams can bring, because these day dreams and night dreams often move us forward to seek change in our life. Perhaps we are not just what we *eat,* but what we *dream*. We can begin to find contentment with our lives by enjoying the benefits of sound sleep.

DAILY EXERCISE

Here is something that costs nothing and brings a multitude of benefits. You do not need special shoes or clothes. You do not need to spend a penny on anything. You simply open your front door and go for a walk.

Exercising everyday will improve your mobility, help keep down your weight, keep your heart and other essential organs fit, release tensions and stress, and lift up your spirits. Walking is something you are born to do. It is an intrinsic human function. Yet, we seem determined to walk as little as possible. Where once men and women walked to work and children to school – and this could mean many miles - today not to take a car or bus seems very odd indeed. With an elevator at hand, many people refuse to climb any stairs – even to the first floor.

When a child I use to sit waiting for breakfast by a large window where I could watch the street below. My favourite time was when a short plump young woman would scurry by. She had a funny walk, slightly swaying from side to side with each step. I found this amusing. Later when I asked my father about her he told me she had five children and every morning walked to her work in the canning factory. *But it's on the other side of town!* I cried. My father replied: *It's only seven miles from start to finish- less than fifteen miles in total.* He did not think it too far or odd or even unusual, because in those days when few people had cars and buses fares were unaffordable on a regular basis, it was normal for the vast majority of people to walk. Gone are such days in Western countries.

Walking which comes naturally to us is our cheapest and most environmentally friendly mode of transportation. We hear an enormous amount about how electric cars will help pollution, but next to nothing about how just using our feet might help save the planet. Thich Nhat Hanh, the famous Buddhist Zen Master says this about walking: *People usually consider walking on water or in thin air a miracle. But I think the real miracle is not to walk either on water or in thin air, but to walk on earth. Every day we are engaged in a miracle which we don't even recognize: a blue sky, white clouds, green leaves, and the curious eyes of a child - our own two eyes. All is a miracle.*

Benefits of regular exercise

More than 2,400 years ago Hippocrates, a Greek, who is considered the Father of Medicine, claimed walking is a man's best medicine. Today we know even a little exercise can have an enormous impact on your health. The physical benefits include keeping your weight down, lowering your blood pressure, making your heart stronger, improving your lung capacity, muscle strength, blood flow, and helping your body to have a raised level of good HDL cholesterol. How right that ancient Greek was in spite of not being able to say *...and research shows it!*

On the mental and emotional aspects, exercise improves your sense of well-being, helps lift depression and generally gives you a more positive view of life. From the spiritual aspect, exercise can bring better mindfulness with a keener awareness of your surroundings and other people. This amazing effect on you means that simple exercising has released you into an operational mode which results in a more complete union of your mind, body and spirit. If you think this sounds too much like a magic cure for all your ills – well, maybe it just is!

How much exercise?

In the final analysis how much you should exercise depends on an individual assessment of your present state of health. Even then there is conflicting information from health experts about just how much exercise we actually need. It is likely that the amount of exercise we need for good health is fairly minimal. Some health experts advise you to do vigorous activity at least three times a week. As to walking, everyday twice a day for 20 minutes seems a good rule of thumb.

A surprising number of people see no point in walking. The trouble seems to be that they are so goal orientated that simply walking around quickly bores them. At a hotel near me, the manager gets in the car and drives to get his daily newspaper – the shop is just two minutes walk away! In America, say in Hollywood, it is possible to drive down a street and see cars but no pedestrians. We make a lot of excuses for using our cars, but we were born with legs and feet and need to use them.

You can make your walking part of your daily life – walk to work, walk to the shops, walk to the train or bus station instead of driving and get off the train or bus just a few stops from your destination and walk the rest of the way home. When you are on your lunch break, take ten minutes of it to walk around, loosen up your muscles, and get your head around something besides what is going on at work. As to rain, a little water will not make you shrink.

At first make it a short walk around the block for the first couple of weeks. This gets you in the habit. When you walk notice what is going on – hopefully you do not live in a dangerous inner city ghetto, but even then there are times when it is safe. Keep your head up, eyes open, arms swinging freely to open your lungs. Ask a friend to join you for your walk. You will find plenty of people who need the exercise and your invitation acts as an encouragement for them to start doing more exercise.

Once you are in good shape you can do more strenuous exercises every day. We are told these should always include stretching and bending and those movements which increase and deepen our breathing, raising our pulse rate somewhat.

If you decide to add this kind of more vigorous exercise to your life, then always warm up before starting after having waited a couple of hours after eating a meal. Wear loose-fitting and comfortable clothes, and drink some water at the end of the activity to replace what you may have lost in sweating. If you feel dizzy or get chest pain and shortness of breath, check it out with a doctor. Finally, do not over exert yourself – this accomplishes nothing.

Today gym and exercise classes are held in most communities. These range from traditional gym workouts to the gentler arts of Yogi and Tai-Chi. The cost is minimal and many are free of charge. The instructors will show you how to do more vigorous exercise that will help you and there are plenty of leaflets, brochures, and online information where you can pick up the detailed advice of professional health experts plus exercise programmes on CD. For the elderly, if you can walk as well as spend some time playing, you can leave the more active stuff to the middle-aged or the young. The important thing is to make your exercise part and parcel of your ordinary day.

Dancing

While regular exercise in whatever form lifts our spirit and makes us feel better, there is nothing like dancing to achieve this result. Every culture has its own variety of dances but no matter how or where you dance you are creating an atmosphere of joy. You are becoming a free spirit. As we skip, step, and whirl through a dance the glad cry of our bodies is *Rejoice! Rejoice!*

From time to time I give a spirituality retreat. The people who attend these are a mixed group of various ages and different kinds of work experience and careers with a variety of spiritual and self-improvement interests. In one of these groups was a seventy-five year old man called Tom. Talking with him privately, it emerged that Tom started his working life as a ballet dancer. A dancing career on stage is short for male ballet dancers so when he had to give up public performances, he started teaching dance. He eventually retired and found life as a widower very lonely. He eventually became depressed and was finding life not worth living. After his beloved wife, the thing he missed most was dancing. No anti-depression drugs and no amount of seeing other people dance either in the theatre or on CDs and TV satisfied his desire for moving to music. His very soul yearned for this expression of his deepest feelings. He told me that one evening as he stared at another senseless bit of entertainment on the television, he suddenly turned it off, got up and started dancing around his sitting room. He stumbled a bit. He felt at one point rather dizzy – but he was moving again. He was dancing! He started doing it every day. He began exercises to improve his muscles and balance. He lost his excess weight and got trim. With all these work-outs his flexibility improved and, unsurprisingly, his depression lifted. He found himself having a ballet exercise bar installed in his bedroom. He worked out every day and soon found he could still turn a nifty leap in the air. No longer depressed, he became more outgoing and started telephoning old friends. One day he chanced on the telephone number of a ballerina he had once danced with in London and New York. On an impulse he telephoned her. This lead to something quite different than what you may think. They did not fall in love. She told him she had been asked to do a walk-on dance part with one of the world's most famous ballet companies and needed to have a partner for the character role she was to dance. Would he do it? From that performance with all its rehearsals and meetings, a new life opened for Tom. Depression became a thing of the past. Through the exercise and art of his dancing he discovered that when we are embodied- that is accepting and living not just in our minds but actively in our bodies - the spirit awakes and joins the play for it too needs exercise.

Lose weight now – exercise helps conquer over-eating

Everybody knows that when you exercise you burn off calories. What is less well understood is that when we exercise it also makes us feel less hungry. The physical exertion makes our body much more sensitive to whether we feel full or not. When we feel full we eat less. This phenomenon shows that exercise plays a vital role in helping solve over-weight by returning the body to a state where we can recognize real hunger and know when it has had enough food. What apparently happens is that an excessive intake of fat in food creates failures in the signaling mechanism which controls feelings of satiety in the brain. These failures result in the person being unable to recognize when they have had enough food and, consequently, they keep eating. Researchers from the University of Campinas in Brazil have demonstrated that exercising increases the protein levels in the brain's hypothalamus. This enhances sensitivity of neurons in recognizing two hormones which control appetite – insulin and leptin. This study has added considerable weight to what we understand about how exercise helps control our weight.

However, reading about such research is not exercising just as reading about a diet is not dieting. The result of you knowing this scientific research about exercise and your brain should be an added incentive to getting on with walking, bicycling or hiking, or whatever exercise you want to do.

Keeping to a exercise programme

As I said in the beginning of this book, scientific research has repeatedly shown that it takes about 21 days to establish a habit. So in the first three weeks of any new way of living your programme or schedule must be designed to help you get through these first few weeks.

The thing is you have to exercise every day, *no matter what.*

This very hard for most people. Excuses abound. I can find a million of them when I don't want to take the time to exercise. It is discipline which is called for until your exercise pattern becomes a set part of your daily life – and you look forward to it with pleasure.

Although a lot of health experts and physical exercise experts tell you it helps, I personally do not think writing down what exercise you take and matching the exercise to lost calories is really something anyone sticks to. In fact, I find it discouraging and so may you. Making a record of exercise may initially give you some motivation and a goal – but will you keep it up or just get bored? My advice is not to waste time and paper. Just make the object of your exercise *pure enjoyment.* The calories will burn. The weight loss will come.

When not to exercise

Do not exercise when you are ill. If you have a fever, stay home and rest. The fever shows your body's immune system is at war with some infection. Do not add exercise to the battle field. Your body needs to get on with its main job. Having a cold does not rule out exercise – but don't go to the gym and give it to other people. Exercising when you have a cold does not make it worse. Skip any kind of exercise if you have the flu. Go to bed. Treat yourself with loving care.

Exercise and medical conditions

If you have any health condition which needs medical supervision and medication, then always check with your health advisor before starting an exercise regime.

If you one of the many people who suffer from asthma or have respiratory flare-ups, then be sure to warm up enough before starting any exercise even brisk walking. If you get tired or get out of breathe or start feeling weak while exercising, stop at once and rest.

Asthma is an increasing problem for children and adults. Perhaps it is lifestyle or pollution but in any case breathing problems not only limits the amount of exercise you take but can dramatically limit your available energy. Some research has shown that asthma sufferers' breathing is at fault. If you suffer from asthma symptoms, there are breathing exercises to help correct this or improve respiratory function. The most current widely medically endorsed non-drug alternative therapy for improved breathing in asthma suffers is the Buteyko Breathing Technique. The celebrated Mayo Clinic in America called it most promising and in the British Thoracic Society's guideline on the management of asthma this technique is suggested as an effective method to help reduce symptoms and the use of bronchodilators. If you can successfully get off drugs in treating your asthmatic symptoms and not spend money on these as well as visits to your doctor, then you have saved on spending while improving your health. This leads to a better quality of life and that brings increased contentment. If you are an asthma sufferer, then discuss the Buteyko method with your medical adviser before undertaking changes to your exercise pattern. Some insurance companies today cover the cost of being instructed in this breathing technique.

Yoga and breathing are inseparable so this ancient practice in its various styles and schools may also help alleviate many respiratory symptoms. There are yoga classes in almost every community and neighbourhood. Many are free or you give a "modest teacher donation" or whatever you feel you can afford.

If you recently suffered a concussion, take great care about exercising even walking. A concussion is a traumatic brain injury, and your brain needs to heal properly. ***Do not start exercises except ordinary walks around the house until and unless your medical specialist tells you it is okay to do more.*** You certainly do not work out at the gym. That is a big *no-no*.

Any sudden pain that does not go away after a few minutes when you exercise requires you to stop what you are doing. If pain persists, seek medical attention.

Extreme or persistent fatigue can be a sign of illness. Do not undertake exercise until you have checked out your condition with a doctor.

If you are pregnant, ask your prenatal clinic, midwife or your doctor for a safe exercise programme. Exercise is good for you and swimming, special yoga classes for expectant mothers, moderate exercise and low-impact movements are beneficial. Daily walking can be ideal for maintaining a healthy pregnancy.

There are many ways of walking

If you thought walking was just about putting one foot in front of the other, think again. There are many ways of walking. Here are just a few and every one of them can be fun. Wear the right shoes or boots and clothes. Leave mobile phones off. Do not plug yourself into your music player. Open eyes, ears, and lungs. Remember life *is* good. Now pick one of these walks and get started.

Strolling is walking along at a goodly pace but still being able to talk to someone or occasionally stop to admire the scenery. You are not in a hurry but you have decided how far to walk.

Sauntering is fairly slow and you pay little attention to getting where you are going. You talk perhaps, you stop and sit down for awhile, and you thoroughly enjoy the journey. This is one of the nicest kinds of walk. I love to saunter. When I go with my *serious walking* friends and I dare to saunter they hate it. *Oh, Come on!* , they say, at *this rate it will take us all day*! I shrug and think: I don't care if it takes all week- I am enjoying the world right now.

Meandering means you are walking nowhere in particular.

Fancy is your guide as to where and how you walk. You may even get lost when you meander.

Hiking is a deliberate setting out for a goal. You have a plan. You are prepared for challenges so out with the walking boots. The hills and the mountains beckon. Hiking can be solo or in a group and it is usually high up on the scale of physical exertion.

Wandering is mystical. You may even be in a bit of a daze. You become one with all that is around you. There are no goals, no boundaries. Time stands still yet you are still moving.

Meditative Walking is movement to still the mind, using your breathe and motion as a deliberate rhythm to help the mind empty. A walking meditation is about paying attention. It helps develop balance and a patient durability of your ability to concentrate. One of the most widely practiced walking meditations is a Buddhist one.

The Venerable Sayadaw U Pandita, one of the foremost living master of Vipassana meditation, is the abbot of Panditãrãma Monastery and Meditation Centre in Rangoon, Burma. He has taught meditation worldwide since 1951 and describes five benefits of walking meditation attributed to The Buddha. While these are intimately linked to Buddhist ethos and sitting meditation practice, they are also quite applicable to those who are not Buddhists. This practice is not contrary to Christian faith.

The first is that walking meditation increases your stamina.

The second is that in bringing mindfulness of the present moment, it helps prepare you for the actual practice of sitting meditation [which I discuss elsewhere in this book.]

Thirdly, the continuous shifting of your body in the walking movements revives muscle tone and stimulates your circulation.

The fourth benefit is to assist digestion – a great benefit these days when so many people complain of poor digestion, lower gut problems, and difficulties with eating many different kinds of food. Good digestion means that your bowels are kept in good working order. This minimizes feelings of fatigue and torpor.

The fifth and last benefit of walking meditation according to the Buddha is that it builds up your ability to concentrate. Such focus is essential if you are to carry out any practices that bring good health.

As I said, you do not have to be a Buddhist to do meditative walking or even have any interest in Buddhism as a spiritual path. Walking meditation practice is so successful for so many people that it is worth you giving it a serious try. Here is a simplified method:

Pick a place inside or out, perhaps not more than 20 steps in length. This walking is not about physically going anywhere. The journey is to use your walking and breathing to go into your inner self. Do not stare down at your feet – you do not want this image floating around your brain. You need to focus yourself on the sensations you are feeling which are not visual – for example, lightness, warmth, coldness. Deliberately take very slow steps. One foot after the other in a line to the far end of your walking space. Turn and walk back. At the end, turn and walk back again. Continue to repeat this pattern. Soon you may feel bored, maybe anxious. Don't worry, it is part of the process. Keep walking this way. Do not try to escape your boredom. Soon it will pass and you will be so into walking up and down that you will begin not to notice the room or outside trees or cars or whatever is there. Keep walking – you should continue in this fashion for a good 20 minutes. Later do it for 30 minutes. Empty the mind. Calm the body. Forget darkness. Become light. Buddhists commonly do a walking meditation for an hour.

The rhythm of this walking and the gentle yet deliberate breathing decidedly clears and stills the mind. Soon you may enter a meditative state. Even if all that happens is that you relax that is a healthy result too. Most people have no idea how just doing the natural thing of lifting up and putting down your feet can be filled with such incredible possibilities.

Try meditative walking the next time you feel stressed at

work. Even a ten minute walking meditation serves to focus the mind. Take your break outside where you can walk up and down undisturbed. Notice only the rhythm of your breathing. Let your worries go. Remember everything is a cycle – ups and downs, downs and ups. All passes. All will be well.

Mindfulness Walking can be the your goal even if the practice is not meditative walking as described above. In mindfulness walking you are trying to focus totally in the present moment of your life. You might decide to do a mindfulness walk because you have just had an argument with your partner or you have burned some cooking or the noise and confusion at home is getting you down. Mindfulness helps us escape the worries about what has already happened or worries about what might happen later or tomorrow. Since the past is gone and the future is unknown everyone knows it does no good to get worried about either- but we all live in the three realms – past, present and future. It is how we balance these elements of our history that counts. When you get too stressed or feel overly anxious then try mindful walking. Focus on what is happening as you walk: How do you feel – legs, arms, head, face, hands? Is your hair blowing in the wind? In fact, is there even a breeze? What does the air smell like? What can you hear? Look at what is around you. Pay close attention to what is going on *now.*

Joy Walks are little pilgrimage somewhere just for the sheer fun of it – through the woods; quality time with the children; exploring a hill; finding a spot of wild flowers to look at- the possibilities for joy walking are endless just like a good fairy tale. The announcement you need to make to yourself and family or friends is: *Let's go for a walk!* Forget exercising – you will be doing that in any case. Forget about any purpose to your walk except pure pleasure. Just walk for joy.

Journeys are serious stuff. You are setting out to get somewhere. It may be the supermarket or it could be a museum on the far side of the city. In any case, you have a plan and you have much determination. You mean to get there. When you come home you will talk about your journey for certain.

Trekking can be a bit like hiking only it is usually in the open country. Camping out or making planned stops on your way as well as carrying a backpack is usually all part of the deal. Being prepared is an important aspect of getting ready to trek. You set out and walk – stomping, struggling, insistently pushing your way through thick and thin, valleys, woods, field, open spaces and all challenges that you meet. You are always aware of nature reserve regulations and the sanctity of wild places. You are walking a planned route. You are making an expedition.

Tramping is a sort of disorganized version of hiking and trekking but beware for tramping means walking firmly, deliberately and with intention to get somewhere – that somewhere is often an unknown place when you start out. Your motto for tramping is: *Walk on! Walk on!*

Pilgrimage is a journey to sacred places motivated by personal devotion, usually with the aim of obtaining spiritual help or as an act of penance or thanksgiving. Such pilgrimages are not confined to the Christian faith and usually involve walking in some form either to get there or as part of the religious ritual at your destination. Two of the most famous places of pilgrimage are the route of Santiago de Compostela in Spain for Christians and many others of no particular faith and, of course, Mecca in Saudi Arabia for Muslims. In the latter pilgrimage, which is called *The Hajj* and is for Muslims only, the pilgrims in religious practice *walk* seven times around the Kaibab which is a cube-shaped building and the most sacred site in Islam, predating the religion itself and said to have been built by the Prophet Abraham. The most famous pilgrimage by walking is undoubtedly the Santiago de Compostela route through France and Spain to the city where the bones of the Apostle Saint James are said to rest. This is an arduous but beautiful walk taking many weeks and has been a pilgrimage for more than a thousand years. The journey is well mapped and it is still possible to follow medieval routes without too much trouble. As in most adventures, it is not the arrival that counts so much as the journey itself.

Political Walking is for a social and political purpose. It is usually a march in public with banners, noise and the specific aim of getting a message across to the public and those in power. My first such political walk was in Tarbes in France. It was about retirement benefits needing to be increased. When the parade came by me, someone in it grabbed my hand, shouting *you are old, so get in here and walk!* I did it and I admit rather proudly. Sometimes if you believe strongly enough in something which affects you and your community, it is good to go on a political walk. This is the privilege of democracy. As to being healthy, walking with like-minded people can bring new friendships and these often enhance our sense of well-being.

Nature Walks are for discovering aspects of the natural world- insects, animals, plants, trees – anything and everything that lives in this world. These are often organized for groups and many are free and usually lead by experts whose knowledge about nature can be fascinating. Your attention is drawn away from self concerns into a larger picture of life. As you nature walk try to make the connection between yourself and all you see and hear. We are one in this universe, intimately linked in a marvelous network of biodiversity. The emotional and physical benefits of our being aware of this connection are enormous. It can bring a sense of reality and urgency to our need to stop mistreating the earth. This awakening is more than an exercise for the body, it is an exercise to open your heart to a clearer and stronger vision of your world – and this vision makes for good living.

Educational Walking is not just for school groups. There are plenty organized for adults. It is about walking to learn. Recently, I was invited to go with friends for a *Dragonfly Walk* in a nature reserve near a big city. Not open to the public except for events like this, the place was a maze of weeds, wild flowers, bridges over little stream, ponds, and secret shadowy places where you could pause and reflect. On an educational walk you can discover and learn new things. For example, I had never known before my walk that a lot of dragonflies indicates that any nearby water is particularly clean or that dragonflies can spend years in the water before emerging on the shore to breed. Educational walks can be wonderful in many ways, stimulating and stretching body and mind.

Companionship Walking is about setting out with a friend. You don't need to chatter. Just walk along enjoying the intimacy of the moment with someone special.

Listen Walking is what you can do that helps a person when they need the warmth and caring of friendship. You need to listen with an open heart, not judging the other person, but really getting to grips with what they are feeling. Don't offer advice. Just walk and listen. If the other person is depressed, then the physical act of walking can stimulate the body's chemistry to lift her emotions. If you are walking solo, you can still do a Listen Walk for you are going to listen to the world –human sounds, noise, and the many sounds of nature. All these and more belong to the concert of sound that is your world. Can you hear a tree whispering?

Dog Walking always raises the question of whether you walk the dog or the dog walks you. Either way a dog forces you to recognize that exercise is essential and if it is good for the dog, then it is good for you. People who have a dog and regularly walk it at least once if not twice a day are earning health points. If you do not own a dog, try borrowing one. You will make a new animal friend and that too helps your health.

Garden Walks are a way of bringing you back from the industrialized world, the consumer marketplace, and the goals of materialism. In a garden you may enter into a place of peace and sanctuary and today millions of people visit a huge variety of garden venues. Walking around looking at plants and trees seems to have a calming effect on most people whether or not they are interested in actually gardening. The Quiet Garden Movement encourages the provision of some 300 local gardens where there is an opportunity to rest and to pray. These are in both private and public places world-wide.

Earth Walking is about taking off your shoes and setting out barefoot. When you walk naked foot to natural ground, you make deep contact with earth. The sensation is one of freedom and at the same time a sense of belonging to nature. Millions of people are going on barefoot walks, inspired by *Born to Run,* a book by Christopher McDougall who tells the story of how a tribe of Indians in Mexico run distances exceeding 100 miles wearing only thin sandals. Running barefoot or in the newly fashionable light barefoot-like running shoes changes the way your foot moves, producing in some cases strain on the foot, calf, and Archilles' tendon. So start slow and let your body get use to earth walking.

Weed Walking is about going into the woods, mountains, hills or by the sea, even in your own garden, and paying close attention to the weeds - those uninvited guests of which there are always plenty at home as every gardener knows and those that grow in the wild where we let them roam. Weed walking is meant to call your attention to the interesting observation that in nature, as in humanity, there is a balance between what we humans deem *good* or *bad*. This is the Ying and Yang balance of life. To look at what we usually think of as *bad* is a way of opening our eyes to what nature deems *good.* Beauty and surprise awaits you. You will see hundreds of details you missed – designs on leaves, fragile tiny flowers, curls of tendrils- a thousand different ways of nature's loveliness. It reminds you that as with the weeds so with yourself and others. Do not judge whether bad or good for each is splendid in its own way.

Wild Walks need to be taken in the mountains or a jungle – somewhere that is savage and strange, maybe even exotic. If you plan a holiday in such place it offers you the chance for a walk on the wild side. Take this unique opportunity– but with someone who knows that mountain or jungle.

Specialty Walking is about a walking plan where you go on an organized tour to see something special. The mode of transportation for the programme is walking. It is almost always arranged for groups. There are, for example, **Film & Fiction Walks.** One such is to walk around where the Harry Potter films were made, seeing the sets and so forth. There is the famous **Hollywood Star Walk** where you walk from place to place reading and looking at the various hand imprints and information about famous film stars on special pavement sections and then go on to see where they live. **Samuel Johnson Walks** take you on a tour of Old London. There are loads of such specialty walks in both city and country and often they cost little or nothing to join.

Game Walks are when you play a game as you walk. You can do this with others or by yourself. This is especially good for you if you are a grumpy person. Since the world seems filled with people who complain about this or that, getting rid of grumpiness is good for your health, bringing a change of mood and an increase of good chemistry in the body. The games you can play are endless. Just to name a few: **Spot the street. Going up hills and down hills. Colours of Houses. Kinds of people on the street. I-Spy!** Whatever game takes your fancy. Most children do not use their bodies enough so going for a game walk is a way to get them outside the house and away from computers, games and television – but make certain the walk is an invitation to fun. When you are walking *and* playing a game, problems of hard times are placed on the back-burner for awhile.

Fitness Walking promotes increased body mobility and a change in body and mind chemistry that brings a sense of well-being. It burns up more calories than ordinary walking and increases body strength and muscle tone while elevating your heart rate in a good way. This kind of walking can be as good as a gym workout – and it costs you nothing.

Lifestyle walking is what we all do every day as we go about our ordinary living. We walk when we are in the house, on the street or when shopping. All of us do lifestyle walking – but all of us need to do more of it.

A final word about walking

The next time you forget that much of good living even in hard times costs you nothing simply open your front door and go for a walk. This will bring you back to the wondrous reality that is life.

FEELING LOVED

Where there is no love, put love and you will find love, wrote St. John of the Cross in a letter in 1591, but he admitted there were obstacles to our being able to act in this way. He felt these barriers arose from our earthly desires and these prevented us from putting love into our lives and into our relationships with others. They prevented us from acquiring the grace of feeling loved, an essential part of true well-being. He claimed our many desires made us uneasy and we became confused about how we really felt. From such confusion our good intentions became soiled. When this happened we were so weakened that darkness was cast over our spirit. We want to love, but somehow it all goes wrong.

It is this basic yearning to love and to feel loved that is the key to the reality of loving and feeling loved. This reality means you live by love, you are defined by love, and your values are those which come from love. This formula for living is not so strange. After all is it not true that whatever it is in our lives that we wish to know well, we must love it? You cannot master music, art or any profession unless you love what you are studying. You will not bake a delicious chocolate cake if you do not like doing it. If you understand this reality, then it is clear that the whole path of love in your life must start in accepting how you really feel. This means you start feeling love by feeling it for yourself. This is not a selfish act. This is not about spoiling yourself with treats and satisfying your desires. It is about loving yourself just as you are. To love yourself in this way is your first generous act that will bring you a feeling of being loved.

The place where we start to learn this loving is by seeking awareness of our true self in all its many shapes, forms, disguises, and ploys. *Know thyself* is a principle of living found within the teachings of all the great religions. The reason is simple: to extend love to others we must first understand ourselves as we are and for what we are – the bad, the good, and the indifferent. Only through such self-acceptance of our own light and dark sides can we stop finding faults with others and simply love them as they are. It takes most people a lifetime to accept the truth about themselves since most of us prefer to ignore this dark side. An old Hindu poem sums our situation: *"Do not let me forget who I am", cries the child in the womb, and forgets at birth.*

In spite of all such forgetting, we must somehow learn to love others if we want to be a person who lives to the full and who is compassionate. There is no other way to survive the human condition of living together, especially in an over-populated and increasingly urban world. Without acceptance of ourselves, we have no tolerance to extend understanding to others. Without such understanding unconditional love becomes impossible and family and friends constantly fall short of our expectations. We are caught in the unhappy trap of judgment where the grace of compassion finds no space to thrive.

The goal of knowing yourself has never been happiness but rather that wisdom which can bring this much needed compassion first for yourself and then for others. It is begins in the acknowledgement that the self is our first love. Saint Bernard of Clairvaux (1090-1153) wrote that we have no feeling which is not for self and asked *Who ever hated his own flesh?* Even the Apostle Paul said love of self was natural and comes even before that love which is spiritual. It is fundamental to our nature and cannot be denied, save in that ultimate act of love when we sacrifice our life to save another. This is the powerful core of the sacrifice of Jesus. It is the act of courage that we honour highest.

However, such wisdom springs from a deep sympathy that our own human condition is shared by everyone we meet or know. Such sympathy is quite simple and not at all difficult to comprehend. It is the discovery that others are not so different from ourselves. Just as we have accepted ourselves as we really are, so we have accepted others as we find them. Such acceptance has no room in it for judgments since we have no expectations. Such acceptance is profound and goes to the very heart of compassion which is unconditional love. It is for the realization of such unconditional love that the holy writings of Judaism, Christianity, and Islam teaches that judgment belongs to God alone.

Sadly, most of the contemporary ways of seeking self understanding are without the supporting framework of a spiritual path or a religion even though many techniques and practices may originally spring from such sources. This lack of a supporting guide to our pilgrimage of the self has lead to even greater emphasis on an individualism that puts you *first* and everyone else *second* in ways which do not lead to much sympathy for others and rarely to compassion. The fashionable aim is most often about seeking self-improvement rather than self-knowledge. Such an aim does not involve loving yourself so you may better love your neighbour. This kind of seeking fits neatly into our consuming materialistic society and the 'me-me' culture. It is probably as well a result of such devotion to consumption and the values of possession. However, this does little for the nourishment and growth of the individual, the family or the community. It is a form of self-love that always makes the object of desire the satisfaction of the senses. It is a self-defeating principle that turns every new discovery of self into a situation where the individual dismisses any knowledge about themselves that doesn't fit in with their preferred self-image – images which are promoted everyday in our lives by self-serving economic interests. We are constantly reminded that all is light and that there is no dark *if only* we behave in this way or that. Since this is not true, we are bound to be disappointed and our sense of guilt grows.

This kind of seeking is a form of self-concern which does not lead to accepting yourself or to loving others and certainly not to any lasting contentment. If it did, people would have ceased to hunt for insight into themselves since their lifestyle and its values would be an expression of such understanding and, thus, result in acceptance of others which is the first step to loving them. Indeed were this the case, our world, full of understanding and not just comprehending love but practicing it, would be less selfish, less corrupt and we would have ended our enslavement to materialism. We would not need any book to tell us about good living in hard times or why we need ethical and moral values or why the expressions of our individuality must be also contribute to the common good. We would already be practicing all the virtues that make such living possible – virtues which are profoundly spiritual in source and do not arise from the habits which are merely external to our inner life and do not reflect what we feel about the meaning of our life. As I said earlier, I believe these values can only arise from the moral and ethical concepts of a defined spiritual path or faith which acts as a supporting framework for our *know thyself* seeking. Once we know what we truly believe and, thus, from that what we truly value we have travelled most of the way toward gaining insight into ourselves.

The foundation of our search

The pillars that form such a supporting framework to encourage us in our search for self revelation must surely be made of faith, hope, and love. These are spiritual values, not mental ideas since the mind like a wild bird flies about the air in swoops of fancy, deciding to land here, there, anywhere. It has been rightly called our *monkey mind*. The Apostle Paul said that the greatest of these three pillars is love. It is from love that our insight, acceptance, and compassion all come into existence. To believe we can understand ourselves or others by some way that does not have a moral and ethical basis does not accord with our human history for it depends not on a shared understanding of the unity of belonging together but on principles of personal esteem and opinion.

Without the pillar of hope we are utterly lost for hope keeps us focused in the present moment which is where we find belief in a better future whilst getting on with the situation we are presently experiencing. The pillar of faith must always be of a mystical nature for even the most fervent religious person must ultimately accept by faith alone that which is invisible and non-provable by human minds. But such hope and faith can not be sustained or indeed even happen without being formed by love.

Yet, this love that may so successfully govern our lives is not only that which we feel toward others. We also need to feel we are loved. Without such consciousness love does not make us *feel* loved. This is why those three words I *love you* are the most meaningful of all the expressions of love in every language around the world. Yet, it is no good hearing such words if in our deepest self we do not believe them. The mind or body responding is not enough. We must deeply believe them. Such belief begins by our loving ourselves because otherwise how could we believe anyone else could love us? So the very first person to whom you need to say *I love you* is to yourself. This is the initial step toward the practice of unconditional love – you have acknowledged the bad, the good, the guilt, the anger, the fear, the resentments, the desires – in fact everything that makes up your life story to date.

If you are with someone who makes you feel loved, then rejoice! If like so many today you still hunger for such a feeling in spite of all you have, then you do not feel loved. Ask yourself why you won't accept that you are loved. Do not fudge this issue for it is of vital importance in living a contented life.

To start with you are probably still lacking that inner insight and acceptance of true self which brings the stability found in confident self-esteem. You are still not at ease with your own history. You may feel it as anxiety or too much stress. You may simply feel a lack of ease as if at any moment something dreadful is about to happen. You are on edge. Call it what you like but you do not yet know enough about yourself. Until you do, you cannot achieve that necessary acceptance of how you actually are. Since we are loved in proportion to the compassion and love we give to others and cannot do this unless we see in others the echoes of our own foibles, this lack of full acceptance of self is a barrier to truly accepting others. This makes it almost impossible to show others that necessary love and compassion which, in turn, will bring us feelings of being loved. Such sentiments toward others cannot, therefore, be superficial. They must resonate with this accepting of our own strengths and weaknesses. Anyone can act, of course, as if they feel sympathy. Anyone can pretend to understand someone. Such politeness masks much shallowness of character on our part and everyday society is full of this seeming acceptance of others which, of course, is utterly vacuous.

While we may never completely forget the feelings of being unloved that we carry, for example from our childhood, this haunting of our life by such long-ago unresolved feelings and situations does nothing to bring us happiness, much less the capacity to love others. We have not forgiven someone important in our story - ourselves. Any lack of forgiveness of ourselves in terms of our life story disables our ability to extend unconditional love and compassion to others. The substitution of good manners for emotional sincerity can be devastating on how we feel about ourselves and how others feel about us. Even the ability to form lasting intimate relationships can be affected. This refusing to let go of yesterday's sorrows and this lack of acceptance of ourselves as we truly are, is the source of our feeling unloved. If you are a person of faith and do not accept yourself then this means at heart you do not accept that God loves you *as you are.* Once again, the art of contentment means the practice of those values which acknowledge we are but the mirror of every living thing.

Sometimes we feel we have exercised compassion toward others by our acts of charity or through spiritual practices such as prayer or at healing circles. Nuns and monks often favour this form of expressing sympathy for others. Unfortunately, it allows them to remain detached from any emotional encounters with those for whom they are praying. While prayer may be helpful for another person, such spiritual acts do not replace real physical and emotional involvement with the person to whom we wish to extend our sympathy. Our words of supplication may reach heavenward but without earthly actions to back them up we have only done half a job.

No one is ordinary

If you lie down with dogs, you get up with fleas is a folk proverb that has been around a long time. This little saying contains a powerful truth in that we are enormously influenced by the people we associate with, yet often believe we are not. The way we envision our life and the value judgments we make are all influenced by the people we meet and especially those we make our friends. In fact we cannot meet anyone, even a stranger on the street, without it influencing us in some way. Everyone would admit that books and television have a considerable influence on our opinions and vision of society and the world. Yet, we most often chose friends by accident or random chance and we are inattentive to what we chose to view or listen to, allowing entertainment or information to pass into us willy-nilly as if it has no influence. Science tells us differently. Above all else it is other people who have the most profound influence on our behaviour and values. We need to choose the company we keep with the greatest care.

Recently I was asked by a close family member who was

irritated with my talk about a friend who seemed to me to be highly talented: *Don't you know any ordinary people? Everyone you mention seems special.*

I did not respond since the person was not seeking my opinion but simply telling me off – but I did carry away his question when we parted and pondered on it. Why did it seem I did not know any ordinary people? I know lots of people and a variety of types of friends from all walks of life. They all couldn't be extra-ordinary, specially talented or gifted could they?

My answer is that I have met delightful people, boring people, powerful people, fragile people, and saints and sinners, but *never* anyone who was not special in their own right. Every single person whose life story I know has proven to be extra-ordinary in some way.

I believe that none of us are ordinary because we all have a history that is unique. We may share the same emotions, such as depression, joy, grief, and loneliness, but each of us experiences these in a slightly different way. Additionally, each of us has different gifts and a personal creativity that belongs to us alone. In terms of creativity and talent, one person may bake a delicious chocolate cake, another has a sympathetic ear for people in trouble, and yet another artistic talents. These may seem unequal gifts for we do not usually put baking the best peanut butter cookies in the same class as painting the Sistine Chapel – but why not? Millions are enthralled by that famous painted ceiling and millions are given pleasure by a mouthful of cookie. Why look for ways to put the talents of people in categories of quality? What they express in their lifetime is not a product but a developing process – *a work of art in progress* as some joke. We become part of that process when we get involved with them. When you dig deep into a person's life story, it is always special and unlike anyone else's.

Since all of what I have said seems to be true, there can be only one answer to the question I was asked: *No, I do not know any ordinary people.*

Consider for a moment your friends. Surely each one is different in some special way. This acknowledgement that everyone is extra-ordinary means you are too. This builds up your self-esteem which is part of good health. It costs nothing but your generosity of heart to yourself and to others. You will feel more loved, because you will discover how very special every life is – and that includes your own.

The nature of friendships

Friendships are like a stone thrown into the water. As the rings of ripples go out so it is with people in your life. The first inner ring is intimacy. Only the loves of one's heart may live there. The next ring are those who form our dearest friends. We offer each other mutual support in every way we can. The next ring in the water are people we see once in a while. They form a community of friendship. The final ring seems endless over the water. It goes out and out until it becomes invisible. In this widest circle is where all the friends are who we will never meet - the unknown brothers and sisters of our common humanity. But what was this stone which is thrown into the water? The stone is our life. The water is the universe of all sentient beings. We make a little splash and a beautiful moment of circles is created. Then it appears to end, but the water and stone are still there. All our friends near and far, known and unknown, remain in the same mystery.

Solitude & intimacy

More and more people today live alone whether by choice or circumstances. Relationships may come and go, divorce is frequent, careers and work move us from one place to another so that we are often living amid strangers in a new place. Loneliness and feeling isolated and rejected are common factors in modern life. While we all like our own space and a bit of peace and quiet, being alone has real challenges and especially when we are living in difficult times. In this situation we have little to distract us from constant worries.

It doesn't have to be this way if we make the spiritual dimension of ourselves a real part of our ordinary life and not something we drag out from time to time for such events as church, self-help groups, shared meditation, or yoga practice. Because we do have this spiritual dimension, our lives are lived in two ways although united in being a single entity of self.

One way we live is in the solitude of the inner self. The other is in our relationship to everyone and everything. Our spiritual life demands we find a balance between these inseparable worlds if we are to be healthy in mind, body and spirit and able to receive and give love. *Alone but not lonely* is what we should aim for, especially if unsolicited solitude is where we find ourselves.

The achievement of this kind of solitary living means acceptance of our situation – but with a heart full of hope. Gladness is not put aside until times are better. Now is almost always the right time for you to be happy. We can live this way by making for ourselves a sound structure of daily living that feeds our soul as well as our body and mind. It is sustainable no matter how difficult our situation because we deem spiritual values and not materialistic ones to be the values by which we live. If you are a person of faith then you have been given the greatest of examples, for instance in Christ and the Buddha. There are many other men and women who by the wonderful example of their love and compassion may serve as models for us.

A solution without price

Sheikh Muzaffer Ozak Al-Jerrahi (1916-1985), a Turkish Sufi master well know in Europe and the United States, declared that

Love solves all problems, opens all closed doors. In one of his most important books, *Blessed Virgin Mary*, this answer for all our problems is his theme. Most people do not believe Sheikh Muzaffer for one instant – or anyone else who would suggest that love can solve the problems of the individual, never mind those of a nation or world. *What about money or illness?* people ask. *Love won't pay the mortgage this month!* Since the world has never tried this solution of love, who can be certain? But if love solved all problems then there would be no wars, no torture, nor any of the other senseless acts of cruelty done in the name of solving a problem. With love we might not get more money or recover from a disease. However, we could at least remain tranquil in the face of our problems whether they are personal or those of our society. Such utopia will probably always remain a dream. Meanwhile problems don't go away. If we stay in a state of loving and compassion about life, if we look at the stars and say *Aren't we lucky!*, if we delight at children playing, if we observe the thousand and one events and things that are blessings in the here and now of our life – then we have a chance of remaining calm no matter what happens. We can be at peace even in facing defeat for our body and mind may have to give way to forces we cannot control but our spirit can remain free in rejoicing that we are alive.

In return for this outward humility, our constancy in offering love as a solution to all problems brings us dignity. Such dignity is a shield against the enemy of fear.

Dignity is a word which has only recently come back in fashion. It was the demand, for example, of those claiming a right to democracy and an end to dictatorships in the Jasmine Revolution of the Middle East. But what does dignity mean in living an ordinary day-to-day life ? The wise Saint Bernard defined dignity in a way which I feel suits not just the individual but a society as a whole. *When I speak of dignity or the worthiness of man*, he wrote, *I mean free will. It is the possession of the power of choice that renders man superior to all other living creatures on the earth.* This is the state of dignity in which we all want to live. To seek it in the face of hard times and to guard it as a precious treasure in the good times is to truly love that which endows ourselves and others with worthiness. This is an act of the highest human generosity. We have no choice then but to put love into all our situations and relationships. In such generosity we are bound to discover that we are loved.

BEING SPIRITUAL

This late October morning I woke to a cold clear day. A time when flowers give one last performance and picnic things are put away until next summer. I took my dog for a walk along the river with its wild ducks. Up by the still fields where cows graze, I see Pascal hand-plowing his large vegetable plot. We wave but do not stop to speak for words would change the pleasant rhythm of our morning peace. Two local men are clearing leaves from a road damp with dew from over-hanging trees. My dog runs with excitement. How blessed was this day for me. This blessing was not just in my vision of such pleasant scenes or in the happy cogitations of my mind. What I felt was something else. The term we have for it is *feeling spiritual.* I was filled with an undefined but strong sense of the world being just right. For a moment, I felt part of that perfect relationship of each thing to everything else. There was no separation. No *me* and *them.* My spirit was dancing with contentment and I wondered yet again why anyone would want to deny the spiritual.

In researching retreats I have met people from all walks of life. They have been aged from sixteen to over eighty and provided a meaningful cross-sample of all generations. There were young mothers and career women, grandfathers and bachelors, factory workers – scarce on the ground these days – and bored civil servants, high flyers and social failures, students and social butterflies, emotionally well-balanced people and those with endless problems, and the unemployed and unemployable. All were searching in some way for a part of themselves that can only be called *spiritual,* because it is not quite the mind or the body but seems so essentially an inseparable aspect of the whole being that makes up a human.

Being spiritual does not mean we have to believe in God – even though this proves helpful to billions of people around the world. Today *God* by any other name seems acceptable just as long as it does not infer going to church or being told what to do. So many people I meet seem to be against the church or against organized religion because, they tell me, it has caused wars or at least grave trouble between people. In any case, it seems they do not want anyone telling them what to believe whether it is from the traditional holy scriptures of a religion or some presiding person in that religion, such as a pope, priest or minister. This is all part of our modern struggle for individualism, a struggle which I think doesn't lead anywhere except to a self-centered view of life and of one's relationship to others. Freedom and the liberty of true self reside in the spirit of each individual. It is fine to have constitutions and laws which allow us freedom- but we do not have to be *given* it. Even a slave can keep a hidden heart that she alone knows. Such a heart is born free no matter humanity's laws. Such a heart may seek the spiritual without claiming a certain belief or the guidance of other people.

The forces and interests of materialism and profit may continue to march us along, destroying the earth and telling us how wonderfully free our lives are. Yet, everyone I meet has that inner feeling that beyond the good and bad of human activities and accomplishments, there is some kind of higher energy – a universal force that pervades all life and is beyond our control and our face-to-face encounter. A power that has nothing to do with the petty concerns of daily living. While some scientists and other "experts" continue to deny the probability of the existence of God, ordinary men and women still seek some meaning to their lives and most must give it a name – a name that signifies something holy and beyond human creation or control. To this end, they look inward only to find they are staring out into the universe. Maybe it is correct to say that we do have a God gene and that we are hand-wired for seeking the spiritual. There is so much that remains a mystery, so why not?

Do you suffer from spiritual bankruptcy?

Why anyone would want to deny the spirituality of her or his humanity has always been incomprehensible to me. Our feeling spiritual is a joyous affair for it does away with feelings of isolation and brings a sense of meaning and unity to our lives. This spiritual element of us remains largely unrecognized by the evaluations of science because it does not fit into the measurements and methods of their investigations. Unless, of course, through some special phenomenon such as meditation, science can attach the existence of what we commonly call *spiritual* to an organic part of the brain or body. It seems if we cannot find and describe it by our contemporary definitions of truth, it doesn't exist. Yet, whatever science and its host of disbelievers in the existence of the spiritual may pronounce, the vast majority of people yearn for that which they call *spiritual*. They may not like institutionalized religions or believe in life after physical death or in dogmas such as a Final Judgment, but almost seventy percent of people interviewed in one British survey admitted to having an experience that they could not define except as spiritual. These people were a random selection of religious disbelievers, agnostics, and atheists as well as people of faith from all walks of life. Other similar surveys in various countries show the same kind of results.

Re-inventing ourselves

Since the beginning of human history, the spiritual has been defined in many ways and forms. Religions and practices, spirit myths and stories abound. Today in the West, we can create our own spirituality, refusing any established spiritual or religious path. A bit of teaching from Buddhism or Christianity, a practice or two like yoga or meditation, and perhaps regular ecological walks to enjoy the pagan richness of Mother Earth – a pick-n-mix bag of spiritual stuff. *If it works for you, why not?* is the modern reaction to anyone reaching out to spiritual concerns. We cultivate a polite indifference – as long as they do not try to convert us to their way of thinking.

I used to think this kind of attitude was a good one, reflecting a tolerance for other people's different spiritual paths and life choices. My thinking this was largely based on Ramakrishna's credo that all our journeys may be different but in the end they all arrive at the same spiritual place of the One God or, put another way, of a universal *Common Ground of Being*. This approach seemed to slot in well with the rather loose boundaries of my Christianity along with my sense of respecting others. The most widely read religious writer of the twentieth century, the Catholic monk Thomas Merton, tried to reconcile this *Common Ground of Being* idea to the dogma of a defined faith in which Christ is God, but failed in practice to melt these two religious visions into a mystical whole.

In principle this idea of different paths but one destiny seems to agree with our contemporary idea of personal choice and democratic rights. However, I am not so sure any longer that this liberal approach to discovering our spirituality really gets us anywhere as individuals or as a cohesive society. We may get spiritually plump on a gourmet platter of spiritual practices but, as with too much body fat, it may not be very good for our spiritual health. Sooner or later, especially in illness, grief, and old age, most of us come to agree with the Old Testament Prophet Baruch when addressing himself to the God of the Jews: *We long to praise you in our exile.* [3:7-8] The problem is we may deliberately persist so long in exile from our spiritual feelings that we forget the nature of our deepest needs. Instead we believe them to rest solely in matters of mind and body, forgetting that not all of our feelings can be explained away by the physical chemistry of these organs.

Everyone may have a democratic right to their own beliefs

but for any sense of morality the community or society must agree on some standards which everyone may satisfactorily follow and which allow them individual dignity. This gives cohesion to individual behaviour within defined boundaries for a social life of equal benefit to all. The profits are in peacefulness and that progress which should be defined by the good health and happiness of its members and not by the present economic ideals which have been foisted on us by the interests of materialism and its goal of monetary gain. If these interests of the market place worked for us and satisfied our spiritual needs, we would not have a pandemic of depression in the West nor suffer slavery to consumerist values. We would not be obese, malcontented, and constantly seeking to displace our inner feelings by entertainment and diversion. We would, instead, be able to enjoy good living no matter the economic times. Quite simply we would perhaps have a chance to be contented.

If you dismiss my claims as too all-encompassing and general then try to recall the last time you noted any spiritual benefit promoted by the economic system which is capitalism.

The importance of our spiritual heritage

If you also think that I exaggerate the importance of the spiritual in the lives of people, then it is helpful to note that recent British research shows the majority of people still admit to or follow an established faith even as Sunday church attendance continues to fall and that the rapid growth of alternative spirituality that found its fashion in the New Age movement has slowed down. If nothing else, the enormous growth in followers of the Islamic and Christian faiths among young adults shows the yearning for the spiritual remains with us.

One problem of putting together a unique package of personal spirituality is that we forget history. This history includes various religious and spirituality understandings. We are surrounded by them in our architecture, art, literature, and daily social mores. The very fibers of any national culture are made from the religious influences of a common spiritual inheritance whether we like it or not and no matter how we strive to diminish its influence through the advancement of secularism. When we dismiss or ignore this spiritual inheritance, we put aside the collective wisdom of our ancestors.

The question that arises is why anyone would want or need to reinvent spirituality for themselves in isolation from their historical inheritance. Such a person surely cannot maintain any cohesive sense of cultural or community continuity. One is shrugging off the whole history of our humanity. This cannot benefit our health for it brings a continuing questioning of what to do or how to act and reassessment of how best to live one's life. What is good or bad in our decision-making? How do we judge what boundaries of personal and community behaviour is needed for maintaining peace and order? There are no models to follow except those celebrities we read about in the popular press or see on TV shows. Millions of young people have few other models for morality and rightfully reject those represented by the worlds of finance and politics. The available models are almost always examples of those who are celebrated for worldly achievement. This leaves out Jesus, Mohammed, and Buddha for a start. In any case, our role models are unreal for we remain ignorant of a current celebrity's real feelings. Certainly, we have no access to knowing how they feel spiritually. Here today and gone out of fashion tomorrow, they are false models for our own lives. They remain figures of entertainment and have no lasting value and provide no lasting guidance toward our happiness. So millions either turn back to an established religion or invent a belief for themselves which they can change whenever they want and that fits in smoothly with contemporary ideas of individual rights or they ignore altogether the spiritual side of their lives, many simply confusing the word *spirituality* with the word *religion.*

The paradox of knowing and not knowing

With this reluctance to incorporate our spiritual history into our daily life, a kind of learned ignorance arises in us. That is, we desire something we do not know, yet we are aware of it. If we were not thus aware, we would not yearn or search for it. *How can the object of desire be spoken of when it is not known?* Saint Augustine asked. *If it were entirely unknown certainly it would not be desired,* he concludes.

We long, therefore, for something we know but do not know. This paradox is one which continues even when you are a person of faith. Faith may give you boundaries and choices to guide your life style, but the final mystery of the exact nature of our spirituality cannot be known. It remains holy and what is holy is perfect. Such perfection is never achieved by humans and must remain in the mystery of what we call *divine* since it is beyond our complete understanding.

This does not mean you must believe in a god or go to church or claim to be a person of faith if you want to realize a sense of the spiritual in your life. What it does mean is that you have accepted that part of yourself is spiritual and that this spiritual feeling needs a home. It may rest in your heart or your soul or your head - but remain with you it will.

If you want to enjoy balanced good health then there is little to be gained from self-argumentation about accepting your inherent spirituality. It only creates disunity within yourself and potentially disharmony with others.

The spiritual mirror of our animals

At the moment we have not yet found out if other creatures also have such a spiritual sense. However we may imagine the life of animals, there is no doubting that they have a high rank in the universe. *Psalm 148,* a cosmic praise of all creation, puts sea creatures, wild and tame beasts, reptiles and birds just after the heavens, sun, moon, and seas – and before even mentioning kings, princes and ordinary men and women. We may believe we are born divine children but in the cosmic scheme of things we appear just as part of universal bio-diversity. If we are star dust then so is the pet cat that sits on your lap or the doe that hides in the forest. Even that medieval theologian Thomas a Kempis told us: *If your heart be straight with God, then every creature shall be to you a mirror of life and a book of holy doctrine, for there is no creature so little or so vile, but that shows and represents the goodness of God.*

When the Bible tries to explain God to us, it repeatedly turns to animals. Jesus refers to himself as a mother hen gathering her chicks (Matthew 23:37), the Prophet Jeremiah says that God can roar like a lion (Jeremiah 25), and when Jesus was baptized we are told the Holy Spirit descended like a dove. Even to this day we use the image of a dove to signify peace. So when the bible speaks of animals in such familiar images as a hen, a lion, a dove or other creature, it is telling us that this invisible universal presence of the mysterious holy is living in everything. Even the empty shell on a beach when held to our ear echoes the ancient Hindu cry, *OM*. Indeed, what is the Noah story about if not the vital importance of all creatures?

Science may still have to spend many years of research to catch up with our sentiments but no one I know would deny that a dog can smile, a horse fall in love, or an elephant swoon with sorrow. If you live in rural France as I do, you are suppose to be able to buy a fine live chicken and wring its neck for the Sunday cooking pot. I don't know about you, but I would have to be on the point of starvation before I could even contemplate such violence. These popular lyrics from the poem-song by Cecil Francis Alexander [1818-1895] and used in part as the title of the best-selling book by the British veterinarian James Harriot come to mind:

All things bright and beautiful,
All creatures, great and small,
All things wise and wonderful,
The Lord God made them all.

So whether you are a person of faith or just a pilgrim going along with life's journey, all living creatures occupy a special place in our environment and commonly in our lives and homes too. This rapport with creatures is not a matter of our mind deciding an affinity. We feel it and such feelings are spiritual in origin whether or not we credit them to religious instruction or scientific information. Our animals, wild and tame, are a spiritual mirror. In seeing them we see the nature of ourselves and this sharing is not just of body or mind but of the spirit too. Let the cat on your lap or the dog barking next door remind you that all *is* bright and beautiful. If you are suffering, go to these wise and wonderful creatures. Hold the sea shell to your ear and listen. Within moments you will find comfort and renewal.

On the right beginning for a spiritual life

The end goal of a spiritual life is not ultimately the observing of a set of commandments or rules however necessary to religion. Such things are the merely the habits of a soul which has not yet reached its highest point until it is transfused and crowned by spiritual joy. The most indispensable of the dimensions of faith is not breathe but depth and, above all, the insight into sanctity and the power to produce saints. When we receive this crown, we put away the practices, rules, and rituals which were such a help on our spiritual pilgrimage. We have become part of the mystery where love is the sole observance. We no longer need to seek for we have found and can be joyous in just *being*. When this spiritual feeling fills us, we enjoy a balanced self. We are whole. This strengthens us with nourishment that money cannot buy.

EATING REAL FOOD

To eat real food means we have complete nourishment suitable for our age and our activity at every meal. It means we care how we eat and what we eat. It means we do not act like grazing cows or like pigs wallowing up to a feed trough or a swallow catching something to eat while winging it. It means our food is not fashion, fad or fast. It means we care that our food is fresh, unprocessed, and cooked and served with respect. To eat such food shows we are glad to be alive. It honours Nature in all her glorious abundance.

Sadly, most people in the West fail to achieve this simple but essential act of living. The results are poor health, a concern more for image than well-being, and a major contribution to dissatisfaction with life. It remains true that we are what we eat.

I hope by the time you have finished reading this chapter you will know why one good quality, non-sprayed, in season naturally grown carrot is cheaper and better than a bunch of low priced ones which have been sprayed, grown under fleece protection, disinfected, flown half around the world, and generally treated as some manufactured item- shaped just right, produced in a brighter orange colour than nature intended, and presented to you under special enhancing lights as " fresh" when it is no such thing.

The food you put in your body can either heal you or kill you

In America obesity and over-weight has reached a crisis point and Britain and the rest of Europe is getting there too. The statistics by any standard of good health are appalling. Right now two out of three Americans are over-weight and one in three is medically obese. These figures are expected to continue to climb rapidly even higher. One in three of Americans already suffers from diabetes and children with this life-threatening disease are increasing very day. Don't even think about the epidemic rate of heart disease. African-Americans have a 50 per cent higher prevalence of obesity and Hispanics are 25 per cent higher when compared with those termed "white" Americans. The future health of Americans and Europeans is dire. Even China, so recently poor, is now facing rising obesity.

Poverty, lack of access to fresh quality food, the cheapness of fast food, and ignorance are the consumer factors which generate this continuing escalation of dangerous eating habits. When you marry these elements with the political and marketing power of the agro-industrial corporations and the mythologies about food supply and quality which they continue to promote, it is not surprising that the average consumer feels defeated and continues along a path to ill health and potentially early death. With some 2.2 billion dollars spent in 2009 on advertising by the American fast food industry and with the insidious political lobbying by industrial-food corporations to minimize regulations and increase their markets, you are going to have to work very hard to eat well in good times, never mind the hard times. But eating real food is possible for everyone and well worth the effort.

You may feel alone in this struggle, especially if you are already on the poverty line. You may even be one out of the eight Americans who rely on food stamps. Even in France, land of glorious eating, people who must use food charity can have little choice outside donated processed food. But none of us should lose hope that things can be changed, that we the consumer will one day be protected from the present excessively intrusive and socially irresponsible food industry who pedal the myth that they care for our health while continuing to fight any regulations that they think might interfere with their freedom of operations. Do not be beguiled, the food industry is *not* your friend.

Sugar, salt and all things nice

We live in a time when sugar, salt, and fats are considered our enemies. Yet, each of these serves us well in preserving, seasoning, and cooking our food. The problem today is that we over-eat them. Snacks, sodas, fast foods, pre-prepared dishes, and processed food all contain more than we need of these normally helpful ingredients. What is it about us that makes us want to eat this way in the first place. Is it culture? Yes, in part. What it is *not* is hunger or appetite.

There seem to be two basic reasons for this modern habit that has lead to such rapidly rising rates of obesity, heart disease, and diabetes. First, we have not eaten a proper meal. Second, we need to put something in our mouth. The psychology of such oral satisfaction is highly complex – but one thing is clear it helps calm us, much as a nipple pacifier stuck in its mouth quiets a baby. Added to this is an increasing need to displace our anxiety and nervousness and for millions the grazing on snack foods serves this purpose. If you eat like this, it is easy to become addicted. As with all addictions, recovery is hard. If you are living on reduced income and worries about money, there is every good reason to want to displace your anxiety, but do not do it by over-dosing on sugar, salt and fats. Try getting over an addiction you no longer can afford. Maybe such recovery also makes us a bit wiser about ourselves, our culture, and why all those swinging bellies and wobbling butts are out there.

What do the words *Good, Powerful* and *Honest* mean in terms of food?

Good food is non-processed fresh food. It is the basic ingedient that you are using, such as a carrot, a lamb chop,or a bunch of turnips. Sometimes it can be a traditional *slow food* such as a Toulouse sausage – but even with such special traditional foods watch out for additives. Such food is hopefully organic certified, or raised locally, and bought as direct as possible from the original producer.

Powerful food is food which is naturally nourishing and healthy for you and which boots up the immune system. If the food you eat is non-processed and fresh, then it probably is powerful in this sense.

Honest food has depth and does not pretend to be what it is not. It does not dress up as something else or parade in the latest dish as some kind of novelty. A few examples, are tomato soup made from scratch, homemade noodles, a beef stew or a loaf of bread which you made yourself. If you eat such honest food, you are not likely to be fat and you will feel better and have more energy.

The lost history of our food

> *Whereas cooking can be merely a mechanical execution of the instructions in a cookery book, eating involves the use of all the senses. Life can be enhanced by the sensual elements in our surroundings. Forgotten memories are evoked by smell throughout life, and what can compare with the everyday smells of freshly roasted coffee and of bread as it is baked, or the delicate scent of plum or cherry jam as it cooks?*
>
> Nathalie Hambro, *Particular Delights.*

The American philosopher-ecologist Wendell Berry claims that these days we can hardly ever know the history of our food. The whole process of growing, harvesting, processing, transportation and marketing is far too complex and global to trace. Such separation from the life story of the food we eat and our subsequent ignorance about it serves the profit goals of the agro-industrial system. Such a food system with its limited regulations, often misleading product presentations, and subtle marketing practices brings in its wake a cascade of health problems of which obesity is but one. With "easy cook," "oven-ready" and other pre-prepared foods, we have lost the history of our own cooking as well as that of the actual food itself. Since food and its cooking and serving are part of the rituals that make up a culture, our loss extends beyond our own kitchen to our community and society. This dislocation of our heritage serves only the profit motives of an economic system based on greed. It has fragmented one of the most important aspects of family life which is the taking of meals together. This latter result may be a social change more profound for society than even the growth of communication technology.

Local farmers markets and the development of regional organic farming helps us to attach some history to the food we buy – but many of us living urban and suburban lives do not always have such options. The supermarket is the default choice for most people. Whether this is a good thing or not depends on what we buy and when we buy it.

Long haul food is dead food

If we insist on buying asparagus out of season where we live but in season some 5,000 miles away, then we are buying asparagus that are as processed as the tinned kind but simply in a different way. For example, I recently watched one of Britain's most popular television celebrity cooks show how to make a strawberry crumble. It was in November and she explained that she knew "it was wrong" to buy strawberries out of season but her recipe would make these otherwise long-haul fruit into a delicious desert. Although apples and pears were abundantly in season where she lived, she chose to tell millions of her fans that it was okay to buy out of season food if that is what they wanted at the moment. This is an act of instant gratification which is one of the aims of food industry marketing. It does not encourage us to appreciate or be aware of what fresh food really means.

This celebrity was endorsing an agro-industrial system, which in changing our purchasing habits from that which nature makes available to that which the present economic system wishes us to buy at a time when it wants, has corrupted most of the world's farming and turned the average person's knowledge of food on its head. Given the enormous influence such celebrity cooks have on the way we think about our food, her recipe gave the wrong message on many scores from the benefits of buying in-season food to the deeper concept that what we eat reflects our awareness of ecological issues. The cook in question should have included the under-lying message that we all have some social irresponsibility about the food we buy in terms of ecology, energy, nutrition and farming. Buying out of season food does not send such a message. In my research I bought an armful of current women's magazines, many themed to that country living *feel good* factor. Time after time I found summer recipes which contained winter seasonal food and summer dishes which were made from winter produce. All the food suggested sounded delicious – but at what price of taste and quality?

To eat real food we first need to buy produce which is in season where we live and which has been grown and harvested as close to our community as possible. This takes effort and time but these are well spent in terms of our health and our pleasure. When we do this kind of buying we are giving ourselves liberty from slavery to an economic system based on profit and not good eating and best nourishment.

Fast food

Fast food has always been around in all countries from the delicious dishes spooned up in the great plaza of Jemaa-el-Fna in Marrakech to our own cities with their hamburgers and fries. There is nothing wrong with such food as long as it is not eaten every day, because we need variety and balance in what we eat. Having said that, the kind of fast food we are eating in the West is not good for us and the huge amount of publicity about this means no one can really claim not to know it.

However, there are other factors about such food that are less well known. For example, a recent study published in the *Journal of Nutrition and Metabolism* showed that eating junk food has a prolonged effect on the body. Just a month's worth of eating such food or frequent binging on any high fat and sugar foods can make it hard to keep your weight down for the next *two years*. Even when this extra weight is lost, there is still an ongoing effect on the way your body stores fat.

So the real price you pay for fast food can be too high in terms of good health. Make it, then, a treat rather than a regular meal – but forget salted and sugared snack foods and soda drinks. These are *not* real food.

Convenience is your enemy

We all know how much effort we must put into something if we want to do it well. You cannot learn to play a violin if you do not practice and practicing means making an effort and spending time doing it. The same is for any activity we want to learn from repairing motorcycles to doing yoga to cooking good food. So if you want to eat well, keep your immune system in tune, and your weight appropriate, then you need to cook. Sure it takes more time, but if you are having trouble making ends meet, then time is not money for you. You are measuring your life by a different system, a set of values which puts you are in charge and no longer a willing victim of big food companies.

Water is your friend

I recently met a woman in a small Welsh village. She was in her forties, happily remarried to an oil engineer, but suffered constant illnesses. In fact, she never felt really well. With three children and a busy husband to look after, she needed the energy of good health. Her doctor and various specialists could find nothing wrong with her. She was not depressed and never felt anxious except about the present state of her health. I suggested maybe she should drink a lot more water, since it has been discovered that many people suffer from insufficient water to maintain smooth running of their bodies. *I don't like water*, she responded. Now whatever could she have meant? If she had said that she preferred tea, coffee or sodas, I might have understood. But not *like* water? We are born to like water since we cannot live without it. She was happy to have endless medical examinations and to take any number of prescription drugs in hopes of easing her discomfort and feeling better – but she did not want to drink any water. This is more than foolish or acting childish and perverse, it is contrary to the nature of being a human for water is our friend, the substance we cannot live without.

When you feel under-the-weather and not up to scratch, try drinking more water. The average person needs about 1 ½ liters every day. This is plain cheap water from your kitchen tap. You don't need it bottled, filtered or in tea, coffee, or soda. Water is a friend who was made absolutely perfect for your good health. Drink it often!

Chicken is for Sundays

Regular balanced meals are the key to good health and there are thousands of books and websites devoted to this message. In the West these messages seem to have had little impact, especially in the face of sophisticated marketing by the food industry and its presence through public relations programmes in public places which were closed to them until very recently. For example, after the Second World War when manufacturers were still not allowed a presence in schools either through product presence or special project sponsorship, they became increasingly eager to get in and cozy up to the generation who would become their adult food shoppers. In consequence, their public relations consultants worked hard to find ways to have a presence in the educational system of America and Britain. On top of these efforts there were powerful political lobbies by candy, sweets, sugar, artificial sweetener manufacturers, various chemical industries related to the food industry, and others involved in the production or growing of food. All had the aim of making their industrialization of food acceptable to the public with as few regulations as possible. Today, such industrialization has a global influence over most food production and processing. The interests of consumers came late to the scene. Such interests continue to have very limited success in the face of the massive financial investment made by the agro-food industry in political lobbying and cultural engineering. One direct result is that our children's health has been sacrificed to the making of money.

As Kevin Moloney in The New York Times recently pointed out in one of his articles, *Factory food took over most American schools in a rolling, greasy wave of chicken nuggets and pre-prepped everything over the last few decades.*

There are some signs of change toward more real food here and there including some schools but it is a continuing story of Jonathan battling Goliath. Just this last week I read that members of the food industry will be on the official committee of the British government which is looking at food regulations. Such industrial representation may appear benign. It promotes the false idea that they are interested in "doing the right thing" for the consumer – but the heart of their motivation is profit and as little government regulation as possible. The history of the agro-food industry shows that they do not and cannot represent your interests or mine as consumers of food.

Returning to the words of Wendell Berry, most of us would

now agree with him that hardly any intelligent person is unaware of the scale of the industrial agriculture business, a scale of abuse so large it cannot be hidden any longer. In his classic essay *The Whole Horse* he says the following which brilliantly sums up our present situation with the food we are eating: *It is virtually impossible now for intelligent consumers to be ignorant of the heartlessness and nastiness of animal confinement operations and their excessive use of antibiotics, of the use of hormones in meat and milk production, of the stenches and pollutants of pig and poultry factories, of the use of toxic chemicals and the waste of soil and soil health in industrial row-cropping, of the mysterious or disturbing or threatening practices associated with industrial food storage, preservation, and processing.* As to the development of organic and community based and supported local food, he claims rightly that such food can never be produced by a global corporation.

We only need take the supermarket chicken as the perfect example of how the food industry has corrupted our access to real food. This has become a boring story told and retold by the media that everyone, as Wendell Berry suggests, supposedly knows about – but I would like to revisit it to stir your memory and, hopefully, to put you off ever buying these poor, factory raised birds *regardless of how little money you have to spend.*

Once the chicken was expensive but very good to eat. Until well into the 1960s it was a weekly Sunday treat in many traditional American homes. With intensive poultry farming, the price came down. We could eat chicken anytime we wanted. It became cheap food. It also became tasteless and more diseased. Today chicken comes in all forms from oven-ready to pop-in-the-micro nuggets. Now if you want to eat good chicken it means paying a premium price. The consumer never wins it would seem – but you *can* win as a consumer by returning to chicken once a week and by buying the very best. This calls for restraint which we are not so good at in these days of instant gratification – but if you are on hard times, restraint goes hand-in-hand with thrift which is what you are trying to practice.

What is a truly complete meal?

A complete meal nourishes the whole of you – the body, the mind and your spirit. It does not depend on fashion or having a lot of money. It begins with recognition that, like the air we breathe and the water we drink, we must have food to live. How we use and enjoy that food depends not just on our economic and social circumstances but on our whole approach to food itself. It includes each of the following things – to harvest, to offer, to taste, to be thankful, to digest, to enjoy.

To harvest

More and more people are trying to grow their own food. In Britain there are waiting lists for allotments and even apartment dwellers are growing fresh herbs on window sills. However, most of us still have to buy the harvest that others have done for us. What we choose to buy, therefore, is what we harvest for our meal. Just like a farmer, you may have a good or bad harvest. Unlike a farmer, which one you have is your choice. It is what we chose that is the modern problem in eating well.

The majority of British and Americans do not eat a daily meal of balanced nourishment of anything. Most people graze. The average French person persists in believing that properly cooked food is vital to a good life and the majority eat at least one cooked meal each day. This meal almost always consists of a balance of different food, including vegetables and salads. This common French practice is scientifically and psychologically sound and yet finds little favour in the cultures of most other Western countries – but sadly even the French are succumbing to processed food and the increasing French obesity rate proves it.

If we did not know where our next meal was coming from like

billions of people in the world today, then when we had food, *any* food, we would take our lucky moment and eat it. If you are reading this book it is unlikely that you are actually in need of food. You might even be on food stamps or discounted cheap foodstuff, but you are *not* starving. Therefore, you do have at least some choice about what you harvest

Most people when interviewed think buying quality fresh food is more expensive than the supermarket stuff. They are right on the ticket price but wrong on the cost to health. The key to making a good harvest is to buy fresh, seasonal, organic, and as much locally or regionally grown food as possible.

To offer hospitality

The Rule of Saint Benedict, used a guide in monasteries for some 1,500 years, tells us that when someone knocks on the monastery door we must greet him or her as Christ himself. This means we offer hospitality to anyone who knocks. These days we are unlikely to invite a stranger into our home for we are consumed by fear for our safety – a fear which often has no reality and is increased in us by the news of crimes which we are constantly fed. It was not always this way with strangers at the door, especially not in America. In my childhood, even a tramp would be given food. To be poor was not to be a loser then for the American dream was thriving and you understood that today's poverty stricken and unemployed could be tomorrow's millionaire. And this did happen in those days when America was still welcoming immigrants from foreign lands to help make the nation strong and rich, because everyone was in the same dream.

As to the urgency for extending such hospitality, Saint Benedict said that when such an opportunity came we were to leave even our prayers and go at once to offer our help and care. The reason for this is because hospitality is an act of love. It is a going out to others, the sharing with them not only what we have but who we are. There is no better example of this in the family than the gathering together at Thanksgiving or Christmas. We need in our everyday lives to offer such hospitality and not wait for a knock on our door. We need to make an effort to be conscious that we are sharing our food. Such sharing binds us together psychologically and at a deep spiritual level. In the New Testament, it is surprising how many times Jesus goes to feasts and celebrations. If you are a person of faith, the idea that Jesus enjoyed himself with food and wine may offer you a fresh vision of the completeness of his humanity.

On every level sharing food with family, friends or strangers is a form of hospitality which strengthens and enriches our lives.

To cook

Cookery means the knowledge of Medea, and of Circe, and of Calypso, and of Helen, and of Rebekah, and of the Queen of Sheba. It means the knowledge of all herbs, and fruits, and balms, and spices; and of all that is healing and sweet in fields and groves, and savoury in meats; it means carefulness, and inventiveness, and watchfulness, and willingness, and readiness of appliance; it means the economy of your great-grandmothers, and the science of modern chemists; it means much tasting, and no wasting; it means English thoroughness, and French art, and Arabian hospitality; and it means, in fine, that everybody has something nice to eat.

John Ruskin, *The Ethics of the Dust*

What are we to make of all the current crop of fashionable cookbooks by celebrities, famous chefs, and food writers? You will lose little by ignoring the ones by celebrities. As to the famous chefs, it is better usually to read them for inspiration than for their recipes. You are not cooking restaurant food and your cupboards should hold essential ingredients, not an expensive carload of stuff you will use perhaps once or twice in a year. As to contemporary food writers, I do not feel very friendly toward them because I think a lot of recipes they offer are inappropriate to family meals or are minor variations of traditional dishes which do not improve them. There are notable exceptions such as the general cookbooks by Delia Smith in Britain and the famous *Joy of Cooking* by Irma S. Rombauer and her family in America. A close inspection of almost all the recipes given by the famous food writer Elizabeth David will prove suitable for family meals, based as they are on traditional French, Italian and English dishes. Otherwise most of today's good books are about fabulous images which turn food into art and the reading about wonderful dishes – not cooking them. Don't waste what money you have on such entertainment.

Cooking is a skill you learn so you start on well-established dishes. It's just like starting to ride a horse. If you never rode before, you start with a tried and true pony that knows his stuff and has been around long enough that faults have been corrected and improvements made. The same is for the recipes you chose to cook. You will be amazed at how your skills and your interest in cooking improve and what satisfaction you feel when you put what you have made on the table for those you love. Here is another way to feel contented.

Finally, pin this notice to your kitchen wall: ***Cooked with care, served with love***

To present

Fine restaurants around the world take very special care of how they present food. The images in cook books and on the internet look fantastic. Most people have never been able to eat such food because it is far too expensive. But when I talk about presenting food I am not saying we should even try to imitate these splendid restaurants with their artistry. I am suggesting that if you want a truly complete meal then you need to pay attention to how you present the food. If we cook with care, then we need to present it with care. You might say *to be mindful of the dish.* It can be simply but carefully arranged on the plate.

Even the religious who praise God for his abundant gifts can be guilty of a disregard of the importance of the food they eat. When I first went to the monastery I was asked to cook the suppers. I did not spend more time or money at it than any other monk there but I took greater care and when I put it on the table it looked appetizing. At first all the brothers were pleased. Then grumbles started. Questions were asked. *Why was I paying so much attention to food? Were we not supposed to be poor? If we were living a simple life why would we worry about what or how we ate and especially how it looked?* After awhile I got tired of this grumbling and with more anger than I like to admit, I asked the other monks: *How can you praise God for all the bounty of the earth and asked for your daily bread and not show respect for what He has provided.* I then rather shouted out the psalm we all sang in chapel about appreciating the good things of this earth. My words were met with silence. After that I continued to produce delectable dishes and the monks continued to enjoy them for we had all seen that the food on our plates was a true thanksgiving which should reflect the many songs of thanksgiving we sang in the chapel – and in due course I learned to be less sensitive about criticism and more considerate of how others might feel.

So it is an important part of eating a complete meal to not only cook the food but to present it with care. When you present it to your family, friends or other guests, remember what is it you are doing - you are serving up a dish of love. If you have not thought of cooking in this way, then this deeper vision of what eating is about will make your food special no matter how limited your budget or how ordinary the ingredients . It will make every meal you share a celebration of the good things of life.

To smell

Smells, scents and odours all trigger responses in our body. Our taste is as much about what we smell as what we have put in our mouth. The cosmetic and food industries rely on this fact. When we are hungry, our appetite is aroused by what we smell. Few people can resist the mouth-watering smell of brewing coffee or freshly baked bread. If we want to have the food you serve smell good then you have got to use fresh oils, spices and other ingredients. Stale food of any kind has given up its ability to entice us.

To taste

If you do not chew your food but gobble it up in a hurry you are losing most of the enjoyment. In fact you are eating like a dog. Since we are not dogs and have been given the ability to taste what we eat, why not slow down and take those few seconds that can bring manifold enjoyments? If you don't think you gulp down your food, put a mirror on the table and just watch yourself. Even more enlightening, watch other diners in a restaurant. People together eat more slowly. Those eating alone will be done with the meal in no time flat. It has become much the accepted manner in Britain and America to eat while walking down the street or popping something in your mouth as you work. Eating in haste makes for little taste. It shows a distain for food.

To be thankful

Nearly one in every six people in the world goes hungry, according to the 2010 Global Hunger Index report, published by the International Food Policy Research Institute. When was the last time you or I went hungry? When we are lucky enough to have a meal, we can give thanks for it without being a person of faith – although at least in the latter case you can feel as if you are directing your message to someone and not just into space. But even if your thanksgiving is just a few words that float around the table and disappear at least in that brief moment you are remembering how good it is to be able to eat some food. You don't have to recall how many billions are starving as you eat for you are giving thanks for what you and your family are receiving at that moment. These short little prayers which are referred to as *saying grace* and ran along the quick lines of *Bless the food we are about to eat. Amen!* were once said at most meals by ordinary people including those who didn't really believe in God. The moment of appreciation was the important thing.

The prayer of thanksgiving which I like best is this one which is credited to a British workman who, when he finally finished digging a very long ditch, looked heavenward and said, *Thanks a lot, Boss!*

These little acts of thanksgiving at table when we are about to eat bring mindfulness of exactly what we are doing. We are focused and reminded that we are nourishing ourselves and, hopefully, we are sharing with others this essential act of nature and spirit. In this way, we are affirming life.

The affirmation which I find most inspiring is this Native American one:

When you rise in the morning,
Give thanks for the morning light.
Give thanks for your life and strength.
Give thanks for your food
And give thanks for the joy of living.

To digest

These days, it is fashionable in the West to be fussy about what you eat. We have gone well beyond just a dislike for a particular food or vegetarian and vegan preferences. The list of what people do not eat or cannot eat or will not eat seems endless as does the reasons they give for such declarations. Everyone seems to have an allergy to this or that food or certain combinations of food. The list is truly endless. In the majority of cases, the problem is not medical. Our body is working properly but we are asking it to cope with chemical and additive over-loads. The less we eat of processed food the happier our bodies are and the less fussy we need to be about our digestive system.

In spite of the massive publicity and material given to diets and nutrition, most people don't know anything about how they digest their food. It goes in one end and comes out the other. What happens in-between remains a mystery to most people. Among other reasons it is this lack of knowledge which makes most of us victims of faddy diets and fashionable allergies. We think digestion is a simple process when, in fact, it is complex.

To start with, most of us do not process the food correctly once it enters our mouths. We bite, munch, graze, smack our lips, and immediately swallow whatever it is – but we hardly ever really *chew* our food. Your saliva glands begin the lengthy process of turning your food into nourishment. If you do not chew your food well, they can not do their work and you have already begun the descent into poor digestion. The secretions of these glands are like the starting kick of a football game for your digestive system. They add enzymes, antibacterial properties, antibodies and other elements into your food – all great stuff for good digestion. Treat your mouth as a very special health provider.

When you swallow this well chewed food, it passes into the magic pot of the stomach where the powerful product of hydrochloric acid (HCL) further prepares the food for assimilation by your body. So powerful is this acid that if the stomach lining did not protect us, the acid would burn straight though it. This marvellous acid does a lot of work, destroying harmful bacteria, keeping the contents of the colon from shifting up into our small intestine tract where it could cause damage, and signalling to the pancreas to produce digestive enzymes and bile. Without enough of these enzymes and bile, we cannot properly digest our food nor absorb the carbohydrates, fats, and protein contained in it. If this happens, the food continues down the digestive tract anyway. The result is upset tummies, unexpected pains in the gut, and food allergies.

An estimated 80 percent of patients seen by doctors today claim to suffer from some degree of impaired stomach acid production levels. So the first culprit for what we think is an allergy may not be the food we have eaten but the way in which we have eaten it.

For those women whose hunger is for a pencil-thin body rather than eating properly, it is worth remembering that the worse your digestion, the more you will age. As we age so does every element in our body and this natural process which includes our digestive tract. The most common thing is that the powerful hypochoric acid in our stomach is under-produced. This happens to about 15 percent of the population in the West and by the age of sixty almost fifty percent of the population are affected. We cannot expect our digestive system to be forever young no more than we can think the same for the rest of our body.

So making the right food choices isn't enough. We also need to have good digestion. If you have heartburn, flatulence, or constipation on a regular basis, and you are eating real food, cooked and served with love, then start paying close attention to *how* you eat. If symptoms persist see your doctor.

To enjoy

We are meant to enjoy eating. It is one of the outstanding pleasures of life. We may not always be able to go to a party and drink and eat merrily with others, but we can enjoy what we have. This enjoyment helps the body, stimulates the mind, and lifts our spirits. The table is where we should find the pleasures of smell, taste, companionship, and thanksgiving, all rolled up in a delicious confection of pure enjoyment. You do not pay for this enjoyment. It costs nothing but your intention to have a complete meal of real food – not lavish, not out of season, not expensive but good, powerful and honest, cooked and served with thanksgiving and love. If you truly wish to live a contented life no matter your economic circumstances, then you cannot achieve it unless you include all that eating real food really means. Start with your next meal.

SLOW TIME

Everyone seems pressed for time these days. There is so much to do and so few hours in which to get it all done. Here, there, everywhere we rush. In effect we are speeding our way through life. What lies behind this situation? Is it that we are forced to be evermore busy by the sheer pressures of modern life? Is it that our generation has more to do than those before? Perhaps there are other reasons than practical ones for our speeding through time – an individual action which has the effect of speeding up time itself as it exists in our life. What may we actually be doing when we live in such a rushed way?

The Swiss philosopher Max Picard (1888-1965) believed that our love of this speeding up of time is a flight from God. It is a way of escaping our pursuit by the holy or what Francis Thompson famously called *The Hound of Heaven.* If we should be caught up by God, what then our beliefs, our way of life, our guilt, our feelings? Indeed, will we suffer a divine judgment on our life at that very moment of capture? This is not a matter just for the religious, because the fear of the vengeful God lurks deeply in the human psyche. In referring to Picard's claim, the Rev. Fulton J. Sheen explained that when the person of faith takes such flight in speeding up time he enters into himself, that is into his interior life, but that today for most people this flight is external, that is into the world. Sheen believed that in such external flight *we try to speed through time in order to fly from our origins and to escape the dread of being driven back into our selves and being confronted by the spirit.*

The end result of this speeding up of time is that humans, believing they are in control, have gained the illusion that all things are subject to them. Since God is in permanence, our attempt to escape this eternal and continuing presence by flight and speed never works. Such action does not bring happiness for we cannot have repose. Without repose we cannot be truly happy since happiness is a peaceful state which has gathered together all our pleasures at being alive. These are those pleasures which dominate our deepest feelings and create our highest aspirations. For example, hope in the future, the possession of truth, and love in all its varied forms. In his sermon *How to Have a Good Time,* Sheen claims that if this is the case, then time is an obstacle to our happiness and that the only way we can be really happy is by completely getting outside time. This means we have transcended time. Time then for us can have no measure, because our true concerns, if we wish to achieve the state of being we may call *contentment,* must lie outside the restrictions of time and reflect eternal values and that permanence which represents lasting truths. Such transcendence of time means we are willing to enter our inner world and to face the dark and light aspects of ourselves. We acknowledge our imperfection. We do not long for an escape into the external world. We do not need time as a fuel to speed us away from facing the awareness of true self nor from getting to grips with the fact we will one day die and have no certainty when that happens as to vengeful or judgmental gods or anything else. This choice of our relationship to time is spiritual and in matters of the spirit time does not exist.

What this means then is that time is not just speeded up so we can escape through it but in doing this we lose the meaning of time itself. Our view narrows as to its true nature. Saint Augustine, who went from infamous sinning to profound holiness and left us a stunning biography of this journey, explained the real meaning of time. Naturally, being a deeply spiritual man, he was not talking about clocks but about time in the sense of endless universes. Augustine's sense of time was that it has no measure *because* he understood it in spiritual terms much along the lines I have discussed above. He realized time is simply not really very important in the greater scheme of things, especially during our short life – a true paradox.

You might think that this cosmic idea of time doesn't have much to do with things like picking up the kids from school or keeping a dental appointment. After all, we all assume this clock time is just a way of organizing our day and seeing that it helps us fit in with the demands of modern life. Yet, we can let this practical use of the measure of time so invade our thinking that we become anxious and stressful. How often we say or hear others proclaim *I don't have time!* and *if only I had more time!*

Many people, especially in Western Europe and America, make time keeping a dominating habit. Some people even make arriving exactly on time almost an art form. A widespread belief is that to be late is impolite or thoughtless of others. In addition, the Christian work ethic, still a powerful cultural undercurrent in our daily life, makes us feel that time not spent usefully is time wasted and that such wastefulness is somehow immoral or wrong. We quickly lose any sense that time is eternal and has no real measure or importance in the more profound aspects of living. We rush here and there in the service of a sense of time we invented and which does nothing for our spirit. It fragments any feelings of unity in our lives. Such time keeping by the clock has become yet another cause of stress in our lives.

Augustine's belief that time is no measure since the eternal is without measure and the reflections of men like Max Picard and Fulton J. Sheen on our speeding up of time as an escape from inner awareness bring us a grander vision of our lives and a sense of the presence of the universal. Such a vision frees us from a view of time which is small and mean and one invented for convenience but which can end up ruling our ordinary living with a pitiless tyranny.

When we do not worry about time and time keeping we slow down inside ourselves. We become more alive to the moment, more present, and more focused. We are able to grasp the concept that our lives are more important than the daily tasks we do. Bearing in mind that our time keeping is simply a practical tool, we can carry out our chores and appointments in a relaxed manner. Meanwhile, regardless of your personal situation you carry with you a greater vision of yourself as a person who is far more important than how efficient you are with time.

In any case, on the purely practical level, why organize yourself around a clock? Will your life be better? Will it change things? Maybe it helps for those who live in chaos, but such people need a whole bag of life skill tools to get it together and not just time adjustments. Getting stressed out about time certainly will change things in your life even if it has no effect on the wider world. You will not be healthy and your life will not feel abundant.

One of the things we have to do every day is to eat and that means buying and preparing food. Here is one of the areas of spending time that many people resent. Magazine and newspaper articles and television food programmes are full of such expressions as *easy, takes no time, quick,* and *fast* – all of which underscore the idea that we contemporary folk simply do not have the time to properly prepare food. When we feel time is short, we tend to grab a frozen or pre-prepared dish and pop it into the micro or buy a take-away. As long as it seems to save us time, it is just what we want.

This approach to food treats it as fuel and so we are unlikely to receive the maximum of enjoyment and nutrition from it. How sad since food is one of the greatest of sources of pleasure and conviviality in life. Raymond Blanc, the celebrated French chef, talks about the time you spend on preparing and serving food in his book, *Cooking for Friends*. This is what Blanc wrote: *What we lose in the convenience of speed are many essentials of our general existence – the joy, the feeling of achievement, the appreciation, the adventure, the curiosity, the trying.* I think we can apply his understanding to many of the other activities of ordinary living that we do every day – it doesn't have to be just about cooking. Try thinking in his terms about house cleaning, making beds, doing the basic shop, or getting the kids off to school.

So take time in everything you do. Leave watching-the-clock worries to one side and practice *slow time*.

This means slowing down and not letting the clock get the upper hand. The next time you feel you must rush somewhere or feel you are going to be late, take five minutes out just to sit still before you carry on. If you are one of those who make time keeping an art form, start a life of slow time by arriving late for appointments. Being on time is not some sacred social code. Five minutes here or there will not matter in the greater scheme of things. Let this be your slogan: *I have all the time in the world!* In those extra few minutes of freedom from rushing, if you *must* think, then meditate on these wise words, which may bring you that calm balance of putting things into perspective and which often easily arises from a few moments of mindful reflection:

> *Look at the lilies and how they grow. They don't work or make their clothing, yet Solomon in all his glory was not dressed as beautifully as they are*. [Luke 12:27]

> *Look at the birds of the air, for they neither sow nor reap nor gather into barns; yet your heavenly Father feeds them. Are you not of more value than they?* [Matthew 6:26]

Aren't you equal to a flower? Doesn't the bird take time to sing? So do not rush for any reason except for the irresistible impulses of love. You want to have a sense of timelessness in all you do.

Augustine's idea of time when applied to daily life is about such timelessness of living – that even if our human life is short on earth, it is in a real sense eternal because we continue even after our physical death. The form of such continuance is not very important – dust to dust, reincarnation, or any of the other ideas of what you believe might be waiting for us. The important point is that this vision of our lives as timeless can help to make us feel the sheer grandeur of being alive.

To experience this sense of timelessness we need to focus on the present moment. It is for this reason that I suggested you stop and sit for five minutes the next time you panic about being late or have an over-whelming feeling of not having enough time. Stop thinking about what you have to do. Be totally alert in the present moment. Look at your hands, feel your face, listen to the sounds of the traffic and humanity nearby or to the silence if it is there. Do anything to bring you into the present moment. Focus on what you are doing when you are doing it. Make no room for the illusion of time passing. When you focus in this way you are mindful. This mindfulness brings an ability to act that is concise and direct. You will accomplish more and not become stressful. You are in a state of interior intent. You are freed from the tyranny of clock time and can be the flower in the field and the bird singing in the tree. Do not worry since worrying has its origin in our fears. Fear contracts a sense of time. It creates pressure on us, a hammer with which our lives are shattered into fragments.

Use the principle of *it is not time that slows down but me that slows down*. By slowing yourself down, you slow down the rate at which your mind takes in things. You increase your perception of where you are. Control is out of the clock and back into your own hands. You have no fear and time expands.

We need to expand this kind of a sense of time until it reaches from our earthly life up to distant stars and becomes a sense of timelessness about life itself. Then we can understand more clearly what Saint Augustine was talking about when he said *Time is no measure for man.* If this sounds too grand, then just remember that nothing is too grand a vision for your life. The grander your vision the more in awe you will be. Awe causes you to take in the fullness of where you are. You pay closer attention to what is going on. Unlike being too fat, this fullness makes for health and good living.

Therefore, act as if you have all the time to do everything you want to do. This is *slow time*. Such a sense of timelessness allows you to accomplish all the practical things that you need to do while helping you to open the way to contentment. Remember that in all of this, you are practicing an art.

PLAYING

Have you forgotten how to play in the pursuit of all the serious things in your life? Forgotten how to really let go? Just fed-up with so much to do and so little time and cash to do it with? If this is the case, play will balance your perspective on your situation.

In the industrial-political financial ethos in which we live, play is not considered productive. That is of itself, it does not generate consumption. Business has tried to turn play into forms of activity that produce economic returns. For example, no sooner are we told that jogging or running or going to gym classes is good for us, than we are told we need certain shoes, certain clothes, a whole list of so called essentials that cost us money. The instruments and equipment of play are big business. Since I am interested in living well in hard times, how we can play without spending any money is what I focus on.

Play is like love

Play is rather like love – most of the time neither has any set purpose. Even if they did, we cannot control or direct the outcome. Reproduction aside, the reason for love is love and play is the same. They are not *useful* in the same sense as, for example, when we tackle cleaning the house or garden or wash the car or drive the kids to school. Love and play do not and should not lead anywhere that makes us money. They do not increase our economic status in society. Play and love are simply states of *being*. The benefits of both are manifold and affect our physical and mental health. We suffer if our lives do not have this wonderful element of play and too often we relegate it to the bottom of our list of activities. It needs to be fairly near the top of our priorities.

Too much work makes Jack a dull boy remains good folk truth. If we forget to play, we become dull in our thinking and weary in our bodies. Brian Sutton-Smith, one of America's foremost scientist on the role and nature of play, claims that the opposite of play is not work but depression. We need work for practical purposes, but we need play more. Play is not just leisure or taking time off from work. Play for an adult should be like play for a child - free, joyful, without regard for anything except the moment, a time for letting go and having fun. Play without fun is just another version of work.

Men and women have always worked hard, often at boring repetitive jobs and in dangerous conditions. Many years ago when Sunday, the traditional day of rest came, the community habit was to make the day not just one of rest but of play. In those pre-television days, play was about games, walks or sport. Playing cards or checkers, scouting for mushrooms in the woods, taking the dog for a run, getting a team of neighbours or friends together for some baseball catch, were just some of the many forms of playful rest – and these did not cost money for money was scarce and wages low. Some would argue that our video games, surfing the net, Facebook, watching TV, and other modern amusements are just as good but the majority of these modern amusements involve little if any physical activity and they cost hard cash. The more our work has become less manual or not manual at all and the more our homes have been mechanized, the more our play has been turned into the concept of leisure. Leisure means not doing much, just being cool about life, being entertained and forgetting about everything except how you are feeling. This kind of non-participatory leisure model has little to do with play for humans. In such leisure, far from doing nothing, we are busy – fully occupied with all the activities and actions that go with the idea of *holiday*. We remain busy, busy, busy.

So most of us do even more on the weekends at home than usual. Our stores, fast food spots, and a multitude of other places are open and geared to keep us busy shopping, eating and drinking. In short, to keep us amused while we spend our money. Shopping is a leisure time activity, even for many a form of self-therapy. Far from hurting us in any way, it is claimed by those with vested interests in it that shopping as a leisure activity gives even marginalized people a sense of self-expression, better self-esteem, and a sense of control over their lives because they are making choices for themselves. Do not be fooled, the shopping malls have placed at your disposal what they chose you to have. Your choice is limited to the interest of business, no matter how amusing and wide the so-called choice may be.

Leisure in all its forms today, lead by modern consumer shopping is just another sector of the commercial market. If you are in hard times, this kind of leisure costs you money, corrupts your liberty, and acts as an expensive diversion in its momentary displacement of your real feelings. Do not fall prey to it.

The kind of play we need

The kind of play we need is available to each of us regardless of our circumstances. It is an important health issue because when we play stress and anxiety levels are reduced and the chemistry of depression alters. These are major reasons for one of the contemporary research ideas that the opposite of play is not work but depression. Hobbies and activities which have no other purpose than to enjoy yourself provide ways to express your creativity, increase your physical and mental skills, and get rid of any suppressed feelings like anger. When we get really involved in a play activity, we enter into a semi-meditative state, a kind of gentle rhythm of the brain. It focuses you on the immediate *now* of life. You become mindful of what you are doing. The body, mind and spirit are all involved in such play.

Almost half of all Americans today commonly define play as being occupied on computers, gaming consoles, mobile phones, and online. Supposedly, the younger you are the more you occupy yourself this way, the older the less. Yet statistically nearly a third of American adults over 65 years play such games every day. If it helps relieve boredom and loneliness, why not? The media and many people often criticize these games and tell us how bad they are for our health. These criticisms usually boil down to the fact we are not physically exercising when we play this way. But there are other aspects perhaps more important than whether we are physically active or not. These have to do with the nature of play itself – what is really happening to us when we are at play.

When we enter fully into a game, we forget ourselves and we concentrate exactly on what we are doing – a time of full mindfulness. Such mindfulness is good for us, because when we are playing like this we actively change the physical state of our brain in a positive way. Maybe we do not get smarter but we get more alert. The brain is stimulated and this increases those biological and neurological states which benefit us. Examining these benefits further, studies show that play brings forth positive emotions which promotes people getting to know one another at a higher rate than normal – much faster than if they were working together. Smiling and laughter are part of any play. This encourages creativity, spontaneity, and a sense of personal autonomy. Play also helps us bond with people. Buddy relationships and group adhesion grow rapidly. This not only helps our individual health but creates a sense of belonging to a neighbourhood and community. This leads us to feeling more comradeship. This comradeship turns us outward and we become more aware of others. It lessens our self-concern. This is mentally and spiritually good for us. A wonderful array of benefits then just from your play.

The best play is free play

Almost every animal in the world engages in some form of play because it is a safe way to release aggressive tensions. We need the same kind of inner release of tensions. Within many games we get the chance to play a "role". This role playing is good for the brain. In the end we usually feel happier and that is good for our health. The psychiatrist Stuart Brown at the Baylor College of Medicine in Houston interviewed some 6,000 people about their childhoods, and his research suggested that a lack of opportunities for unstructured, imaginative play can keep children from growing into happy, well-adjusted adults. In adults, role playing and free unstructured play also has the effect of helping us to be well adjusted.

So the very best kind of play you can do is free play -just playing around, not organized or structured in any way. Nothing could be cheaper to do nor give you a greater sense of liberty in your body, mind and spirit.

I thought I could dance all night

It seems to me that one of the best kinds of such free play must be dancing. I have talked about dancing in the section on *Daily Exercise* in this book but from the exercise point of view. Here, I want to look at the play aspects of this important aspect of our human expression, because dance is always more than exercise, changing as it does the biochemistry of our brain and touching in us that which is spiritual.

Both the Old and New Testament have many references to dance as a form of joyous celebration and worship, especially and very directly in several of the Psalms: *Let them praise his name with dancing and make music with timbrel and harp.* (Psalm 149:3)

Starting in the Hebrew religious tradition dance was understood as medium of prayer and an approved way of praising

God. It was often interpreted as a mediating bridge between people and God. In the Hebrew language of the forty-four words for dance only *one* is a possible reference to secular dancing with no religious connotations. In the Aramaic language which Jesus spoke, the word for *rejoice* and *dance* are the same. Hence, we are commended to dancing in the Spirit (Luke 10:21). So it is not surprising that in the last fifty years or so dance as a form of worship has been rediscovered by a broad spectrum of Christian churches.

The spirit of dance

The most frequent type of dance that the Israelites used was circular, either in procession or in a circle. We are told this was the kind of dancing that King David and his troops did before the Ark (OT 2 Samuel 6:14) But they had a third type of dancing which included whirling.

The most famous dance of this kind is the whirling dance done by the Order of the Whirling Dervishes. This is only one branch of the vast Sufi tradition of Islam. Its origin and roots lie in the life and practices of the Prophet of Islam, blessed be his name, and the Qur'an. Among other worthy goals, Sufism is a well-founded interpretation of Islam which focuses on love, tolerance, and worship of God. The dancing is performed for the purpose of reaching a spiritual state and not, as many people assume, to reach some kind of religious ecstasy. The Whirling Dervish is a mystical dancer, one who dances between our material known earthly world and the cosmic unknown universe. His dance is a sacred ceremony in which he displaces all inward mental thoughts, and the revolving of his body turns every cell in his body, just as everything on Heaven and Earth revolves and changes. This emptying of self results in a trance which unifies the dancer with the nature of the universe – a universe which is in a constant state of movement from the cells in our body to the tiniest particles that compose matter. Everything revolves and so the Sufi dances to cosmic forces. At the deepest level when you dance around the room, just letting yourself go in such liberation of mind and body, you too are dancing to the cosmos. When we forget ourselves in this way, the ego loosens its terrible hold over our life. Such play may often make us appear us a little foolish. This is the kind of foolishness that is amazingly good for us. It gives us liberty at least for a few minutes from the tyranny of our self-centered concerns and fears. It puts us squarely in the present. We can transcend our worries and anxieties. We are refusing the blandishments of a modern consuming society. We are no longer afraid. We simply do not care! We are at play in holy fields, burning bright with life. Every cell in your body says, *I love to play!*

THINGS THAT MAKE YOU RICH

SEX

This could be the shortest chapter in this book or the longest. Sex and talking about it in one form or another is the theme of most of our conversations and entertainments from neighborhood gossip to TV realty shows. The reason is simply that our sexuality involves every aspect of our mind, body and soul. It is the one aspect of our humanity that compels us to conclude that in sex we are holistic whether we want to be or not and utterly dependent on the interplay of mind, body and spirit that such intimacy brings. With sex all is possible.

It is not useful to talk here about the mechanisms or hormonal drives of our sexuality. All this and more is available in any number of books and online. There is little about sex that you cannot easily find out today.

This is suppose to have liberated us – but has it? If it had everyone reading this book would know how to fully enjoy their sexuality and would accept that it is one of the jewels of life, the brilliance shining out of loving relationships, the rapture point of pleasure, and a bridge over which we may walk together to resolve emotional feelings that nothing else can achieve except this deep giving of ourselves. If we are to live a life that is rich in freedom of mind, body and spirit, we need to accept and express our sexuality in a way that results in this understanding of our sexuality.

Each of us is unique in what attracts us sexually and in how we ourselves are sexually attractive. When we apply this understanding to our lives it means we do not have to be worried or confused about our sexuality – we are as we are. Such acknowledgement enriches our lives because it can help remove sexual anxieties and bring us tolerance of the sexuality of others. If we do not accept our sexuality, we will never be really contented with our life.

Good sex is honest

Sometimes we think that if we have sexual relations with someone else, we'll feel less lonely. But the truth is that such sex doesn't relieve the feeling of loneliness; it makes it worse. Sexuality should be accompanied by understanding and love. Without understanding and love, sex is empty. With understanding and love, sex can be holy.

Thich Nhat Hanh

All of us quite rightly guard with care the sexual aspects of ourselves because when we are sexual we are completely exposed in body, emotions, and spirit. This means that good sex is when we freely give ourselves to another. If your heart is not in it, sex is apt to be less than satisfactory. We may all joke about the woman who mentally makes up her shopping list while having intercourse and no man is *absolutely* certain whether or not the organism of his female partner is real, since screams and moans are part of our vocabulary of lying. This means good sex is honest and truthful about how we are feeling physically and emotionally and is about giving all of ourselves to our love making. In sex we should be united in joy *and* in honesty.

So we could say that bad sex is about being phony in an area of your life that calls for giving yourself freely, putting all of yourself into the action, and being utterly real. There still remains the fact that good sex is what one believes it to be.

Being in love

Falling in love is as much in our heads as our hearts for there is a bio-chemical basis for romantic love. Helen E. Fisher, a biological anthropologist in the Department of Anthropology at Rutgers University, maintains that humans have evolved three core brain systems for mating and reproduction: Lust which is our sex drive; Romantic Attraction or what we call romantic love; *and* Attachment which is our deep feelings of union with a long term partner. She describes how brain scans of people who feel rejection in a relationship suggested they secrete excess dopamine and cortisol during the initial phase of being rejected. Dopamine is the chemical in the brain that produces the effects of romantic love and the sensations that accompany falling in love. But when such love is thwarted, the very chemical that contributes to such wonderful feelings becomes more potent, impelling us to want to hang on to the person and save our love and sexual situation at all costs.

So brain chemistry helps explains both the romantic and sexual feelings we have as well as the intense anger we can experience when rejected or always kept on the brink of such rejection. This is why we can wildly swing between love and hate when in the throes of being rejected by the other person in a relationship. If he or she should be a manipulator, then we are kept in such a state of emotional ups and downs all the time. This is unhealthy. Hard times are tough enough without carrying the baggage of an unworkable relationship with a partner who pulls you down.

The right to our own sexuality

The control over our sexuality and whatever we determine it to be is an inherent right of every human. Progress in the liberation and equality of women, especially in their right to *all* decisions about their bodies, and of same sex preference people has gone a long way toward acceptance in the West. It means we determine our relationships, their beginnings and their endings. No higher authority in society or religion should enjoy the privilege or right of a final say in our sexuality unless we chose to follow their teachings as individuals. Laws about sexuality need only be there for the sexual protection of everyone who should need them.

Global progress in such tolerance continues, but too slowly. Meanwhile, we have choices, of course, but it is illusion to image that we will ever keep our established ways, habits, thinking or the people we love. Such must and does always change if only through death. If you wish to claim such a natural right to your own sexuality then you must acknowledge that right in others whether they are your friends or family – including your adult children.

Our sexuality is not defined by our gender

When I was a child, men were imprisoned for being gay and hanged for sodomy and now in some places they can marry. Lesbian women were often forced through social custom to marry and live unfulfilled and deeply unhappy lives. The lesson has been that our sexuality is not defined by our gender. We often think we are tolerant, yet our knowledge and understanding of others is often poor and generates no real understanding.

This was brought home to me once when I was giving a spiritual retreat in England. I talked about gender equality and Holy Scriptures, relating the story of Buddhist nun friends who had told me of their struggles in their spiritual studies to transcend the male dominated Buddhist writings. I told them this was also true for some of my Christian nun friends with regard to the bible. I concluded my retreat talk with the familiar Christian apostolic teaching that in God there was neither male nor female. That evening one of the group, a young man in his thirties, asked to see me. He asked me what I thought of Holy Scripture study problems for trans-sexual persons. *I don't think I know anything about it,* I confessed. He replied in a gentle voice, *Maybe you should if you are going to talk about there being no male and female in God which pretty much leaves transsexual people like me out of the picture.* Jimmy had once been Jane and he taught me that sexual equality and justice means no one is left out.

Celibacy

Choosing not to be sexually active for whatever reason is a choice we also may make. It is the reasons for such a choice that determines whether we are contented with our decision or not. Turning away from the overt physical expressions of our sexuality because we have problems with it solves nothing and leads to discontent with our lives. We wear a sort of mental chastity belt against what we don't like or don't understand about our feelings. If this is the case for you, then seek professional counseling because celibacy should be a balanced choice made for sound personal reasons. These may be religious or simply because we have found we are happier not being involved in this way with other people. Many people today are celibate from time to time for a variety of reasons. Not making love does not mean you are no longer a sexual person. It does not mean you do not have desires. It means you have chosen for this time in your life to remain chaste. There is absolutely nothing wrong in this life style as long as it was made freely and for reasons which to you make good sense. Then your celibacy is part of your contentment with your life.

The flesh of our incarnate gods

There is a strong undercurrent of sexuality in most mystical and other spiritual writing. In Christianity expressions such as *embracing God* or *holding onto Jesus* are not uncommon and the spiritual ecstasy of many female saints are often as close to a description of a female sexual orgasm as you are likely to read in contemporary fiction or in medical definitions.

Much of the language of religion, whether of mystics or not, is charged with physicality and, hence, inherently with sexuality.

The celebrated Cardinal John Henry Newman (1801-1890) admitted that *reason is God's gift but so are the passions.* If our sexuality, the most powerful of all our passions, is a gift from God then we ignore its rightful place in our lives at the peril of diminishing the richness of living that is our natural inheritance.

This natural aspect of being human is something we are apt to forget in our apparent need to elevate our gods above the nature of our humanity. In doing this we forget the experience of the mystics and saints and make of our gods a distant object of desire devoid of sexuality and, therefore, empty of one of the most salient connections to our own humanity.

Jesus, created human and having lived as a man, is a totally different proposition. When Christians embrace Jesus Christ, they acknowledge him as divine *and* incarnated in the flesh.

Nevertheless, I challenge you to recall the last time you saw a portrayal of Jesus *completely* nude on the Cross. Images of his genitals, save in a few rare exceptions, are always covered – not for the sake of modesty, not for any spiritual or biblical reason, and not even out of some kind of misplaced respect but because we refuse to treat our own sexuality as good and the expression of it as a wonderful gift. Even today in a Western world where modesty, humility, and boundaries of moral behavior are in very short supply, we rarely if ever mention the sexuality of Jesus as a legitimate subject of ordinary discussion among Christians. Masturbation? Nocturnal emissions? Erections? Can you even imagine a church which took the question of the sexuality of Jesus as a legitimate subject for a Sunday sermon or bible study subject? Such seemingly immodest questions about Jesus the man are not disrespectful but can be honest attempts to understand the human cost of his divine sacrifice. Unless Christians embrace the full humanity of Jesus as well as his divinity, then his death and resurrection cannot be complete in meaning.

The importance of our sexuality as a gift of the spirit

This separation of our sexuality from the rest of our being, whether in our incarnated gods or not, leads away from the deeper spiritual recognition that we are one with other creatures and the earth. It is not enough to say that we share the will to live but need to claim that we share the will to live *and* to reproduce. These are so inseparable in all life that we should place our sexuality in the highest regard. Indeed, we must treat it as divine in its expression and purpose.

If our sexuality is such a divine gift, then I say again that we ignore its rightful place in our lives at the peril of diminishing the richness of living that is our natural inheritance. It does not matter if we are single or with a partner or celibate or sexually active whenever the opportunity presents itself. What matters is that we remain conscious that we are sexual beings and that this state is natural, good, and to be welcomed. How we express our sexuality should remain our individual privilege. Moral codes based on religious beliefs work well for many but these are only valid if you truly and happily consent to such boundaries of the expression of your sexuality. This means that you have retained all the privileges of your sexuality but express it in ways which bring contentment, emotional balance, and positive feelings about yourself.

If you want a rich life then your sexuality is a big part of it in one form or another. An important aspect of learning to live a contented life is to understand and accept your sexuality whether overtly physically expressed or not.

CONVERSATION

One of the greatest pleasures in life is conversation.
Rev. Sydney Smith (1771-1845)

At the moment we are born we cry out. This first sound signals our entrance into the social world in which language is the primary tool of conscious communication. This is the opening cry that announces the beginning of our life's journey. But we are without speech and must communicate by moans, cries, groans, and physical signals what we feel and want. Indeed, the very word *infancy* is derived from a Latin word which means the period of life without speech. Inside us are all the physiological and psychological mechanisms waiting to develop into language. Once we start with words we then never shut up.

Conversation can be on any subject and it consists of words and body movement. Words are powerful. They can be creative or destructive, as superficial as a babbling brook or as deep as the sea. Words in some mouths have the power of life and death. Even our lips closed in silence can condemn by unspoken words. Our words are the necessary bridge of our basic social networking at every level of our life from home to work to life in our community.

The saying that no man or woman is an island is true because we humans are social animals. We are inherently programmed to be with others of our kind. Some of us need the company and companionship that conversation affords more than others. Everyone is different about how much social intercourse they need or want. Even the celebrated early Christian Desert Fathers who were hermits talked to each other from time to time. We know this from the record of their many wise words to each other. When faced with a problem a monk would pose the situation to an older monk and ask his advice. After this conversation, the older monk would almost always advise the younger one to return to his room and pray on the matter. This kind of praying offered the problem up to God which freed the monk's mind from anxious worries. It was a way of liberation. In due time, of course, the problem would be resolved, usually without much action on the worried monk's part because the passing of time solves most things if we give it a chance. Like the young monk, we discuss our worries with a partner, close friend or member of our family and so use conversation to ease our minds, to get rid of anxious feelings, and to reassure ourselves about any decisions or choices we are going to make.

Theories still abound about how we acquire language and researchers still pursue a definitive understanding of such basic questions as why a child babbles or how does a word acquire its meaning. It is assumed that all children in the world start by having the inherent capacity for making all speech sounds and some develop from the external language sounds they hear and some seem to disappear because they are not part of the child's verbal environment.

Most except that the younger a child learns a second language the better. In today's Western inter-nationality and inter-racial marriages and the mobility necessary for many jobs means that increasing numbers of children not only are bi-lingual because of their parents' native languages, but they also acquire fluency in a third, even a fourth, language. As we pass youth, the ability to learn a new language becomes more and more difficult for most people. In my own case my foreign accent can be too great a hurdle for many French people. My mouth remains essentially American, the language environment in which I first learned to speak. Only last week I asked Jeremy who helps me with the garden if he could help me stack winter wood for the stove, but what I actually said was *Can you help me with wood for the chickens?* I had not drawn back my lips into the right shape to say the French word for stove so out came the similar sounding word for chicken. Needless to say, my young helper thought it was all hilarious. This does not mean, however, that I am not communicating. My French friend understood I needed help.

Body language

One of the reasons Jeremy understood I needed his help was that in spite of my words I unconsciously used body language. Some researchers claim that as much as 93 percent of our communication is body language and the remaining 7 percent our words. In any case, the majority of investigators into this question seem to suggest that at least 60 percent of all meaning is derived from non-verbal behavior. This unspoken language is called *paralinguistic clues* which provide information as to the attitude or state of mind the speaker is in. These clues may indicate aggression, attentiveness, boredom, relaxation, pleasure, excitement, anxiety, amusement or other emotional states. Even when we shut up, we continue to communicate.

One of the world's best known authorities on the relative importance of verbal and non-verbal communication is Albert Mehrabian, Professor Emeritus of Psychology, at the University of California, Los Angeles. He finds when we try to communicate our feelings or attitudes that about 7 percent is our actual words with some additional 38 percent just being vocal *sound.* The remaining 55 percent of our communication is in our facial expressions. Most would probably agree with Professor Mehrabian that we frequently react to the *tone* of what someone is saying more than their actual words. Moreover, everyone reacts to the expression on the face of the person speaking. We cannot help these intuitive and unconscious interpretations. Even the tiniest changes in our face can signal how we are feeling. Such almost imperceptible changes have been called Micro Expressions and, of course, science is busy investigating them.

The importance of our micro-expressions

Named by the American Psychological Association as one of the most influential psychologists of the 20th century, Dr. Paul Ekman has built his reputation in the field of Neuropsychiatric research by focusing on the meaning of facial expressions. These expressions are brief, fleeting, and involuntary even when we try to suppress emotions. After studied people all over the world [and chimpanzees as well], Dr. Ekman identified these seven basic facial expressions:

Happiness: *raised lip corners and cheeks, narrowing of the eyelids to produce crow's feet in the corners.*
Sadness: *narrowing eyes with the eyebrows brought together, mouth turned down at the corners with the chin pulled up.*
Fear: *mouth and eyes open, eyebrows raised with nostrils flared at times.*
Anger: *lowered eyebrows, wrinkled forehead, tensed eyelids and lips.*
Disgust: *nose scrunching, upper lip raised eyebrows downcast with eye narrowing.*
Surprise: *dropped jaw, relaxed lips and mouth, eyes wide open with slightly raised eyelids and eyebrows.*
Contempt: *side of mouth raise into a sneer or smirk.*

Since such micro expressions last only a fraction of a second we are hardly aware of them, but they register deep within us at the sub-conscious level. Our subconscious, always at work, sends interpretations of these quickly vanishing subtle expressions given by the other person to our conscious mind. I am not sure what other facial expressions Dr. Ekman investigated but in some countries even a twitch of your nostrils can be full of meaning.

Most of us recognize a lot of other body language signs. Here are a few examples:

Brisk erect walk = confidence
Standing with hands on hips = readiness
Open hand = sincerity, friendliness
Sitting with foot kicking slightly = boredom
Hand to cheek = evaluation, thinking
Walking with shoulders hunched = dejection
Arms crossed on chest = defensiveness

Hence, when we make conversation the truth is written all over our face and our body. Our conversation can build up or tear down, make the people we speak to happy or sad, let the world know we are full of self-pity or joy. If you want to live fully in good times or bad ones, then your conversation – the very words you speak, the subtle expressions on your face, all the details of your inner life – can make you as rich as King Solomon in all that really counts for a happy life. We can all be the angels of good tidings, giving away more than mere money can buy.

Two essentials for good conversation

The key essentials for creating positive and life-enhancing conversations are sincerity and thanksgiving.

Sincerity is an attitude of the heart, and The Prophet Mohammed, peace and blessings be upon him, declared: *Assuredly, God does not consider your bodies or your appearances. Rather, He considers your hearts.* This reminds us that in all our conversations we need to be truly sincere in mind and spirit if we are to create happiness for ourselves and others. Nothing less will do, because anything less is not truth and is not freedom. As we face difficulties that freedom which is sincerity enriches our lives and lessens the burden our worries. It also pleases God.

Thanksgiving is to remember our blessings. There are always many blessings in our lives no matter our circumstances if we but look for them. They don't need to be big ones like winning a lottery or getting a job. They can be small like someone giving you a nice smile or finding a new friend or having someone tell you are looking great. The characteristic that all blessings have in common is that they are about good news. When we express our thankfulness for them we are having a conversation with the Universe or, if we are people of faith, with God. Either way we are articulating a joy. This conversation of thanksgiving does us a power of good. It helps us to see the positive side of life. It puts things in a more balanced perspective. When we express our thanksgiving in conversations with other people we give them hope for what we have to say encourages them about the positive side of living.

How we look is part of our conversation

When we make conversation there is one element to which we react that just seems part of being human. This is about how the other person is dressed. While you may think you haven't ever judged a person based solely on their clothing, you probably have. Before you even hear them speak or know anything about them, you probably make certain assumptions about a person based on their clothing. They are probably doing the same thing looking at you. First impressions are very important and clothing is one of the biggest factors in first impressions. We are more often wrong than right in such judgments.

The confusion about the importance of clothes starts with ourselves. I suggest we should take a radical approach to our clothes when we are facing hard times and money is scarce. There is no better time to clean-out our closets and cupboard. Take the stuff you have not worn in years, which probably no longer fits you anyway, to the local charity shop or recycling centre. Get your shoes in good repair. It is a little money well spent. Finally, even for those that don't sew and this means most people today, learn to thread a needle and make do and mend. You have spent a lot of money on your clothes so treat them as an investment. The old advice on being thrifty to make do and mend has recently come back into favour. When you dress, forget about the latest fashion which you can't afford anyway. Dress to look your best whether going to the shops or just waiting at home for the kids, because how you look is part and parcel of communicating. It is understandably difficult not to want to be fashionable but if times are hard you need to opt for neatness, freshness and appropriateness.

Affirming your life by what you talk about

When we recall the blessings in our lives they become affirmations. Affirmations are powerful tools for positive living and for keeping us going in good times or hard ones. Our lives can often seem boring and unrewarding or overfilled with responsibilities that keep us far too busy and fragment our sense of life's natural unity. But somewhere in our activities are blessings of one sort or another. Affirmations do not have to be about big events. Even something that pleased you is an occasion for an affirmation. It could be an email from a friend or the success of a batch of cupcakes or finding the car doesn't need new tires after all. Whatever you find to be good and glad in your life pin it in your heart. Affirmations of love, hope, faith, joy and even foolishness all help us feel life is worth living. Learning to affirm your life is a tonic for your self-esteem.

Our self-esteem is a fragile thing at best and in hard times it takes a lot of bashing. When you are feeling deep blue and life seems hopeless is the best time to get affirmations going. Practice affirming only one thing at a time. Don't crowd your mind with a lot of them - give each one real time to work. Think of your affirmations as seeds. You are planting them one by one in the garden that is your mind, body and spirit. There they grow together and give you a positive view of your life. Say aloud your affirmation, making a conversation with yourself. Never mind if others wonder why you are mumbling. Do not affirm what you *think* may happen in the future but stay in the present. Be mindful of reality. For example, don't say *I'll get that promotion next month,* but say what is happening now: *I have a good job now.* Don't say, *I'll get a bigger house soon,* but instead say, *where I live is just fine.* Affirm only what is good and don't hide little secret wishes in your affirmation. Say, for example, *Our relationship is loving* instead of *Our relationship is getting better.* Affirm what is wholly positive, making where you are and what is happening to you now in this present moment into your affirmations. How you are *now* is what is real. No matter how much or how little you have, this is the way to have dignity about yourself.

Since blessings are essentially spiritual because they contain the element of hope, constantly reminding yourself of them keeps your spirit joyful. If you pray or meditate, take time regularly each day to do this. If you find peace and rest in nature, take a walk to some trees and tell them how beautiful they are. These can things make you feel good and this affirms your life as it is now which is the only real place you can be.

Keep talking and delight in good conversation but make what you say true, sincere, and positive.

HOSPITALITY

Recently I was walking in the Atlas Mountains in southern Morocco. This is a beautiful region but sparsely populated and very poor. The villages are made of adobe and people scrape a hard living from poor soil, clustering themselves in small groups around the few rivers and wells, for water is precious and good rains infrequent. We had been walking down a dusty road when we entered a village of perhaps a dozen houses. Two small boys were kicking around a football and I joined them for the fun. My two women walking companions sat gratefully by a wall in the shade watching us. When heat and running got too much we stopped playing and the two boys invited us home to meet their family. Their house was a small sand and mud affair with one glassless window with a cloth curtain and an open entrance, the precious wooden door being stored until winter. As soon as they heard us, the mother of one of the boys came out with two of her daughters and an old grandmother. They warmly welcomed us. Mint tea is the national drink of Morocco and the mother went inside to make us some. In a few minutes she came to the entrance and beckoned us inside. Muslim custom dictated that as a man I should not enter because her husband or another adult male member of the family was not present. So I squatted outside against the house wall in a bit of shade with the boys while my two female companions went inside to drink their tea. The grandmother scurried out and pressed a beautifully decorated glass of tea into my hand.

Now what is important about this hospitality is that all these women could offer as a welcome to their village was some sweet mint tea and that the glass I was given and those of my companions, so wonderfully decorated with scrolls and flourishes of gold lines on pale lavender glass, were the very best they owned. Here was the warmth of sincere hospitality. So the next time there is an unexpected guest do not panic and feel inadequate but put the kettle on and find a tea bag or a spoon of instant coffee. Don't apologize if you don't have a biscuit or cookie to offer.

No one lacks the means of hospitality no matter how little they have or how hard the times on which they have fallen. There is no household anywhere so poor that it cannot afford hospitality, because true hospitality is not about how lavish, elegant or plentiful your hospitality is but about sharing whatever you may have. It may just be a cup of coffee or simply giving the other person your time in listening and conversation. This courtesy was clearly understood in the old days and was almost universally practiced as a social and religious custom in almost all cultures- east, west, north and south.

Hospitality is still understood in this traditional way in many countries, especially in Africa and the Middle East. If your cupboard like old Mother Hubbard's is bare, do not fret when someone unexpected knocks on your door. Invite them in and offer them a chair. If it is close to a meal time, share whatever you have. If you have only enough soup for one, divide it in smaller bowls than usual. If fresh bread is scarce, cut the loaf into small pieces. The portion you serve may be small but offer it with real warmth of heart. Even in these days of so much material abundance, offering a glass of cold water can still be a sign of hospitality.

While the practice of hospitality will enrich your life whether you are drowning in money or just keeping your head above the financial waters, it is true that we must not allow guests to take undue advantage of our hospitality and disrupt our normal household routines and personal habits. The ancient Romans knew this and so do we. Titus Maccius Plautus, who lived about 200 years before Christ, put it this way: *No one can be so welcome a guest that he will not become an annoyance when he has stayed three continuous days in a friend's house.* We always need to keep a balance in what we do and this includes our hospitality, but remembering that a guest and a fish both go off after three days.

To give you an example of how hospitality can take many forms and does not necessarily include either food, drink or even any words, I return to my adventure in Morocco.

We were in a valley high up in the Atlas Mountains. Wild roses grew magnificently here and each year tons of petals were harvested to be sent to make rose water and oil of rose for the markets of the world. Although the scent of roses perfumed the air, we had not thought we could possibly be lucky enough to be there on the one day the annual rose festival was held, because it was always a different day depending on the harvest. This unpredictability kept tourists and the media away. We found ourselves foreigners in rare luck.

At four in the afternoon we walked down the long road toward the village where the celebrations were to be held. The road was filled with dozens of men and women dressed in different regional and tribal costumes. Children would run up and laugh at us in curious delight or try to shout something in French but the adults just politely smiled and otherwise seemed indifferent to our presence. Finally we arrived at a small enclosure rather like a Spanish bullfighting arena. In the Islamic tradition the men and women were separated. We stood waiting, not being able to decide if we should divide up by our gender or stand between the two groups. By now the arena was filled with perhaps a thousand or more people. In the center on the left was an open tent where local tribal leaders and a prince of the royal family were seated. Suddenly, a woman came up to us and taking the arm of one of my companions lead us to the women's side, indicating I should also come. This was the start of their hospitality.

The arena seating was simply continuous concrete circles like a Roman amphitheatre, perhaps even originally having been one. The women lead us to the women's section and then without discussion some of the seated women moved, creating a space for us to sit. The women in the row in front of us moved too so we had room for our legs in comfort. Looking around we realized there were no other foreigners. At the blast of a horn everyone was silent. A man dressed in flowing blue robes come to the centre and bowed first to the open tent of the powerful guests, then to the people on each side of the arena. Finally he walked directly in front of us and bowed to us. With the perfume of roses in the air, music, dancing, amazing head gear and clothes, royal awards for special rose harvest services were finally given out. Sunset brought a golden end to the festival.

These people had all offered us hospitality in the form of the one thing that they could afford to give: the space for us to sit. They had shown us that hospitality which is generous of spirit, without judgment or prejudice, and in keeping with the highest of religious traditions. It comes from the heart and not from money or social position.

Even in the toughest financial and personal times, you too can offer some form of hospitality to others. When you do you will feel that emotional lift that almost always comes when we help others or make them happy.

The tradition of hospitality

The English writer Max Beerbohm, speaking of the kind of insincere hospitality that can arise in a society given to superficial social habits for reasons of status, declared that when hospitality becomes an art it loses its very soul. Those two words *hospitality* and *soul* are intimately linked because what we offer is never just something material or even the time we spare for someone. What we give is ourselves. It is the warmth of our welcome and the manner in which we give it that counts. This idea of the importance of hospitality is a spiritual one and arises from religious understandings of what is believed to please God and from the subsequent social customs that follow it as part of our communal living habit. For this reason, hospitality is important in all the world's great religions.

Hindu Holy Scripture teaches that the unexpected guest be treated as God and that hospitality, no matter how poor one is, should always include at least the offering of charming words, a place to sit down, and the refreshment of a glass of water. A flower garland is often offered as well. All these actions are symbolic of the affection and kindness which should be naturally a part of hospitality.

Hospitality is one of the Divine tests of belief in Allah and the Last Day according to the sayings of the Prophet, upon him be blessings and peace: *Whoever believes in Allah and the Last Day should be hospitable with his or her guests*. If you are a Muslim it is understood that hospitality is part of good manners and the etiquette of Islam, reflecting the high character and spiritual wisdom of Prophets and the Righteous. The deeper religious meaning of such hospitality is understood to be our being in need of God's help and that God supports such a person's need and saves them from self-centered living by sending him or her a guest. In this way our acts of hospitality are prompted by God for our own benefit as well as for the good of our guest. Once again we are led to understand that we are not separate from each other and that acts of compassion to others is to our own good as well.

One of the traditional duties of a Buddhist lay person is to offer food, accommodation and help to guests. A kind of hospitality common in the Buddhist world is to make provisions for travelers and pilgrims by building and equipping rest accommodation in villages and towns or along a pilgrim road. The Buddha himself declared that planting trees, building bridges, digging wells, giving water to wayfarers, and making resting places were all deeds of great merit. This tradition is not confined just to Asia or to Buddhists. It exists today in my own village. We are on the pilgrims' route of Santiago de Compostela which stretches all the way from Northern Europe down to the Atlantic end of Spain where in the vast cathedral of Santiago de Compostela the bones of the Apostle James rest. We have many households who welcome pilgrims with a free bed and a meal. In our local camping grounds we have several log cabins especially for passing pilgrims.

Most Christians understand that hospitality as written about in the bible is not just something you do from time to time but a way of life which is comprehensive and challenging. In the bible strangers in need, angels, and Jesus are all welcomed into people's homes and through such unexpected encounters the people offering this hospitality were transformed in spirit and character. This is because hospitality is more than the offering of food, drink and shelter. It affirms and honours the shared humanity of people. For Christians hospitality becomes a way of making an effective witness of their faith to the world, because when a committed Christian invites another person into his or her home they put on display their life values which reflect the precepts of their religion. In this way Christian hospitality is intimately linked to evangelism and mission.

Peter Morales, president of the Unitarian Universalist Association defined religious hospitality in this way: *Hospitality, true hospitality, is emotionally powerful. It touches something very deep in us—our profound human longing to feel accepted, to belong, to be loved, to feel safe, to be valued and respected. Hospitality is not something to be proclaimed; it must be lived. Hospitality is both a spiritual discipline and an expression of spiritual health. If I feel angry, hurt, unloved, or alienated I cannot offer a warm welcome. Conversely, if I am at peace, filled with joy at being alive, aware of those around me with compassion in my heart, then hospitality flows naturally and inevitably from the depths of my being.*

Why sharing food is so important

When we sit down at table and share a meal we unconsciously are bonding with the others around us. This begins the moment our mothers cradled us to feed at her breast. Nursing is our first and most intimate feeding experience and it is a shared one.

There are many obvious benefits to sharing food. When we share meals and cook for others, we are more likely to eat full meals and to have a more diverse diet. Our conversation at tables helps our digestive system because we have eaten slower, mixing talk with putting the food into our mouths. In these days when more and more people are looking for sustainable food sources and trying to support local food producers, sharing a meal is likely to include talking about the food you are sharing. This easily leads into a discussion as to where it was bought and other comments related to food sourcing. It is claimed that more than a tenth of Americans, for example, have limited or uncertain access to food so sharing a meal can mean better food to those gathered together. Finally, while our food is an essential source of life like water and air, it is also one of our greatest natural pleasures and sharing a pleasure increases its enjoyment.

Wherever we look in our religions, festivals, and private celebrations the sharing of food and drink are involved. This sharing whether between friends or in the family or even at a neighbourhood street party cements our sense of community. We feel we belong together. This strengthens us individually and as a social group and is good for our mental, physical and spiritual health. The most famous of all food sharing is the Last Supper of Jesus and his Apostles. At this historic and spiritual moment the key ritual of the Christian faith was established in the breaking of bread and the drinking of wine in memory of Christ.

Sadly, family meals regularly taken together have fallen out of fashion and social habit in much of America and Britain. Now, food is eaten alone or together in front of the television or computer or with mobile phones in hand so there can be no or little interplay of personalities and conversation. Sunday is often the only day that many people can manage for a shared meal by all the family members, but that day is often devoted to entertainment -shopping, sports, or other outings which in themselves give a sense of the togetherness that comes from sharing. Yet these lack the power of the ritual of sharing food which historically is deeply ingrained in our psyche.

What makes your hospitality special is that you are showing respect to your guest. One reward is to feel contented with what you have in your life right now. Sharing what you have increases your sense of well-being. You become very rich.

RESPECT

Respect has great importance in daily living. Money cannot buy it. Even the most powerful and wealthy, though they command servants, service, goods and influence, may not enjoy the personal respect of others. People may have respect for their power but not for them as an individual man or woman. We can all sense whether we are respected or not and when we are we feel better.

Ordinary respect for others springs from our generosity of heart and our williness to accept that others, although perhaps different in many ways from ourselves, are still part of the human society to which we all belong. Our willingness to act in this way builds up our positive feelings about life in general. Through respect we are better able to appreciate everything around us. Such understanding results in love, because we better comprehend how we are part of the same fabric of universal life. In the end we see a bigger picture than our own story.

When we respect, we are consenting to a person, a thing, event, or an idea. Respect covers a lot of daily living territory and so it is an important aspect if we are to live well. Respect surrounds us with an environment of care and kindness and this is positive for the health of our mind, body and soul.

Everyday good manners build up a better life

Everyone forgets from time to time to respect local customs and laws. Driving over the speed limit is a classic example of ignoring the law. However, common courtesy costs nothing. Good manners which are the result of mutual respect between people have fallen much out of favour and, hence, custom in many countries. In cities and large towns, we often do not bother to greet those who pass us because they are strangers. We also spend a lot of time in our cars cut off from contact with other people.

Saying *Good Morning* or *Good Evening* even to people you do not know is still considered common courtesy in many countries. Where I live in a rural farming town even the children wheeling past on their bikes say *Hello!* These brief greetings pay huge dividends because they make people feel they belong where they live. Such feelings are perhaps taken for granted but the cumulative effect is this sense of belonging. This helps enormously to weave the invisible threads that form the fabric of a community.

Some researchers who ponder the human condition think this kind of communication is not a sign of respect at all. They feel such use of language through our brief greetings, comments on the weather, and other very impersonal social communication to be a way of maintaining social relations through language rituals which are empty of any personal meaning. They even have given it a name: *phatic communication*. On the other hand, perhaps they are wrong and such apparent emptiness is not emptiness after all but a way of maintaining our sense of community. It seems to reaffirm our recognition of each other as part of the local landscape Surely, as we always affect each other in some way, maintaining such awareness is an important part of respect.

Many countries now strive for multiculturalism. This is paraded as tolerance for others, encouraging different minorities to maintain their cultural identity and customs in the hopes that over time integration will somehow happen and people will achieve a shared national identity. Recent history throughout Europe indicates that multiculturalism seems to have done little to diminish our apparently natural suspicion of people who are "different." Recently the French President Nicholas Sarkozy claimed multiculturalism had failed. He publically announced: *If you come to France, you accept melting into a single community, which is the national community, and if you do not want to accept that, you cannot be welcome in France.* Strong words indeed, and in many countries certainly not considered "politically correct" – but his sentiments were also echoed at the time by the German Chancellor Angela Merkel. What multiculturalism seems to have achieved is a sort of an intellectual tolerance which is too distant from any person to person communication to count as real respect.

The philosopher, Slavoj Žižek, who always turns things on their head and shakes out a new vision for us to grapple with, believes today's more liberal tolerance toward others and our general openness to this concept of respect is balanced on the opposite end by our obsessive fear of being harassed. It is okay for other people to be different and we can respect that – but only if such difference does not intrude into our own lives. The concept being that I respect you, but just don't get to close to me with your ideas, customs, or culture. Žižek claims that *what increasingly emerges as the central human right in late-capitalist society is the right not to be harassed, which is a right to remain at a safe distance from others.*

You may well think there is nothing awkward or wrong about this idea of respect as a safe distance from others, but how are we to love our neighbor if we actually do not know and understand them? Without some understanding of the other person's ideas, customs, and culture what is it we are respecting? Leaving people alone, isolating ourselves from others, and making sure there is always a safe distance between us and others hardly counts as respect in a social, spiritual, or moral sense. Fear of harassment cannot be a component of real respect, because we have a closed heart, a heart not willing to be vulnerable to disappointment, misunderstanding or hurt. A closed heart gives nothing to the other person and cements you more firmly in a state of fear.

It is not difficult to show respect to another person. You just need to concentrate on him or her and not on yourself. When you meet someone ask her how she feels. Empathize with her. Show through your facial expressions and your words that you care about how she feels. Seek out some understanding about why she is feeling this way - what these feelings mean to her. As you converse don't start mixing up her problems with your own. You are not starting up a self-help group. For example, if she is having a down-in-the-dumps day, don't start directing the conversation to your own current problems on the mistaken belief that misery loves company. It doesn't help or show respect.

Self-respect

If we do not respect others, how can we respect ourselves? Without such self-respect, we stumble around all our lives looking for answers to such questions about ourselves such as *Who am I?* – or else we keep running away from our real feelings. Meanwhile, we use quick fixes to keep us going. These quick fixes can be emotional, intellectual, or physical and range from other people to over-consumption to all kinds of addiction, distraction, and substitution. The list is endless. When we do finally give ourselves self-respect it means we know the good and bad about ourselves and have accepted our strengths and weaknesses. We have accepted responsibility for our own life. We may not know many if any answers to those big question but we *are* grown-up. Our individuality is acceptable to us and because of this we can accept others as they are. This gives respect all around.

If you have fallen on hard times, had to down-size or even lose your home, have gotten fired or remain unemployed, self-respect usually goes out the window. The result is lower self-esteem. Low self-esteem is like a virus that destroys our vitality. It changes us in ways we don't really like. It makes us withdraw and in that way we create even more distance between ourselves and other people. Thus, our everyday communications do not provide us with the kind of nourishment we need.

If we are in such a situation, then we need to find some kind of pride – a pride in ourselves that does not depend on what kind of home we live in, job we do, or the amount of money in our bank account. We need to be proud of who we are without any material or social trappings.

Years ago when my children were very young I sweated my way through unemployment and living in dead-cheap rented accommodation. I had no work and all we could manage was a single room. At the time I felt ashamed at finding myself and my kids in such a situation. When I finally got a job and some cash, I bought some flowers, remembering the old French saying: *If you only have two pennies, buy bread with one and flowers with the other.* That bouquet reminded me that beauty is as necessary to our human happiness as bread. I felt a deep sense of self-respect because I had put right the balance of life values that I knew I believed in and which I had momentarily lost in my worry over poverty and the future. Unless we maintain our self-respect, our courage in facing difficulties will fail. Since self-respect does not depend on how rich you are or the job you have or your religion, nationality, race or physical perfection, it is a treasure waiting for you to claim. It clears the path to contented living.

The will to live – a vision for our times

Respect as part of a full and happy life is not confined just to other people and ourselves. Our respect must extend to our surroundings, planet, and all other living creatures. While we do not need to follow the Hindu or Buddhist traditions and refuse even to swat a fly, we do need to be aware that we depend on the natural world. This does not mean that we respect only those parts of the natural world we need, but that we respect *all* life. When we do this exactly what are we respecting?

In the twentieth a talented German called Albert Schweitzer

followed his heart into the study of music and became a world class organist and composer. Next, he decided to study religion and won acclaim and professorships as a Christian theologian. He published papers in philosophy. Still young, he studied the wider world and there, just as in our day, he found shocking poverty and illness. This filled him with compassion to help so he studied medicine. Eventually, Dr. Schweitzer went to the poorest place in Africa and set up a small free hospital. Over the years he worked there and his fame as a man of humanity, a great musician, a profound theologian, and a philosopher made him world famous. He believed that all life was sacred because all life contained within it a will to live and this was divinely given. In a speech at Mansfield College, Oxford in 1923, Dr. Schweitzer said, *The time is coming when people will be astonished that mankind needed so long a time to regard thoughtless injury to life as incompatible with ethics.* This reverence for all life was the cornerstone of Schweitzer's philosophy and he considered it to be his greatest contribution to mankind. He believed that Western civilization was falling into ruin because it had lost its respect for life as an ethical basis for daily living. In 1952, he received the Nobel Peace Prize for his philosophy of *Reverence for Life.*

Over the years as the planet was plundered and polluted by the global expansion of capitalism, his ideas fell from favour with academics and the informed public. Then with climate change and our increased awareness of the human causes of damage to the earth's eco-system and bio-diversity, Dr. Schweitzer's vision, like similar ideas of the American writer David Henry Thoreau in his famous *Walden Pond,* become widely popular among those concerned with environmental and ecological issues.

Whether any of us can translate such a philosophy of respect for all life into a collective action that will have a positive impact on Mother Earth and her resources seems doubtful in the face of our continuing human greed and the lack of will of our politicians. However, if you are still living a life where consuming the planet and following a moral code that says *more is better,* then please stop now. Start getting respect for where you live. This place is called Earth. There is only one available for you and *all* life on it is important. The practice of such respect is profound because it is an integral part of the process of love. Your next door neighbor is as good a place as any to start.

ADMIRATION

In our Celebrity Age it is sometimes hard to recall what real admiration is about. It is not some fleeting attention to a film actor or pop star. The reason this is not admiration is because you are very unlikely to personally know such people. To admire is to know someone – the real person. Political figures, influential financial wizards, CEO's of global corporations, and the whole passing parade of celebrities have public personas which are most unlikely to be what or who they are in private. In any case in an over-populated world where competition to succeed in worldly terms is diamond sharp, whoever heard of someone getting to the top of the pile because he or she was a *nice* person? We might like their talents or style but we don't actually know them.

Don't think for a second that this false admiration is only for teenagers who are searching for role models. Women in late middle age regularly buy magazines which follow the dramas of their latest celebrity. A close friend who is seventy years old still buys fashion glamour magazines. When I asked her why, she told me, *I need to keep up*. As she has a naturally aged body, no money for expensive clothes and no place to wear them if she could afford them, where is her need? It is in her head. She still holds the image of herself when young. This means my friend is living in yesterday and not making the most of what and whom she is today. She does not accept that she now belongs to a different part of society with more age appropriate interests. Just look around you at all the women and men who have become sheep dressed up as lambs because we insist that youth is always best, that being sexy is appropriate for everyone at every age, and that appearance triumphs character. Such admiration is hollow and makes you discontented.

If you are to make a rich life you need to admire people you have met or know. It is this more intimate knowledge of personality and character that gives you grounds for your admiration since admiration involves an approval which arises from knowledge.

Admiration and flattery

Pleasure, esteem, approval, and respect are all emotions we enjoy having and which we much appreciate when they are directed to ourselves. So how do we know when someone pretends to admire us but is actually only flattering us?

Sincerity is what makes the difference. Each of us has to judge for themselves whether a person who compliments us is simply flattering our ego or actually admiring us. Some people need a diet of flattery and actively seek it if it is not freely given. They promote questions or comments that prompt others to comment on their appearance or life or children or style of living or possessions. The list of what we can find to flatter about a person is endless. We don't have to be sincere at all. In fact often a person flatters someone they don't even like much less admire. So honesty in how you feel is what makes you sincere when you compliment another person.

Flattery is a false emotion and, since most of us know when we are being flattered, it makes us distrust the other person. You suspect you are being manipulated for some reason since flattery and manipulation go hand-in-hand.

We do not need people around us who flatter us. We need friends who are sincere and who have character traits we admire. This makes our friendships health, loving, and mutually enriching.

Become what you admire in others

Like the wax that makes a good piece of furniture shine so too does admiration add gloss to our lives. Yet we shouldn't stop at just noticing other people's good traits. We should try to imitate what we admire in other people. If you have a friend who always lights up your day with smiles and humour, try spreading around some of the same stuff yourself. If you have a partner who is always supportive, ask yourself if you act the same. If you have a family member who always phones when you are unwell, do you do the same for them? If you are pleased with the way a friend always takes care when they dress, do you take the same care for the sake of others? We have a capacity to admire and we have an equal capacity to imitate what we respect. So becoming what you admire in others is a way of improving your own personality, appearance, and standing with family and friends. None of this need cost you a penny.

Admiration is good for relationships

Admiration is great cement for relationships. Over time we often forget this – for example in remembering to occasionally tell our partner, members of our family, and close friends how much we appreciate and admire them. We have forgotten to build them up. We have taken their deeper needs for granted usually because we are too busy with work or children or just running our lives. Practice admiration the most with the person you share your life with - and don't forget the kids. Teenagers especially need to know that they are *Okay* because adolescent years are filled with self doubts, wobbly self-esteem and a great need for reassurance. If you claim to your friends that your partner is wonderful that is great – but telling the person herself or himself how you feel is even better. Bring them your admiration.

It is suggested by some studies that men for their emotional health, even more than most women, need a feeling of being admired. Continuing studies in sociology and psychological medicine suggest this aspect of men is probably correct. It is generally agreed that the majority of men are goal orientated and competitive with much of their personal identity and sense of self-esteem tied to their talents, work success, and leadership qualities. While including his family, these relate more to a man's life in the world of other men. Both men and women need to be esteemed and special in their own right and not just for the money earned or the rank in society achieved.

How little time and effort it takes to say once in a while to the other person in your life, *Thank you!* Let them know you are glad he or she is around and that you really appreciate the effort, care, and work they do that helps make you comfortable and happy. We are all good at criticizing but usually forget to admire. When you face a tough problem at work or with a friend or relative, discuss it with your significant other. Ask her or his advice. This is a form of admiration. Finally, include the person you love in important decision making. All these actions demonstrate your honour and respect for the man or woman in your life. It also does not hurt to ask your adolescent or grown children what they think. They too have wisdom to share as well as a need for words of admiration.

You can spread sincere admiration around. It costs you nothing but love. You will feel great.

Keeping dignity going

When we feel admired our self-esteem is strengthened. There is hardly a better time for this then when we are faced with hard times and living is not easy. Depression and a loss of self-esteem are well-known factors in people who are unemployed. The longer they are unemployed, the greater their feelings of not being worthy. This is especially true of the bread-winner in the family. Depression easily sets in. Not sleeping, drinking or eating too much, or being easily angry or upset are all common to the long-term unemployed. If you are in such a situation yourself or your loved one, then admiration is much needed. When we are feeling low and worthless we need more than ever to feel loved, respected, and honour. We need our sense of dignity back. Admiration can bring that even if times are tough. When we have dignity we become strong and can rediscovery hope and courage.

HONESTY

We have separated the ethical and moral values of honesty from ideas of being rich because to be rich has come to only have material connotations and the possession of powerful connections. People who control our wealth and politics almost always forget in their actions and decisions the common good and are concerned only with personal self advancement. Honesty should mean you are a person of moral character. Integrity, truthfulness and fairness make up such character. This does not mean you cannot also have loads of money in the bank or occupy a position of authority. Of course, it is hard to make being rich and being honest compatible but that is the challenge we ought to face in being citizens together in a society. Freedom from deceit can be included too in what being honest means – but what about all those little white lies that we utter from time to time? We might protest that white lies are really not being dishonest but rather just a way of avoiding hurting someone else. Yet to paraphrase Gertrude Stein: *a lie is a lie is a lie*. If only honesty was that simple.

So honesty as a moral concept sounds fine but the reality can be quite different. Sometimes we lie and say it is okay. At other times we go for the unvarnished truth. This is especially true today when in Western society we no longer have any widely accepted way to behave socially. We decide as we go along how we chose to conduct ourselves with little regard for the consequences for our wider society. But confusingly this is not always the case.

First, most of us think a person honest if we find they seem to always be telling us the truth. They do not dissemble or skirt an issue but try to be frank. Being too frank has its problems too. When your partner dresses up to go to a party and asks if she or he looks alright, we all know it is wise to say, *You look lovely!* or *You're a handsome guy!* - no matter what you may actually think.

Relationships often include such little white lies to help make the road smoother. On the other hand if asked, for example, if you like her or him wearing orange, a colour you dislike, there is no reason not to tell the truth.

So honesty is always a balancing act between being completely truthful and molding what we say to the specific occasion. This is not to put aside our integrity but to do a bit of blending of kindness to the recipe for honesty.

The environment of dishonesty

Once upon a long time ago, naive or idealist Americans might have believed that politicians did not lie to the public at least all of the time and did not accept back-handers or do deals with lobbyists representing commercial interests. Even more that a handshake of agreement would be binding. Today people would probably think you were crazy even to suggest these things could be true. Not prepared for the dishonesty of the world, we arrive at adulthood to find we are living in an environment today in which we must question the honesty and truthfulness of everything from what is in a tin of peas to the activities of our banks. Life teaches us to mistrust because so much that happens is remote, the evil people do is always before us in the media, and traditional role models are either shallow or proven dishonest.

Actually, this was not always so and it can be inspiring to remember it. When Britain was at the peak of its world empire, the word of an Englishman was rarely questioned. If he was British that was enough evidence of personal honesty. An English friend, Scotland Liddell who had been sent to Russia just months before the 1917 revolution as cub reporter, found such national reputation for honesty saved his life. When fighting broke out in St. Petersburg, he found himself caught up in the conflict. The Bolshevik forces took him captive considering him an enemy since he was both foreign and a journalist. They bundled him onto a train heading to Siberia. With quick wit he slipped from his captors, opened the nearest outside door just as the train started and stepped over into another train. The new train moved out of the station in the opposite direction. With nothing but good luck and the clothes on his back, he had managed to escape onto the last train headed to Finland before Russia fell to the revolutionaries. Penniless in Helsinki with his passport still in the hands of his former captives, he found a travel agent, declared in his clipped English accent that he was British, needed a ship going to England, and promised to send the fare back when he arrived home. On his word alone he got the ticket. Then, he next visited a tailor for a new suit and coat, a luggage shop, and finally stayed in a hotel with a restaurant until it was time to embark on his ship – all on credit because he was an Englishman who, of course, was understood in those days to always honour his word. He arrived in London, wrote his story up for *The Times* newspaper and was launched on a lifetime career as an author and journalist. And, yes, he did repay all his creditors.

Unfortunately, those days are gone as we endure the duplicity of those who would lead us and the dissembling scenarios of corporate business. This affects how we view being honest as individuals for if the rich and powerful among us lie and cheat why should we bother to be honest?

Yet for all that, we continue to hunger for truth and follow with concerned interest investigations such as those of Michael Moore, Julian Assange, and others in uncovering the truth to improve political, corporate and military transparency. We desperately need to rediscover for ourselves a sense of honesty so that we become conscious that our individual decisions and actions have a wider effect on the common good. Honesty gives us a firm ground on which to base our ethical and moral values. Without following religious teachings or good role models by societies' leaders and media, we can but hope that by making ourselves an example of individual honesty we will influence others to do the same. Above all, we must hold firm and not succumb to the values of people who would be our leaders once we recognize that how they behave does harm to the common good.

Emotional honesty

Honesty is not just about telling the truth to others. It is also about telling the truth to yourselves. This is what makes us feel rich. Such emotional honesty means we try to express our true feelings, first with ourselves and then with others insofar as what we say brings mutual understanding and not conflict. To possess emotional honesty we first have to be aware of how we actually feel. This calls for a self examination which accurately identifies our true feelings. Many people find it hard to have this kind of personal insight and often simply do not know how they truly feel about something or some situation. A recovered alcoholic who lives up the hill from me put insight into perspective for me when he was telling me his life story and finished it by declaring, *What I learned was that for the first forty years of my life I knew what I wanted but not what I needed.* He was not alone for most of us rarely know what we really need physically, emotionally or spiritually. We read articles and watch programmes about lifestyles from health to food to sex which are great for telling us about what we need and the choices we can make but when the crunch comes we find it hard to change ourselves. However sooner or later we may be forced to live values that mean change and with them may come a new clarity about our life. We may better understand what we need. This personal insight about ourselves can bring the emotional honesty which provides the necessary discernment between these two often conflicting aspects about what we need and what we want.

The practice of insight can be a way forward

Insight is a term often invoked when discussing both traditional religions and alternative spiritualities. However, such deep understanding of the self involves emotional intelligence and attention to the body which can have nothing to do with religion or spiritual practices. Emotional intelligence means deliberately investigating how we really feel and not fudging the issues. We *think* about our feelings and do not just *feel* them. This insight can bring emotional honesty. It also means we pay deliberate attention to the signals our body is sending us. We may then regain a recognition of when we are beginning to feel stress. We discern the difference between feeling hungry and just using food as comfort. We give our body the respect it deserves through healthy eating, exercise, and weight control. It is no longer just a surface to be decorated by fashion. We accept how our body is and think it good. This too is emotional honesty. In the Buddhist tradition insight plays a direct and important part. It means looking into the nature of reality. A Buddhist song puts it this way: *May I generate the flower of insight.* [Lord Milarepal]

One of the world's most ancient meditation techniques is called *Vipassana* which is the practice of self-transformation through self-observation. In English *Vipassana* is called *insight meditation*. This introspection is a way to emotional honesty.

The beginning of this insight practice involves elements we can all use to our advantage. It includes observation of bodily sensations, analytical thinking, and observations about our experience of living. These reflect our aims of better emotional intelligence and a keen awareness of our body which I mentioned above.

Insight meditation begins by focusing and calming ourselves. As we calm ourselves we begin to concentrate. That is, we begin to be mindful of where we are, how we feel, the various fleeting thoughts which come and go in our heads. We are entering more fully into the present moment, the *now* of life. We are preparing to get insight but have not yet found it.

The practice of this particular insight meditation is a unification which has three steps. First, we practice being tranquility, then secondly we practice insight, and finally in the third phase we bring together the first two elements. Such practice done on a regular basis is a powerful step toward achieving full emotional honesty about yourself.

These insight meditation techniques are not difficult to learn and should not conflict with your religion if you are a person of faith. However, it is preferable at first that you have the help of an experienced teacher. If such teaching is not conveniently available where you live or too expensive, then you can begin your practice by reading about it and following the instructions. You have nothing to lose by trying it.

How society discourages emotional honesty

Without doubt, it takes courage and self-confidence to share our personal insights about ourselves with others because we run the risk of being rejected. Society teaches us from childhood that it is better to ignore, repress, lie or deny how we really feel. Somehow this is considered more polite, safer, and less likely to upset other people. For example, when someone who is not a very close friend or member of our family asks us how we feel, most of us reply "fine" or "good," or " okay" even if that is not true and we are feeling depressed, sad, angry, or ill. We learn as we grow up that it just doesn't seem to pay to express one's true feelings. We are taught to guard our feelings like private property. Expressing them exposes us to gossip but since people always gossip about something, why fear it?

Being dishonest about our feelings in this way does not help us live a better or richer life. This continually hiding of ourselves does not serve our emotional well-being or our spiritual progress.

It takes a lot of psychic energy to dissemble in this way and it disregards the value of our natural feelings. In such a scenario we are swimming against the tide of truth. We eventually sink in a soup of non-authenticity and falseness that does nothing to create a better life for ourselves or those around us. It supports an insincere society in which our little collective untruths cover up the collective social insights we won't face.

Even if we try to be honest, it can be hard to find out exactly how honesty is defined by other people. For example, 15,000 people in England and Wales took part in a web-based study, *Honesty Lab*, organised by two criminologists from Brunel University in conjunction with the British Science Association. Their research found no common standard of dishonesty in today's society. There is also apparently a further disparity between the genders with another recent study revealing wide differences in what men and women view as to what was dishonest. Amazingly, the research suggested that women are more likely to judge it more dishonest to cheat a clothing shop than to cheat an elderly patient in a care home. Most men had a similar attitude with over 80 per cent thinking it was morally wrong to pretend to borrow a dress from the shop when you were actually intending to keep it but only 37 per cent of them disapproving of taking advantage of someone who was elderly and infirm. It is not just that we do not share a common definition of what honesty means in our society but that we don't even seem to understand the moral concept of the idea behind most of our laws. This has grave implication for justice as these findings suggest that if a jury of twelve men and women was asked to pass a verdict on a care home nurse who was up on charges of patient neglect or taking undue advantage of an elderly person, only four in the jury would want to convict.

So being honest has problems, but in the end it is vital to making effective lifestyle changes which make our lives contented. You are worthy of respect and honesty has a key role to play in building such a good reputation. As Mark Twain wrote, *When in doubt tell the truth.* Your life will become richer and more real for being honest.

KINDNESS

Kindness is the golden chain by which society is bound together.
Johann Wolfgang von Goethe [1749-1832]

Born in the Mount Everest region of remote Nepal, the Venerable Lama Thubten Zopa Rinpoche is a Buddhist monk of great wisdom. He has helped ordinary people around the world to gain greater insight into their lives. Such insight has brought thousands of men and women greater peace through a better understanding of the nature of human life. Central to his spiritual guidance and, indeed to all Buddhist spiritual doctrine, is the concept and practice of compassion. Here is where we find the powerful element of kindness, because compassion incorporates all the attributes and activities of love and love in any of its various forms must always include kindness. You cannot love without being kind at the same time.

In his book, *Practicing the Good Heart,* Lama Zopa Rinpoche tells us why our acts of kindness make our lives richer and more meaningful: *Even if we own diamonds or dollars equal to the number of atoms of the earth, if our heart is empty of compassion for others, our life is empty. Even with that much wealth, our life is empty; there is no happiness. However, even if we do not own one atom of diamond or one dollar, if we have compassion for all beings, there is great peace and happiness in our everyday life.*

The nature of kindness

Our acknowledgement that a state of suffering is natural to all humans does not mean that we have to remain in such a sad place. Recognizing this shared experience of life is the first step in freeing ourselves from it. Thinking more deeply about suffering - not just about some passing unhappy event but in the overall picture of the human condition - leads us to realize that the people all around us suffer exactly the same as we do. It is this recognition that underlies one of the most famous teachings of Jesus: *Do unto others as you would have them do unto you.* [NT: Luke VI.31]

Whether you are a person of faith or not, this teaching opens the heart, changes the way we see other people, and practiced as part of the way we live, makes us rich in ways that worldly success cannot. If you can have such a treasure through the practice of kindness, why would you want to stay marooned in the desert of suffering?

The good medicine of kindness

The American comedian Bob Hope whose hilarious comments on life frequently contained a kernel of wisdom said this about the importance of kindness: *Every act of compassion makes a difference! If you haven't any charity in your heart, you have the worst kind of heart trouble.* With the lightest touch and perhaps almost unknowingly, he indentified the link between being kind and good health. Being kind works to help us in this way because when you are kind the emotions are positive. This changes your body chemistry in a way that is healthy- blood pressure drops, stress lessens, and the body stops gearing up for emotional war. The opposite happens when we are filled with anger and hate. So being compassionate is the practice of kindness in thought and deed and it contributes to better health. This better health is not just physical and emotional for ourselves but affects all those around us. Kindness is spiritual medicine.

Healing the wounds of love

What may block us from freely and fully expressing feelings of compassion is when we remain too emotionally wounded. We have not yet healed the negative past that is part of our story. Often, it is easier to be kind to strangers than to those near us. Strangers may be able to physically harm us, but those we love, who know us so well, are the ones who can really hurt us – sometimes so badly we may carry the wound for years after the event. Unfortunately such personal wounds influence how we see and respond to others.

There are two significant ways to heal ourselves so we can act with the kindness of compassion. These are through the powers of forgiveness and reconciliation.

Forgiveness

To err is human, to forgive, divine.
Alexander Pope [1688-1744]

Forgiveness has the power of new beginnings. When two people make peace with each other, there is redemption made historic and visible. This reflects the redemption of Christ who while dying for all humanity paradoxically made his sacrifice for each person individually.

We forgive individually person by person and usually find it impossible to make forgiveness a global affair. It is difficult enough to forgive one person let alone a whole world. Still, when we forgive one person the effect spreads out like a stone thrown into a pond. Our making peace has far wider implications than just peace between two people.

The American psychologist, Margaret Gramatky Alter, once described the nature of forgiveness in this way: *As any counselor knows, change begins as love and forgiveness penetrate the human heart. The counselor's question is not, Should this person be forgiven? but, How can I reach into the despair before me and communicate the tenderness of God to this suffering person?*

So our forgiveness is an act of love as well as a new beginning.

When we forgive we enter a new future. We have turned a page. In this way, forgiveness is an act of hope as well as renewal. Forgiveness is always transcendent in nature and related to ultimate reality where self disappears into the oneness of the universe. Your forgiving someone and reaching out with tenderness, is really an action which is truly that grand.

Redemption

We are redeemed when we forgive for that resentment and anger which rested uneasily in our inner world is at last slain. The actions of forgiveness and redemption involve a re-interpretation of our own past actions and this re-orientates us toward a more positive future. The Dutch theologian, E. Schillebeeckx, whose contributions to the Second Vatican Council made him known throughout the world, claimed that such reconciliation is never in the service of self-justification. He felt it belonged within all spiritual life since our forgiveness, redemption and reconciliation was entirely a spiritual process.

These powers of forgiveness, redemption, and reconciliation are the tools by which we may clear the way for living a contented life because we are no longer carrying anger and anguish from the past in ourselves. We have put down this heavy burden and taken up the way of compassion. In such a life kindness comes first because we earnestly know that a life lived with love as the final judge of what is morally right and wrong makes us rich beyond the treasures of King Solomon. Such a moral principle as part of our daily life strengthens us whether we live in material luxury or the breadline is staring us in the face. The Russian novelist, Fyodor Dostoyevsky, claimed that compassion was the chief law of human existence. Without it, we could not survive either as individuals or as a community.

A Buddhist inspired meditation of compassion

Taking the time to reflect about the deeper meaning of the practice of a new life style value often gives us added courage to take it up. The following three ideas about our human nature from a Buddhist perspective may bring that reflection which can lead you to a deeper understanding of the significance of what you are undertaking when you practice a life of kindness. I suggest you read these comments on human nature and then try the short meditation given after them.

The nature of emptiness

Emptiness in a Buddhist sense is very different to what we ordinarily mean by this word. In Buddhism it refers to the fact that no thing, including human existence, has ultimate substantiality. This means that no thing is permanent and no thing is totally independent of everything else. In other words, everything in this world is interconnected and in constant change. Appreciating this concept of emptiness can save us from the suffering caused by our egos, our attachments, and our resistance to change and loss. This place of emptiness or oneness is called in all the great religions: *the common ground of being.*

The nature of the universe

From the atoms that compose the cells of your body to the matter of the stars in the heavens, everything is in a state of flux. Everything is constantly changing. So how can we fear change since it is the nature of everything in the universe?

The nature of wisdom

To be wise is to be empty of all illusion, expectations, and ideas of you separate from everything else. Since you are not separate, it follows that you alone prevent yourself from attaining wisdom. Why do you wish to struggle against a state of wisdom? Why do you wish to continue to suffer?

Ten Step Meditation of Compassion

1. Set your kitchen timer for 15 minutes. Then sit comfortably, back straight but with a relaxed body, your head inclined slightly downward. Close your eyes.
2. Let all thoughts, ideas and sensations come and go. Do not concern yourself with them.
3. Begin first to become conscious of your breathing in and out.
4. Concentrate gently on breathing in and out.
5. As you breathe in become aware of your body, part by part, feel love for it.
6. As you breathe out, send your breath like a gentle breeze outward to someone else, a person you have seen in the street, a person you met or read about, a person you know.
7. Now let your inward breathe be of love for yourself.
8. As you breathe out, send loving compassion to all sentient beings. Continue this breathing of compassion.
9. If it happens, allow yourself to drift deeper into your meditation where you become empty, where there is no conscious awareness.
10. When the timer sounds, the meditation has ended. Open your eyes, and then begin to move but very slowly and gently.

Do not wait to begin compassion

Beginning this very moment to treat everyone you meet as if they were going to be dead by midnight. Extend to them all the care, kindness, forgiveness and understanding you can muster. Do it with no thought of reward now or in the future. If you practice such compassion your life will never be the same again.

SHARING

It can be great fun to share what you have as every philanthropist discovers. We can all be philanthropists even if we have to tailor what we share to the scale of our modest living. Perhaps we cannot donate great works of art or give vast sums of money for charitable purposes, but what we can do is share our time and a little of what we have with those who are in need. As most volunteer charity workers know, the paradox of sharing is that the more you share the more you increase the satisfaction with your own life. Since this appears true in so many cases, perhaps recipients of charity ought to be included with those who dispense it.

The generation is mostly gone that can remember the depression of the 1930s when ordinary middle-class people were thrown out of their homes and lived hand-to-mouth and often begged on the street. It will come as a great shock if this is seen again by the new generations of Americans who have been raised in years of plenty. When people become hungry, private security like gated communities don't work. We have become accustomed to keeping the poor and needy at arm's length. Nowadays, our sharing is usually done in the form of charities where our money goes into a general fund. This is impersonal and means we do not have to come face to face with people in need. We can see them on television, hear about them at church, or get a mail drop leaflet in our mail box urging us to donate. While all our charity is worthwhile, no matter how much we give or may feel sorry for people, this form of sharing keeps us at a safe emotional and physical distance from those in need of our help.

A Belgium nun, Thérèse-Marie Dupagne, once pointed out that with all the social and other communication now in our lives, we still distance ourselves from much of the reality around us if it makes us uncomfortable. *We are ready to pass out information,* she wrote, *but are we ready to enter into relationships? In a world in which communication is emphasized, are we in communion?* If we are only connected to each other by some form of virtual reality then we cannot completely know the person who needs us. However, what we can understand through communication is their need whether that is a material one like food and shelter or a political one such as the Occupy Wall Street demonstrations for financial reform and political transparency. We must then decide in what way we chose to be in communion with them.

Even in affluent countries, the poor are often treated as second class citizens as if their need was entirely their own fault. When we now have third generation poor and unemployed in our great cities perhaps this is a new Western form of an untouchable class. We might help them as long as they do not enter our personal space, come to the door of our home, or stop us on the street. If strangers approach us we are afraid they will harm us in some way. Besides, to be poor and need help means the person is unsuccessful. As far as most of us are concerned they cannot possibly be our neighbour. They remain *the stranger* or even *the failed stranger*.

Jesus had strong words to say about such thinking. In fact, our sharing or the lack of it is so important that in the Last Judgment it becomes the scale upon which our whole life will be weighed and judged, because to share is to love. The words in the *New Testament* about this weighing up of how we have lived are salutary reading for people of all faiths and those of none, because what is said goes deeply into the nature of our williness to acknowledge our common humanity. It defines whether we have truly loved or not. It really does not depend on you being a believer. Wisdom is not defined by your faith or lack of it. It does not depend on whether or not you are agnostic or atheist or if you believe in a doctrine of a Last Judgment – so please read on.

When the Son of Man comes in his glory, and all the angels with him, he will sit on his glorious throne. All the nations will be gathered before him, and he will separate the people one from another as a shepherd separates the sheep from the goats. He will put the sheep on his right and the goats on his left.

Then the King will say to those on his right, 'Come, you who are blessed by my Father; take your inheritance, the kingdom prepared for you since the creation of the world. For I was hungry and you gave me something to eat, I was thirsty and you gave me something to drink, I was a stranger and you invited me in, I needed clothes and you clothed me, I was sick and you looked after me, I was in prison and you came to visit me.'

Then the righteous will answer him, "Lord, when did we see you hungry and feed you, or thirsty and give you something to drink? When did we see you a stranger and invite you in or needing clothes and clothe you? When did we see you sick or in prison and go to visit you?"

The King will reply, "Truly I tell you, whatever you did for one of the least of these brothers and sisters of mine, you did for me."

It is by such recognition that no one is a stranger but a fellow human who shares our common humanity and suffering and our will to live. Such acknowledgement and the compassion that follows it, enables us to rise above our self-concern and fearfulness and extend the love that waits in our hearts.

The story of a stranger

We never know who may be the stranger waiting to enter our lives. Here is a true tale of a stranger who was once befriended through the natural goodness of a child and the generosity of a famous man, both of whom shared something they possessed. In this case, power and prestige. This also is a story of wisdom.

In the American Civil War, both the father and the only brother of a soldier in the Federal Army were killed. The soldier worried about how his widowed mother and his sister would manage back home on their small farm. He asked his commanding officer if he could have enough leave to go home and sow the spring corn so his remaining family might have enough to eat. His request was denied so he ran away. He travelled as best he could to get to Washington D.C. to seek permission to go home from the President of the United States, but at the gates of the White House he was refused admission. In misery he strolled over to the nearby park and sat on a bench. His eyes filled with tears and he wondered what to do next. After a while a small boy came up and asked what the matter was. He told the child his sad story.

I think I can help you, *the boy said and, taking him by the hand, he walked back up to the White House. The sentry opened the gate without comment, and they walked up the drive to the front entrance where a tall guard clicked his heals and opened the door for them. They walked down corridors, past important offices, till they came to a door marked* PRESIDENT. *The small boy opened the door and walked straight in. There, behind the large desk, was Abraham Lincoln with some of his advisers.*

Hello, Todd, *said the President,* Who's your friend? *Todd Lincoln explained to his father the story told him by the stranger on the park bench, whereupon President Lincoln granted immediate permission for the soldier to return home and care for the family farm.*

So the next time you pass a stranger begging on the street or someone stops you to ask for a handout do not hurry by or brush them aside. Do not consider whether they are honestly in need or not, but see yourself in them as in a mirror.

This way you can really get to grips with the fact that someone out there really is your brother or sister in this struggle of living and they *are* suffering – never mind the reasons why. Noticing someone is suffering more than ourselves and who is in greater need stirs not just our compassion but puts our own situation into perspective.

How the wisdom of sharing may be sustained

Over 1,500 years ago a hermit monk, Saint Benedict of Nursia (480-547 CE) wrote a set of rules or principles for living together in community. This guide, which was designed for peaceful monastic living in accord with Christian scripture, has been a great influence on my life and I feel it has much to offer us if we seek a way of life based on ethical and moral values that bring us contentment. Millions find in his rules help to achieve that peacefulness and purpose in living which serves the aims of mental, physical and spiritual well-being. These rules have been called *an epitome of Christianity* since it is a learned abridgement of all the doctrines of the Gospel, all the institutions of the Early Church Fathers, and all the counsels of spiritual life. For Saint Benedict the perfect human was Christ so he made him into the stranger who knocks on your door. Thus, he decreed in his Rule: *Let all guests who arrive be received as Christ, because He will say: "I was a stranger and you took me in"* (NT Matthew 25:35).

Even if you are not a person of faith or claimed God did not exist, would you knowingly turn away the stranger begging or knocking on your door if you knew it was Jesus? Indeed, we may well call this guideline by Saint Benedict *a counsel of spiritual perfection* for it can guide us into a profound hope in *all* life and not just in that which concerns humanity. Our sharing is this important for it is the key to entering communion with the universal oneness of life. Without such awareness and action we remain incomplete. With such sharing of ourselves we grow as rich as the legendary King Midas, not in gold we may count but in the good health of our mind, body and spirit.

LAUGHTER

Nothing can compare with laughing. Just look at what laughter can do: lifts your mood, helps make friends, renews relationships, prolongs your life, reduces stress, and improves your immune system. It is a balm for mind, body and spirit, soothing and lifting each aspect of you up into realms where *feeling good* dwells. Since joy is an essential measure of how satisfactory your life is, laughter is the yeast that rises up a life into contentment. Without doubt laughter is the best medicine.

Joyfulness now

Laughing, dancing, singing, playing, and listening to a happy or funny story – any and all of these can trigger a sense of joy – that all is okay with life. It may be a fleeting feeling before you seem to come down to earth, but in those few seconds or minutes when you feel joy you are alive in the present moment. You are in the state you should be in most of the time but usually aren't. Joy is a real physical phenomenon with your body truly involved. When we are joyful biochemical changes take place in the body which create a sense of well-being. This feeling alters our negative vision of life and puts aside for a little while the challenges we may be facing.

What is laughter?

You guessed it – there is a science of laughter and it is called *Gelotology*. Researchers still only know very little about how and why we laugh, but so far it appears the major mental benefit of laughing seems to be that it helps us cope with life. I think we all knew that anyway.

However, lets note what they have found out about our

laughing: the main physical health benefits are a decrease in blood pressure, an increased blood flow in your veins and arteries, increased oxygen in your blood, gives your muscles a workout, strengthens your immune system, and triggers the release of endorphins – the body's natural feel-good chemicals. Life has proven to most of us that nothing works faster than a good laugh to bring balance to our body and emotions and to lighten our everyday woes. It gives us a sense of hope and keeps us grounded in that ever needed *present moment*.

People generally believe laughing is the result of something that strikes us as funny but this does not have to be so. What we find funny depends on our intellect and culture and varies from person to person. Children laugh freely and a whole string of ordinary happenings can make them laugh. Sadly, as adults learn to repress feelings, spontaneous laughter can be one of them. This is to our detriment. If you want a full life in hard times then you have got to start laughing more.

When you laugh others find it contagious. So the next time you meet a friend keep it light, stop talking about your problems, and get laughing. Your friend will soon join in. The good feeling that you get when you have laughed remains with you, lifting your mood and that of your friend. If you cannot laugh, then try smiling. Even that will make you feel better as well as foster the bond of your friendship and help act as a buffer against anxiety, stress, and disagreements.

You may feel laughing is impossible at this moment in your life. You are wrong. You can laugh even in the midst of a complete physical and emotional muddle. Here are some ways to start:

Smile. This is the beginning of laughter. When you look at someone or see something even slightly pleasing, then smile.

Count your blessings. If you can't think of any, you are not trying. For example, you *are* alive. Start there.

Move toward the laughter. If you hear someone laughing, get moving toward this lovely sound. Even if you only stand on the sidelines you will probably wind up laughing. Don't be shy as most people when laughing like as many others as possible to join in. You can easily tell if it is a private joke demanding your respectful distance.

Spend more time with happy people. Did you know that children laugh on average 300 to 400 times in a day while adults laugh only about 10 to 15 times? When you release your inner child, you will find you are laughing much more. So we should make friends with more people who love having fun and laugh easily and freely.

Find opportunities to laugh. There are plenty of chances to laugh. For a start watch funny movies or TV shows and give the sad, cruel, scary and violent ones a miss. Avoid the front page of your newspaper and go straight to the comic strips. *Felix the cat* and *Donald Duck* and *The Simpsons* will do more for you than some jargon-filled science report or television crime story. Pick up a few amusing novels at your local library. Find some table games and invite over a few friends. Joining others and playing games can lighten as well as light up your day. Take time to play with your pet if you have one – or even visit a friend who has a pet and enjoy that companionship. Finally, just act silly once in a while. You do not always have to be *a serious grown-up*.

Take yourself less seriously. Acting silly means you take yourself less seriously and this is great for your morale. Some events in life are clearly sad and need to be taken seriously but most things that happen to us in daily living do not call for us to be sad or glad- they just happen as the ordinary routine stuff of living, neither great nor very important. They just *are*. If we want life to be more fun, then it is up to us to make it happen. Our sense of humour and our laughter is the driving gear for having fun.

Laughter Yoga

Our emotions directly affect our breathing. When we are upset or under stress, our breathing pattern changes. It becomes faster, shallow and irregular. When relaxed it becomes deeper and slower. We know now that many victims of asthma can bring this disease under control and improve their prognosis by changing the way they breathe from irregularity and shallowness to regular deeper breathing. Breathing is the only function of the Autonomic Nervous System which works independent of our control but that can be consciously regulated. By changing the way you breathe, you can change your state of mind. The combination of deeper and therefore better breathing with yoga inspired techniques has resulted in a school of yoga called *Laughter Yoga*.

Laughter Yoga helps to cultivate a more childlike playfulness as well as teaching you to breathe more correctly for good health. This playfulness by people in a group almost always results in laughter at one another. It is a natural outcome of everyone's deliberate, playful silliness.

Just 10-20 minutes of even fake laughter can have a profound benefit on the human body. Add the well established health benefits and better breathing exercises in yogic practice and a yoga system like Laughter Yoga makes real sense. Laughter Yoga was founded by Dr. Madan Kataria and Madhuri Kataria and uses the intimate connections of body and mind to actually change the physical state of the brain itself through repetitive physical gestures such as clapping and chanting. It is well known in Western medicine that voluntary repetitive gestures like these do have a neurological effect on the brain- an effect recognized for thousands of years in many Asian religions but only accepted in the West recently with better understanding of brain processes. The effect of *Laughter Yoga* is so powerful that thousands of people with depression have benefited. If you discover a *Laughter Yoga* group near where you live, do try it. The yoga group will provide you with a way of breaking down your reserve and allowing that inner child out to play – the child who once laughed up to 400 times every day.

Rubbing the belly

Swat! Swat !
The escaping fly buzzes
with laughter.

Issa - Japanese haiku poetry tradition

If you visit Asia you will probably see lots of statues of the Laughing Buddha. He is called the *Friendly One*. These statues grace many restaurants, temples, gardens, and houses. You really cannot miss him with his big pot belly, bald head, and his cheerful smile. He carries a sack over one shoulder and this is symbolically filled with food, sweets, and plants to help children, the poor, and the weak. According to his legend, if one rubs his great round belly, it brings good luck and prosperity into your life. This tradition is a folk practice, however, not a Buddhist teaching.

If you should chance upon a statue of the Laughing Buddha try to acquire it for your home because rubbing his belly when you are feeling blue may make you smile and that could help you take life just a little less seriously. Perhaps this will help you see that all situations do change and do pass and that hope, the great cure for most situations, is waiting for you to have its tummy tickled just like the Laughing Buddha.

If you cannot find a statue of the Laughing Buddha, then

pulled up your shirt and tickle your own belly. It is so silly an activity that you are bound to smile. This is good. This helps make your life rich.

THE ENDLESS VISION

THE ENDLESS VISION

If we are to avoid what makes us poor and do what makes us healthy and rich, we must above all else open our hearts to life. We must see with the vision of our spirit the world within us and the endless universe around us. We must see that which is at first invisible in ourselves so that we may discover the hidden qualities in everything else. As the little boy asked the sculptor, *How did you know that there was a lion in the marble?*, the perennial question we need to ask ourselves is this: *Am I missing something when I look at people and objects?* Could there be courage there or hope, charity and need?

What opens this inner eye is goodness and love. There are no substitutes. These are the well-springs of all those things that make you healthy and rich in living your life. They form the moral and ethical base for the values you hold that determine how you act. In this way, you will call Wisdom your beloved friend and become an artist of contentment. You are awake to the sheer joy of just being alive.

On the practice of goodness

A remarkable little monk, who lived centuries ago and was known as Brother Lawrence, left us a way of keeping in the present moment. He referred to it as *the practice of living in the presence of God.* The letters Br. Lawrence wrote in which he talked about this spiritual practice are still widely read. His practice was a way of being focused on the work in hand and not drifting about in yesterday or what you were going to do later in the day or sometime in the future or dwelling in worries and anxieties or just being uneasy in yourself. It was a way of stilling the heart to the benefit of the mind and body and still getting on with the job in hand, yet open to the spiritual. It is the ultimate state of mindfulness.

This being present to God does not have to be some religious matter centered on a deity, as was the case for Brother Lawrence. It can be *the practice of living in the presence of Good* for that which is goodness brings harmony. Such harmony is a song of love where goodness and God is the same thing.

Since goodness is love, Br. Lawrence's practice helped him to be focused on it. Famously, he wrote that he remembered to be in the presence of this universal goodness even as he scrambled his eggs at the monastery stove. What mattered was that he did not fall away from this union with love which is the ultimate union of your mind, body and spirit with the universal and the eternal.

Thus, our practice of the presence of God is the practice of the presence of Good. It will help you in everything you undertake – including scrambling the eggs – because you will be focused and united with the moment in which you are living. That is *always* good for this is the spiritual nourishment we need for our body and our mind.

On the practice of love

The practice of loving is very difficult for we are all filled with self-importance and self-interest and this is a great hindrance to love. Our desires confuse how we really feel and our habits of over- consumption or anger may mask our deep need for love and understanding.

Often we simply do not know what it is we love. This makes living a life dictated by love a continuous challenge because it demands we understand the reality of our strengths and weaknesses and accept them and that we embrace the same realities we find in others without judging them. This is to recognize human failings and not see them as faults. It is to see loving yourself as right and as a precondition for loving others. To love in this way is to be faithful to your true self and to allow that right to others.

Loving is also both connection and separation in our daily lives. It can be sweet in the intimacy of close relationships, for example, but bitter when letting go of failed ones. It can open up your talents without you using them as a means of control over others. It can bring you the wisdom that makes your sexuality a deeply nourishing gift to another because it is the giving of yourself. Love takes so many forms that it evades our definition but it has a heart of compassion which yearns for the triumph of all that is good.

Believe that true love exists if not now, then sometime in the future. Your belief will give you hope and hope will open your heart to love. You will be able to achieve that morally and ethically based life which brings contentment and holds dignity and high self-esteem. However, to have an open heart is to be willing to be vulnerable, a willingness to be wounded by others. It is a great risk but surely the best one in life to take, for love is all.

So believe in true love without reservation – no strings attached, no rules, and no conditions. Isn't that what you would really like love to be about?

Awake every moment of the day

Positive thinking decoupled from positive action is going to get you nowhere. It is just like reading about a diet in a magazine. Unless you actually do it the fat won't go away. So don't just read about the things in this book that make you poor or rich or healthy, but do them as best you can. Make discipline and discernment your best friends but let them be governed by a happy and loving heart.

You need to be awake every moment of every day – for happiness, for pleasure, for the love of life itself. Everyday means *today*, the time you are in *right now*. In the Islamic tradition it is said that Jesus summed it up this way: *The world consists of three days: yesterday which has passed, from which you have nothing in your hand; tomorrow of which you do not know whether you will reach it or not; and today in which you are, so avail yourself of it.*

Compassion is the expression of our love

In offering compassion we should try often to revisit its deepest meaning. We need to do this from time to time in order not to forget the true reason we express our love in this way and remember that our feelings are not just an emotional reaction to someone suffering. Compassion is the profound recognition of the reality of suffering as the state of being human. Everyone suffers, some more, some less, some physically, others emotionally. In realizing this natural state of humanity, we are enabled to share in another's suffering. This intimate identification brings forth our compassion because we see ourselves in that other person.

This sense of oneness makes us act with love. When we send such love to others, we are compassionate. At such a moment we transcend from the ordinary to the universal. We share in the enlightenment of the Buddha. We are witnesses to the salvation sacrifice of Christ. We have petitioned for God's mercy and grace. We have exalted that which is most holy – unconditional love.

In doing this we become bringers of peace and hope to ourselves and to all who meet us. They see by our example that there is good living to be found in the hardest times

Compassion, then, is the jewel in the crown of your life because it is in this expression of the harmony of love that you most reflect all that is divine in being a human.

All endings are beginnings

There is nothing I can give you which you do not already have, but there is much that you can take for your happiness if you will hunt for the purity and mercy which lies within you. It does not matter who you are, what you have, or how you have lived before this moment for the purity you hold is in your spirit, untainted by your failures or your successes. The handmaiden of such purity is your mercy for you were made for forgiveness and love.

So I would urge you above all to take peace with yourself and the world for nothing lies in your future which is not hidden in this present moment. Do not be discouraged anymore for behind the suffering and darkness of this world, yet within our reach, is joy. You will find in joy the fullest awareness of life itself. You will be glad just to be alive. This is to be awakened. Embrace it and be thankful because this life is the greatest of all gifts. It is so full of meaning, purpose, and beauty in its many forms that you will find that your life on earth is also your heaven. This heaven is here and now. It is your treasure without price. Guard this place where love lives. Here is where you will find that contentment which is the balanced union of mind, body and spirit.

Find courage then to claim this heaven with the certain knowledge that we all equally share hope and love and joy.